In a society where we are encourage[...]
lenges us to develop the rare quali[...]
feminist ideology need guidance. [...]
resources for making decisions that result in a richer relationship with God.

—BEVERLY LAHAYE
Chairman and Founder
Concerned Women for America

The pursuit of godliness is a process of learning discernment and choosing rightly. Here's some practical yet profound help for women seeking to glorify God with right choices. Donna Morley writes with clarity, wit, and keen insight. Best of all, she faithfully handles Scripture, unpacking the important truths and distilling them in simple, easily applicable principles. This is a superb resource for women.

—JOHN F. MACARTHUR
Senior Pastor, Grace Community Church

If there was ever a time when America was ripe for a return to godliness, it is now. Donna Morley is uniquely qualified by education, by professional experience, and by a powerful spiritual motivation to confront Christians with a call to discernment about the choices that govern their lives. Her message is one that resonates especially with women. *Choices That Lead to Godliness* is not a theoretical or theological approach, but a thoroughly practical guidebook for making the daily decisions that determine the character and destiny of our lives. Urgently recommended reading for women, for men, for believers and nonbelievers alike.

—DR. D. JAMES KENNEDY
Senior Minister, Coral Ridge Presbyterian Church

I have known Donna Morley for several years and consider her a godly woman with an excellent gift of spiritual discernment. Her knowledge of the Scriptures, of the needs of women, and of how to communicate effectively equip her well to write this book. Her subject is most timely. I don't recall having seen any book like this. I highly recommend *Choices That Lead to Godliness*.

—DR. LOWELL SAUNDERS
Adjunct Professor, Biola University
Author of numerous books, including Great Days Ahead

Donna Morley's practical, down-to-earth book touches so many areas of our lives. Her questions at the end of each chapter help apply the insights in a very personal way. Not only does she show us how to base daily decisions on God's Word, but also she delves deep within to the choices that affect our souls. Investing time in her book is without a doubt the right choice for every woman who wants to be closer to God through Christlikeness.

—ELLEN PARKER
Women's Ministries, Missionary, EVLA
(Evangelical Vision from Latin America), Mexico

Choices That Lead to Godliness is an investigation into a seeking woman's journey with her Father God. Out of Donna Morley's intimate walk with God comes a book that challenges every area of a woman's life—her thoughts, motivations, and deepest desires. Balanced instructions with encouragement equip and enable the reader to be all that God intended her to be. I highly recommend this book for every Christian woman, especially those who desire to be godly.

> —SHARON GIVENS
> *Wife of Senior Pastor*
> *Grace Baptist Church of Santa Clarita*

Biblical discernment, a lost element in today's society, can be yours. In Donna's lively and personal style, she captures the essence of God's teaching for today's woman. No matter where you are in your walk with God, *Choices That Lead to Godliness* will lift you up and give you a virtuous path in which to walk.

> —JOY LAND
> *Director of Women's Ministry*
> *Grace Baptist Church of Santa Clarita*

In a world that lacks wisdom and discernment, *Choices That Lead to Godliness* gives insightful, biblical discernment and wisdom. This is well-researched material that will help women be Christlike in everyday living. I would hope every woman in America would read and live out this Christ-honoring material. This is the best book I have read to help women be godly in their walk with Christ.

> —DR. J. MICHAEL BROYLES
> *Church Training Consultant*
> *Evangelical Training Association*

Women pursuing godliness will greatly appreciate Donna's book. With her love for the truth of the Bible, her delightful sense of humor, and her creative approaches, Donna helps women know how they can spend more time in God's Word, how they can better encourage and edify their friends, how they can make wise words a habit in their conversations, and much more.

> —BETTY PRICE
> *Women's Bible Teacher and Speaker*
> *Associate Dean of Students,*
> *Master's College, Santa Clarita, CA*

CHOICES
THAT LEAD TO
GODLINESS

DONNA
MORLEY

CROSSWAY BOOKS • WHEATON, ILLINOIS
A DIVISION OF GOOD NEWS PUBLISHERS

To my loving husband,

whose life continually brings me

closer to Christ

———

Choices That Lead to Godliness

Copyright © 1999 by Donna Morley

Published by Crossway Books
    a division of Good News Publishers
    1300 Crescent Street
    Wheaton, Illinois 60187

Cover design: D² DesignWorks

Cover photo: Tony Stone Images / Brigitte Merle

First printing 1999

Printed in the United States of America

Unless otherwise designated, Scripture quotations are taken from the New American Standard Bible® Copyright © The Lockman Foundation 1960, 1962, 1963, 1968, 1971, 1972, 1973, 1975, 1977. Used by permission.

Scripture taken from the King James Version is identified KJV.

Scripture taken from the Holy Bible: New International Version® is identified NIV. Copyright © 1973, 1978, 1984 by International Bible Society. Used by permission of Zondervan Publishing House. All rights reserved.

The "NIV" and "New International Version" trademarks are registered in the United States Patent and Trademark Office by International Bible Society. Use of either trademark requires the permission of International Bible Society.

Library of Congress Cataloging-in-Publication Data
Morley, Donna, 1959-
    Choices that lead to godliness / Donna Morley.
      p.   cm.
    ISBN 1-58134-062-1 (tpb : alk. paper)
    1. Christian life.   2. Choice (Psychology)—Religious aspects—
Christianity. I. Title.
    BV4501.M58535   1999
    248.4—dc21
                                98-52540
                                    CIP

15	14	13	12	11	10	09	08	07	06	05	04	03	02	01	00	99
15	14	13	12	11	10	9	8	7	6	5	4	3	2	1		

CONTENTS

ACKNOWLEDGMENTS

I would like to express my thanks and appreciation to all who have helped me in one way or another to write this book.

To my husband, Dr. Brian Morley, for your advice, guidance, and editorial assistance—most of all, for your support. When I was discouraged and wanted to quit, you simply asked, "Is that what God would want?" Who knows if there would be a book today without that simple question?

To Lila Bishop for your editorial honing, which has made this book more effective.

To Dr. Brenda Gilardone, Cindee Grant, Randy Jahns, Sharron Minchella, Marvin Padgett, Maryann Olofsson, Dr. Lowell and Carol Saunders, Erika Smith, Wendy Simpson, and Rev. Eric and Barbara Thomas who kindly shared their critiques.

To Steve Miller and Joanne Heim for your editorial assistance before this book had a publishing "home." And to you both, along with Carolyn McCready, for your steady confidence that this book merited publication. Lastly, Steve, I appreciated tremendously the many writing lessons. You taught me so much!

To Cynthia Buchan and Traci Harris for your sustained interest and encouragement during the arduous four-year trek.

To Phil Johnson whose behind-the-scenes ministry will be known and rewarded only in eternity.

To Dr. John MacArthur and Rev. Tom Givens for your impact on my life, teaching me accurately the Word of God. And to Dr. Mike Broyles whose enthusiastic faith in this project has been a great encouragement.

To those people who are used as illustrations. A few names and circumstances have been changed to protect identities.

To Elisabeth Elliot, Francis and Edith Schaeffer, and Puritan writers Thomas Manton and Stephen Charnock who through their writings have influenced me deeply.

To the countless people who faithfully prayed for this book. I especially thank Paul and Paula Gilbert, who have prayed for me daily since we first met in July 1983. Your life of prayer is an inspiration.

To my father-in-law John Morley whose genuine interest encouraged me along the way. To my sister-in-law Barbara Morley whose spiritual friendship has added to my life. To my family members, especially Dan and Erika Laubacher whose cheering encouragement came all the way from Vienna, Austria. And to my father, Eugene Laubacher, who started my journey with the question: "Don't you have any discernment?"

To my children, Michelle and Johnathan, whose tender young love for Jesus is my constant delight.

Lastly to my Lord and Savior, Jesus Christ—without Him and His Word, there wouldn't be anything worth writing.

> *My heart overflows with a good theme;*
> *I address my verses to the King,*
> *My tongue is the pen of a ready writer.*
>
> —PSALM 45:1

A CRY

FOR DISCERNMENT

My heart beat rapidly, and I gasped for breath as I made a fast dash to the time clock. I snatched the time card and put it in just as I heard the clock tick. *Whew . . . made it in the nick of time!* I caught my breath, straightened my skirt, and put on a "composed look" as I walked into work at the dietetics department of the hospital.

Having spent most of the previous evening studying for college exams, I was tired and not ready for the busy day ahead. I settled at my desk and shuffled the pile of paperwork. *I've got to run my life better.* Little did I know that a call waiting on my phone extension would show me just how true that was!

"Hi, Donna, this is Fred! I'm sorry I haven't called in a while, but I've been terribly busy. I'm calling to find out if I can take you to dinner this Friday night at The Charthouse. It would be great to catch up!"

My mind was racing. *Fred . . . Fred . . . who in the world is Fred? Obviously he knows me, or he wouldn't have my work number. Could he be one of the medical interns?* Not wanting to hurt his feelings, I pretended to know him. "Oh yes, Fred, it's great to hear from you. Yes, I'm free this Friday."

Excited, Fred said, "Great!" Then he paused and added, "Heh, I forgot your address. Can you give it to me?" I did, and he said he would pick me up at six o'clock.

On Friday evening before Fred came to the house, my father noticed I was getting ready for a date. "Who are you going out with?"

"Fred," was all I said. The one-word answer aroused his curiosity. "Fred who?"

Rushing quickly in an attempt to evade any more questions, I said, "Oh, I don't recall his last name."

That stirred my father's protective instincts. Following me into the kitchen, he asked, "What does he look like?"

Coming from my father, this was an odd question because he seldom expressed interest in a person's appearance. Though I could sense tension building between us, I chose to give him a vague answer: "Well, ah, he's taller than me . . . ah, I'm sure."

My dad quickly snapped back, "Donna, everyone is taller than you!"

Just then the doorbell rang. *Saved by the bell!* I thought. I ran to the door, but my father got there first. He opened the door, and I looked at Fred. Then I looked at my father. Both faces were equally frightening. Fred was about thirty years older than I, looked as if he lived on the street, and had eyes that jittered constantly. My father, who was twenty-five years older than I, began to twitch his hands as if contemplating wringing someone's neck; I didn't know if it was Fred's or mine.

Seeing Fred made me wish I could stay home, but again, not wanting to hurt his feelings, I quickly kissed my father on the cheek, told him where we were going, and off we went.

At dinner I confessed, "Fred, I have to be honest with you. I don't recall ever meeting you. How do you know me?"

"Well," Fred said in a hushed, sinister voice, "I was a patient in the psychiatric ward at the hospital where you work. I was on an elevator the same time you were and got your name and department from your name tag. Ever since I first saw you, I've been waiting for the day I could get out of that prison to ask you out on a date." He continued with the details of his life's story while I tried to hide the fact that I was becoming very uncomfortable and scared! I quickly ate my dinner, refused dessert and a movie, and asked that he take me home.

I knew my father would be waiting for me when I arrived. I opened the front door, and there he was, sitting on the couch. He glanced quickly at the clock; I could tell he had been watching it. Then he looked at me, ready to hear about the evening's events.

As I told him what happened, his face turned progressively deeper shades of angry red. He shook his finger at me and said something I never forgot: "Don't you have any discernment?"

Since that day my ambition in life has been to develop a "discerning eye" that would help me avoid potentially troublesome situations. And when I came into a personal relationship with Jesus Christ the following year, a new dimension of understanding was added, as I realized the great value of discernment and how truly precious it is from God's perspective.

A DESIRABLE TREASURE

King Solomon, Israel's greatest monarch, said we should cry for discernment and lift our voice for understanding. He urged us to seek discernment as for silver and search for her as for hidden treasures. Then we will discern the fear of the Lord, and discover the knowledge of God (Proverbs 2:3-5).

At the beginning of Solomon's reign over Israel, God came to him in a dream and said, "Ask what you wish me to give you" (1 Kings 3:5). How tempting it must have been for Solomon to ask for riches or fame or a long life or revenge on his enemies (1 Kings 3:11). Instead, he asked for a great treasure: discernment. God gladly granted it (1 Kings 3:12).

Discernment enabled Solomon to judge the most difficult court cases, such as the one in which two women claimed to be the mother of the same baby (1 Kings 3:16-28). When Solomon's ingenious verdict was handed down, everyone "feared the king; for they saw that the wisdom of God was in him" (1 Kings 3:28).

With his discernment, Solomon led the nation of Israel to enjoy the most prosperous years it had ever known. Because of his wisdom, "his fame was known in all the surrounding nations" (1 Kings 4:31). Wealth and fame could never have brought him discernment, yet with discernment came prosperity and recognition.

DEFINING DISCERNMENT

What is discernment?

Discernment is the ability to distinguish between things that differ. It enables us to bypass the better and choose the best. Discernment helps us to make choices—choices that lead to:

- greater intimacy with God.
- a more satisfying prayer life.
- words that are fitting for the moment at hand.
- thoughts that are true, pure, and lovely.
- actions that seek the best for others.
- stronger relationships with loved ones.
- friendships that build, comfort, and encourage.
- setting the right goals for your life and achieving them.
- the best use of your time, money, and possessions.
- the best use of your spiritual gifts.

Discernment can help us to draw closer to our marriage partners, have wisdom in raising our children, equip us to handle our workload more effectively, and make the best decision when we're confronted with a variety of choices. It helps us to choose right from wrong and to know God's will for our lives. Most important, discernment is the ability to grasp and apply God's truth, a skill that equips us for all areas of life.

No wonder the apostle Paul yearned for the beloved church at Philippi to have discernment: "This I pray, that your love may abound still more and more in real knowledge and all discernment, so that you may approve the things that are excellent, in order to be sincere and blameless until the day of Christ" (Philippians 1:9-10).

As we grow in discernment, we'll notice there are always new and different choices to make. Discernment is an ability we can sharpen through constant usage. By contrast, without continual cultivation of this skill, we can end up like Solomon in the latter years of his reign, when tragically he failed to use the discernment God had granted him.

EVERY CHOICE COUNTS

Each time we make a right or better choice, our discernment grows. This process works not just in the big life-changing issues, but also in the small, everyday routines of life. When we take the attitude that every choice counts, we allow wisdom to permeate in every area of our life. Inviting discernment to be our constant friend will remove the uncertainty, worry, and fear that often come when we're standing at the crossroads of a decision. Considering the many decisions we struggle with daily, discernment is essential. It can do much to help make our lives less complicated . . . and more fulfilling. Wouldn't you like that to be true of your life?

As we journey together through this book, we'll see that our choices shape us. They determine what we are. They shape our lives and destiny. And we'll discover—as the apostle Paul tells us in Philippians 1:9-10—that when we seek to make the best choices, we do what is excellent—and pleasing to God.

Won't you join me, then, as we take a closer look at the choices that lead to godliness?

Part One

Choices
in Our Outer Life

Chapter One

AVOIDING WORDS
THAT WOUND

I shouldn't have said it! I've replayed the situation in my mind hundreds of times and wish the ending could be different. But it can't. The damage has been done. Oh, how I regret those words! It all happened so innocently.

I was reading a book on the living room couch, and my husband, Brian, was in the study. When the phone rang, I answered it. The caller asked for Brian in a thick French accent. Thinking it was our friend Gary, who has a great sense of humor and is the world's best imitator of voices, I decided to have a little fun.

I told the foreign voice, "Brian is not home."

"When will he be back?" he asked.

"Never!" I replied. "He took all of our money out of the bank and ran away with another woman."

The voice was alarmed and insisted on getting in touch with Brian *immediately!*

I told him, "Good luck!"

Still thinking it was our fun-loving friend, I told the voice to please start speaking English, reminding him he was in America, not France. I added, "On second thought, your accent is such a lousy imitation of the real thing you would be a disgrace if you went back to France!" The caller sharply hung up the phone.

As it began to dawn on me that this might not have been Gary, I felt a creeping sense of horror. To reassure myself, I called Gary and asked whether he had just called. Curious, he asked, "Why?" After telling him what happened, he laughed and apologetically said, "No, that wasn't me." I had a sinking feeling. I knew I was in trouble!

I darted to the study with my tongue flapping like a banner in a breeze, nervously trying to explain to Brian what had happened. Leaning back in his chair, my even-tempered husband stared, frozen in silence. Then with a look of disbelief Brian said, "Donna, I had been expecting that phone call. You just insulted one of the men supervising my doctoral degree, not to mention, a Belgian priest!"

I shuffled back to the couch and buried my head in the pillows. Lying there, I felt horrible, but the worst part was realizing that I had mocked and humiliated the priest. Anxious thoughts began racing through my mind such as, *Will this jeopardize all of Brian's hard work at Claremont Graduate School? Did I damage his testimony, to say nothing of my own?*

My compassionate husband didn't allow me to despair for long. He quickly called back the professor and tried to patch things up. But it took him awhile to convince the priest that he had not left me for another woman and that his wife was quite a nice person once you got to know her. That incredibly embarrassing lesson taught me the damage that can be done with words.

So what else can words do? Soft words sung in a lullaby can put a child to sleep. Slanderous words can wound like bullets. Virtuous words, like those of Moses, can inspire and lead a nation. Explosive words can incite a mob to violence. Encouraging words can lift up the discouraged and brokenhearted. Angry words can tear families apart. And God's words of forgiveness will bring the repentant to Him.[1]

Yes, words are powerful! Powerful enough to mold a child's outlook on life, as the sculptor molds clay. Powerful enough to shape those around us. Powerful enough to outlive us.

It's been said that "life is a great whispering gallery that sends back echoes of the words we send out."[2] Those echoing words can be beautiful or ugly. Too often, without much thought, we say what is ugly. Who hasn't at one time said something she has regretted? Who hasn't struggled with gossip or let words burst out in anger or frustration?

Shakespeare's play *King Lear* has a line that I believe sums up a major source of tragedy in the drama: "Speak what we feel; not what we ought to say."[3] The character was emphasizing the need for sincerity, but today this advice is a comment on the way society wrongly values feelings over self-control. Scripture tells us the reason we are to be discerning with our words and to choose them carefully is so they will be "helpful for building others up according to their needs, that it may benefit those who listen" (Ephesians 4:29 NIV). This is the beginning of godly speech.

What then can hinder our pursuit of godly speech? Of the many things, perhaps the greatest is gossip. Gossip created problems even for those living in the time of Christ. Hospitality was important in Middle Eastern culture, and it was common for hosts to provide entertainment during and after a meal. People read poetry and prose, and they danced. Afterwards guests would talk and tell stories and often indulge in local gossip. Because gossip became such a problem, the Bible had to give special warnings against it (Matthew 12:36; Ephesians 5:4).[4] Scripture also identifies gossip quite graphically and tells us to avoid it.

As women pursuing godly speech, we can benefit greatly from understanding Scripture's warnings about wrong uses of the tongue and how to avoid words that wound.

THE GOSSIPING TONGUE

One day four women met for fellowship. One said, "Scripture tells us to 'confess your faults one to another'" (James 5:16 KJV). "Would you all like to do that now?" In due time they agreed. One confessed she was addicted to watching soap operas most of her day. The second confessed to a habit of smoking; she just couldn't seem to break it. The third confessed to spending too much of the grocery money on lottery tickets. But when it was the fourth woman's turn, she wouldn't confess. The others pressed her, saying, "Come on, we confessed ours. What is your secret sin?" Finally she answered, "It is gossiping, and I can hardly wait to get out of here and tell my friends!"[5]

Ever felt like the fourth woman? You hear some news you just "can't believe," and you can hardly wait to pass it on to someone else?

If so, you have company. Many of us Christian women have struggled with gossip at some time or other.

How many have ever heard or said one of the following phrases: "I heard . . ." "Everybody says . . ." "Have you heard . . ." "Did you hear . . ." "Isn't it awful . . ." "People say . . ." "Did you ever . . ." "Somebody said . . ." "Would you think . . ." "Don't say I told you . . ." "Oh, I think it is terrible . . ."[6]

Whether at a friend's table or a church-related gathering, we carelessly use one or more of these phrases to share the latest news about people we know. We add "what I heard" to our friend's "what I heard," and we make the two equal truth. Gossiping is as easy as throwing mud against a clean wall—though it doesn't stick, it leaves behind a stain.[7]

Scripture identifies three types of gossipers. The first is the loose talker, the "whisperer" or "talebearer" (Greek *psithyristas*[8]). Telling secrets or repeating the latest scandal (Proverbs 11:13), this person has mastered the art of saying nothing but leaving nothing unsaid.[9] Because she fails to respect the confidences of others, she is not trustworthy. Her talk is so powerful she can even separate intimate friends (Proverbs 17:9).

The second type of gossiper is the slanderer (Greek *katalalous*[10]). This person's talk damages another person's reputation, whether intentionally or unintentionally. He or she may even say things known to be false. Jezebel, for example, secretly hid her coveting heart as she wrote letters to the nobles, lying about Naboth, and signing the king's name (1 Kings 21:8-14). Scripture says of people like this, "He who conceals hatred has lying lips, and he who spreads slander is a fool" (Proverbs 10:18).

The third gossiper (Greek *loidoros*[11]) insults, abuses, or reviles. Possibly because the reviler herself has been hurt, she strikes back to wound the feelings or self-respect of those who caused her pain. Paul the apostle told believers not to associate with supposed Christians who were "revilers" (1 Corinthians 5:11). He commanded believers to "put . . . abusive speech from your mouth" (Colossians 3:8).

All types of gossip cause pain and grief and often result in unexpected consequences. Job was tormented and crushed by the many insults from Bildad (Job 19:2-3), and who knows the grief Abigail experienced when she risked her life to prevent the bloodshed prompted by her husband's insults (1 Samuel 25:23-42).

FROM GOSSIP TO GODLY SPEECH

Because gossip has created problems since the beginning of sin itself, Paul dealt with it head on, especially when he addressed the women in the church. Those who wished to be deaconesses, he wrote, must be an example to other women. They must not be gossips, but dignified, temperate, and faithful in all things (1 Timothy 3:11). He encouraged the young widows to remarry so they would not be idle and gossip from house to house, "talking about things not proper to mention" (1 Timothy 5:13-14). The older women he exhorted to be reverent in their behavior, not "malicious gossips," and to teach what is good to the younger women (Titus 2:3-5).

James, too, was concerned about gossip. The tongue, he warned, could set "on fire the course of our life, and is set on fire by hell" (James 3:6). The Greek word James used for hell was *Gehenna*, the name of Jerusalem's garbage dump. Gehenna was in the Valley of Hinnom, located west and south of Jerusalem. There all the filth of the city would be disposed of, including dead bodies of animals and executed criminals.[12] Because of the mounds of garbage, the stench, and defilement, the fire had to burn continually. The destructive fire ignited by the tongue, James maintains, can ruin lives, homes, churches, and places of employment. So how can we avoid words that wound and instead grow in godly speech?

Ways to Avoid Hurting Others

It would be wonderful if people said only good and true things about others. But not everyone does. I have had to ask myself, "How can I avoid listening to or promoting gossip? And how can I, in those rare cases when there is a legitimate reason to talk about someone's shortcomings, avoid crossing the line into gossiping?

A KEY DISTINCTION

In trying to answer these questions for myself, I first had to decide what gossip is not. It is not gossip to share facts confidentially with a person who can help another person. (But even then I should share only what is necessary.) If I know of a believer at my church who is in habitual sin, and private confrontation doesn't bring her to repentance, it is not gossip to go to an elder or the pastor in an effort to help her. Nor would it be gossiping to share information that protects others from harm. In a sense, that is what happens when church leaders bring the name of a sinning believer before a congregation for church discipline. It puts loving pressure on the sinner to repent. If unrepentant, the sinner is separated from the rest of the body so that others will not be tainted (Matthew 18:17; 1 Corinthians 5:13).

If I have to share something negative about someone, I can protect that person's identity by not using her real name or saying anything that would identify her.

BREAKING THE GRAPEVINE

From the beginning, it seems, people have had a hard time speaking well of each other. Even great men of history have tried to destroy one another with words. The hatred of Plato and Xenophon is as immortal as their works. So is the spite between Voltaire and Rousseau. Charles Lamb and Samuel Coleridge were schoolmates, but as adults they were enemies. They used their pens as daggers to attack each other. Coleridge also mocked DeQuincy because, while they both used opium, Coleridge says DeQuincy used it for pleasure, while he, Coleridge, took it to relieve pain.[13]

Although it may be easy for any of us to be critical of a person who commits their low opinion of another to posterity in literary form, we can easily become a part of the same process, done verbally. Without realizing it, we can become part of a grapevine, a verbal publication of a bad opinion. But we also have the ability to break a grapevine. When a complaint about another comes our way, and we know we can't be of help, we can recommend that the person talk instead to someone who can help, such as a pastor, elder, or counselor. If this suggestion is not appropriate, then we can ask, "Are you sure it is okay for me to know this?"

If someone asks us for information that would then become part of the gossip, it might be best to say, "Well, I probably shouldn't go into that," or, "I don't think it would help in this case to know the details."

If we are unable to stop the gossip, then we can try to be constructive and offer a different interpretation of the matter. For example, if our friend claims that someone was lying, we can suggest to her that perhaps the person was merely misinformed and had no intention to deceive. If the conversation brings up something that a person did "wrong," perhaps we could suggest that the person might have had good intentions but that his or her actions turned out for the worse. After all, we want to be cautious about misinterpreting another person's actions.

By playing the "devil's advocate," we can stop gossip and keep ourselves from spreading error that may end up hurting someone's reputation. Reputations can take a lifetime to build, and we want to avoid destroying them with words that take only moments to speak.

Watch out for the seven "mis-es." By name, they are misinterpretation, misinformation, misquotation, misrepresentation, misconstruction, misconception, and misunderstanding.[14]

One pastor had to respond to his church in a letter because the "mis-es" got out of hand. He said that he had been greatly troubled by a rumor going around that his wife had attended a meeting of a heretical group, and that while she was there, he had dragged her out by the hair and beat her when they got home. He assured his congregation that he had neither dragged his wife out by the hair nor beaten her. He added that his wife had never attended the meeting in the first place. He closed the letter by reminding the congregation that he was a bachelor and had never been married.[15]

DOUBLE-CHECKING THE FACTS

Not only can we exercise care about what we hear verbally, but we want to be cautious of what we read in print as well. Perhaps you know of magazines or newspapers that will misrepresent people or events. I personally knew someone whose entire career was ruined and family devastated because of misrepresentation in the newspapers. Because of this tragedy, I have learned that sometimes it's best not to say anything at all about what I hear or read about someone. I've also found that it's worthwhile to double-check my facts. It was the sleuth Sherlock Holmes who said, "Pictures can hide the truth." He was right—things are not always what they appear to be.

Scripture encourages us to check on our facts before we jump to conclusions: "If you hear . . . anyone saying that . . . then you shall investigate and search out and inquire thoroughly. And if it is true . . ." (Deuteronomy 13:12, 14).

Whenever I'm about to share information, I try to remember my accountability to God's Word and ask myself, *Did I investigate? Did I search out the facts? Did I inquire thoroughly? Did I try to find out if the story is true?* By asking these questions, I can avoid repeating hearsay.

THINK BEFORE YOU SPEAK

Another time to be cautious is when talking about a person who has wronged us in the past. From having been terribly wounded by the words and actions of a few, I know the temptation to retaliate against them through an unkind word. What has kept me from succumbing is to ask myself, *Do I really need to tell others who has wronged me? Is what I am saying kind? Is what I am about to say confidential? Is it edifying? Is it necessary? And if so, am I the one who should say it?*

THE CODE OF SILENCE

We all know that "the mouth speaks out of that which fills the heart" (Matthew 12:34). Nothing reveals who we are better than our words. And the more we talk, the greater the likelihood that something unwanted will come out because, "when there are many words, transgression is unavoidable" (Proverbs 10:19).

All of us have to be aware of a few special temptations. Untruthfulness, for example, comes disguised as exaggeration. We embellish a conversation and make the story more interesting and dramatic. The built-up story can quickly circulate and cause great damage precisely because it is interesting and dramatic.

Words can cloak unkindness. Things can be said that needlessly question a person's motives or actions. Since the person we are talking about is usually absent, he or she is not able to repair damage done by our words. Without meaning to, we can create an attitude of distrust toward the person. Instead, we ought to be supportive. As one wise person pointed out, most of us regret having said harsh words, but no one regrets having said kind words.

When we hear something negative about a person, we have to be on guard against distrusting him or her on insufficient grounds. For example, a neighbor who casually says, "There is something strange about the Smiths" could remind us of late-night movie scenarios such as *The Burbs* where ghoulish neighbors were secretly running a crematorium in their basement. You may have thought the Smiths were a nice family, but your neighbor's offhand remark could leave you suspicious of them. Journalist Andy Rooney once said, "A great many people do not have a right to their own opinions because they don't know what they are talking about."[16] Whether or not this statement is accurate, there are times when we should discern whether the person making the comment has good reason for it. But before believing any comment—again we must check out the facts.

The key to helping us win over these verbal temptations is, in one word, *love*. It "covers a multitude of sins" (1 Peter 4:8), hiding from view what does not need to be revealed. And it "believes all things" (1 Corinthians 13:7), assuming the best about a person unless the evidence proves otherwise. As fifteenth-century theologian William Struther would remind us, "At tables or meetings I cannot stop the mouths of others, yet may I close mine own ears, and by a heavenly soul-speech with God divert my mind from fruitless talking. Though I be among them, I shall as little partake their prattling as they do my meditation."[17]

Struther took on what I would call "the code of silence"—an ally that can help us out of these awkward situations. Scripture commends those who can keep their tongues as being wise (Proverbs

10:19) and says that "even a fool, when he keeps silent, is considered wise" (Proverbs 17:28).

Other benefits to being silent are that we'll have fewer words to regret, and we won't have to eat "humble pie." Because silence often convicts others, gossipy conversations will end much sooner. Also, our reputation is enhanced, because when we keep silent, we become known as a tight-lipped person who can be trusted with confidential matters. Consequently, when people need to talk privately, they will look for us.

Being silent when a friend is speaking about someone else isn't that difficult. But what about when others are criticizing you? Abraham Lincoln suggests that it's "better to remain silent and be thought a fool than to speak out and remove all doubt."[18] Certainly silence is one way to respond, but I believe there are times when situations require us to defend ourselves. So how can we know when to keep silent and when to speak up?

To Defend or Not to Defend?

Why did Moses pray rather than defend himself when the people of Israel wanted to stone him? Why was Christ silent before Pilate, who was amazed Jesus did not defend Himself (Matthew 27:13-14)? On the other hand, why did Paul defend himself before the Ephesian elders, saying, "I have coveted no one's silver or gold or clothes. You yourselves know that these hands ministered to my own needs and to the men who were with me" (Acts 20:33-34)?

Moses and Christ would not defend themselves because they knew that doing so would do no good in their situations. But Paul defended himself in order to protect the credibility he needed to continue ministering. When there was suspicion that he was in ministry for money, he pointed out that he not only worked for a living, but he even supplied the needs of others. Yet it's important to note that Paul was unconcerned about his reputation for its own sake, not bothered by what people thought of him personally (Philippians 1:17-18; 1 Corinthians 4:3).

So when speaking up will do no good or when nothing is at stake, we can keep silent. But when our credibility for ministry is in jeopardy, we should humbly set the record straight.

Whether we keep silent or defend ourselves, we need to love those who are troubling us. As Christ exhorted, "I say to you . . . love your enemies, do good to those who hate you, bless those who curse you, pray for those who mistreat you" (Luke 6:27-28).

Abraham Lincoln had his enemies. Edwin M. Stanton despised Lincoln and often insulted him publicly. Once he called Lincoln "a low, cunning clown."[19] He said it was ridiculous for people to go to Africa to find a gorilla when they could easily find one in Springfield, Illinois.[20] Stanton described Lincoln, a man of humble means, as "wearing a dirty linen duster for a coat, with perspiration stains on it that resembled a dirty map of the continent."[21]

Yet Lincoln never retaliated. He just went about his duties. When it came time to choose the country's war minister, he surprised everyone by appointing none other than Stanton. When asked why he had chosen his vicious opponent, he replied that Stanton was the best man for the job.[22]

Lincoln's gesture did not change Stanton's dislike for the president. The war minister once received an official order from the president and flatly refused to obey it. "But we have the president's order," said the messenger.

"The president is a fool," blurted Stanton.

When Lincoln heard what had happened, he asked, "Did Stanton say I was a fool?"

"He used that very word," replied the indignant messenger.

"Stanton is usually right," Lincoln said humbly. "I will slip over and see him." Lincoln went, and Stanton convinced him that the course he had intended to follow was indeed inadvisable.[23]

Over time Stanton could not help but admire Lincoln. The night Lincoln was shot and lay struggling for his life, Stanton stood over him gazing silently into his rugged face. Through tears he said, "There lies the greatest ruler of men the world has ever seen."[24]

Stanton never accepted Lincoln's politics, but he came to respect his humility and nonretaliating spirit. Most people in Lincoln's position would have fired Stanton for insubordination. Lincoln didn't because he chose a better way. We can, too.

In the face of criticism, we can:

- Commit the matter at once to the Lord. We can ask Him to remove from us all bitterness or desire to retaliate, to teach us the hidden lessons to be learned.
- We can realize we are forming godly character when we restrain ourselves from talking about others, even though they may be talking about us. We are told in Scripture to remember the example of Christ, who, "while being reviled, He did not revile in return; while suffering, He uttered no threats, but kept entrusting Himself to Him who judges righteously" (1 Peter 2:23; 1 Corinthians 4:12).
- If we must defend our position, then let's ask God to help us do it gently, since gentle answers calm things down, while harsh answers stir things up (Proverbs 15:1).
- When we struggle with criticism from others, it's helpful to remind ourselves of our own sinful nature and of God's grace and wisdom. His grace is free (Ephesians 2:8), and His wisdom to deal with the situation is there for the asking (Proverbs 2:2-7).
- This is an opportunity to be honest with ourselves. Regardless of how vicious we may believe the criticism to be, we might pause momentarily and be humble enough to admit to ourselves, and others if necessary, if there is *any* truth in the criticism.

And, no matter what happens, God's Word reminds us not to dwell on our hurts or failures. Instead, forgetting what lies behind, let's reach forward to what lies ahead (Philippians 3:13).

BLESSINGS AHEAD

Our words can be the greatest blessing we bestow on others. Everyone benefits from them. We ourselves receive a personal reward as we see the good our words have done. The person listening to us gains something money can't buy—our love manifested through our words. Like Christ's Sermon on the Mount, our words can cheer the sorrowful, encourage the heartbroken, guide the perplexed, strengthen the doubting, and inspire the discouraged.

Though most of us will never speak to a multitude of people at one time, over a lifetime we will speak to perhaps several thousand. Because Christ lives in us (Galatians 2:20), we can have a great impact on other people's lives. This is the beginning of pleasing God with our speech.

The woman who pleases God with her tongue has learned not only to avoid words that wound, but she has as well learned to control her temper. Taming the temper has been my own greatest challenge, especially on those days when I have felt like Dr. Jekyll/Mr. Hyde, the man in R. L. Stevenson's story whose charming side was sometimes overwhelmed by a dark, monstrous side. We can have victory over that harsh side. By giving our attitudes completely over to God, we can receive His help to speak with grace and season our words "with salt" so that we can know how to respond to each person (Colossians 4:6). We can build people up even when there is tension in the air, when discipline is in order, or when a flare-up is on the horizon. As we shall see in the next chapter, by learning to tame our temper even as we endure the stresses of life, we can have a tongue that pleases God.

Thinking It Over

1.   What are the three types of gossip?

2.   What are ways you can personally avoid words that wound?

3.   What are ways you can break the "grapevine" when you are among your friends and find yourself caught in the middle of gossip?

4.   What will you do when you face criticism directed at you?

Chapter Two

TAMING

THE TEMPER

My day started normally enough. The kids got up all smiles and hugs. At the breakfast table, they gulped down all their oatmeal and then asked to be excused. With a smile, I nodded to them, and off they went to play. As I mopped the kitchen floor, I thought how blessed I was to have such adorable children.

Just then my thoughts were interrupted by three-and-a-half-year-old Michelle. "Mommy, can I have a pencil to draw a picture?" I got a pencil, and, reminding her to draw only on the paper, I went back to my housework.

A short time later, I heard Johnathan, not yet two, screaming, "It's mine!" and Michelle screaming back, "No, it's mine!"

When I entered the room to settle the matter, I went into shock. Juice from Michelle's "spill-proof" cup was all over the video recorder and carpet. With her little hands she quickly tried to hide the evidence by brushing the sticky liquid into the vents of the VCR. Johnathan, with pencil in hand, had just finished some unauthorized decorating—a mural on the walls, the heater, and the attractively grained light-wood door. To top it off, Michelle had brought in a whole bucket of small pebbles from outdoors, and just then Johnathan tripped over it. The handle of the bucket caught on his foot, and as he tried to flee the crime scene, the pebbles—which were just the size that gets stuck in the vacuum cleaner—sprayed all over the rug. As I stood there quickly reaching my boiling point, Michelle saw that her brother still had the disputed pencil and began to chase him. Two bundles of childish energy ran screaming in every direction. I struggled to stay calm but found myself hollering even to be heard.

Does this scene sound familiar? Our nerves can get frazzled, and we lose control, not thinking about what we are saying. A woman given to outbursts of anger told evangelist Billy Sunday about her problem, but she excused it by saying that it was all over in a minute. He replied, "So is a shotgun, but it blows everything to pieces."[1]

The apostle James compares the control of a horse to the way our tongues influence our lives. "If we put the bits into the horses' mouths so that they may obey us, we direct their entire body as well" (James 3:3). Though the tongue's power can be used for good or evil (v. 9), few of us can really control our tongues (v. 8), and those who do so are truly mature (v. 2).

INCREASING OUR INTERNAL RESTRAINTS

Since that living room episode, I have sought better ways of communicating that don't include hollering. One way I have grown in this area is by adopting principles that help me discern each situation and to think, analyze, and reason with others in a way that is pleasing to God. For all of us who desire to communicate in a godly way, we begin by seeking understanding.

Understanding the Situation

It helps to make an extra effort to look beyond first impressions and see the situation for what it is. Though I don't condone Michelle's feeding the VCR or Johnathan's scribbling on the wall, I have to remind myself that children sometimes act their age. No one is perfect, especially children who are in the earliest training stage of life.

Resisting our first reaction and instead seeking to understand a situation can help us to stay calm. And that is especially important with children because we can make matters worse if we try to discipline them when we ourselves are out of control.

One way to be more empathetic is to recall our own faults. Had I reminded myself of my own childhood mistakes—like the time I took my mother's deep-red lipstick and drew all over my parents' white bedroom walls—I would have been more understanding with my children's failures. Of course, we don't even have to reach back as far as our childhood; we can just be aware of our current daily faults.

A deeper look at a situation can help us have a more discerning response. Proverbs sums up the benefits: "Understanding is a fountain of life to him who has it" (Proverbs 16:22).

Abstain from Blaming

When we continually find fault with someone, whether our child, husband, friend, or coworker, we are implying that we are somehow better—that we do not make such mistakes. This attitude causes tension and hostility in our home or workplace.

By henpecking a person, we gradually inoculate him or her against constructive criticism. Then when it comes time to share something important, the person is not interested. The best way to help shape someone's behavior is not through criticism but through encouragement.

Build Through Encouragement

While continual criticism dulls the listener's ears, encouraging words get his or her attention. Even when you feel you must confront a person, you can still encourage in the process. I personally use what I call the "sandwich" method. The two pieces of bread are the encouragement, and the meat in the center is the problem at issue. By starting and ending with something encouraging, we avoid undiluted criticism as well as keep tempers tame. Let me share with you what I mean.

Let's say my friend Mary calls daily with the latest news, and it's always bad things about other people—things that do not need to be said. This continues to the point that I feel I need to say something about it lovingly to Mary (Proverbs 25:11). I start with a slice of encouragement, telling her what I admire in her life: "Mary, I admire the way you are trying to put God first in your life," or "I have learned so much from you about service. I appreciate how much you help at church—you have such a giving spirit!" This lightens the conversation and takes a lot of the sting out of the rebuke I must share.

After the encouragement I add the meat—in this case, the gossip problem. It would be easy to tear down Mary with condescending advice such as, "Mary, if I were you, I would . . ." or, "Mary, you need to . . ." But it would be better to be empathetic by expressing things from her viewpoint. I might say, "Mary, you're always so informed; you know the latest about everything. I like to be informed, too." At this point my words become crucial, and I need to take time to give them some thought, because I don't want to devastate someone. I might say, "Mary, I look forward to your phone calls, but I think sometimes you and I mention things about people that would be better left unsaid. I sometimes imagine Jesus listening in; what can we do to be sure He would always be pleased?"

By including myself, I no longer put Mary on the spot. Together we come up with a solution, such as sharing with each other what we are learning from God's Word or each doing a topical study on gossip and then sharing the results.

Then I add the remaining slice of encouragement to the sandwich, ending with "I am glad God put you in my life," or, "I love you, my friend." With a little discernment, our words can be as welcome as "apples of gold in settings of silver" (Proverbs 25:11).

With all the encouragement we desire to give, it's best that when dealing with a major problem, we prepare the person for the talk by setting an appointment. I've known people who have been hurt unnecessarily because they, without warning, were hastily reproved at church or given a quick phone call. One person no longer attends church because of a few insensitive words. Rather than crush a person, our goal is to help the tottering to stand and to strengthen feeble knees (Job 4:4).

Listen Instead of Hollering

The Bible tells us that the key to being slow to speak and slow to anger is being "quick to hear" (James 1:19). Listening is a lost art, yet it is one of the most loving things we can do for another person. Listening enables us to "rejoice with those who rejoice, and weep with those who weep" (Romans 12:15). Also listening helps us become more compassionate while getting the "other side" of the story.

We can become skilled listeners (especially in stressful situations) using five techniques:

1. *Listen with your whole heart, soul, and mind.* Block out distractions such as children laughing, snow falling, the fly that keeps beating against the window, or Susie's piano lesson later that day.

Our care for the person will show as we give her full eye contact and an occasional nod and a response, showing that we understand and feel something of what she feels. Our full attention is enhanced when we sit in a way that shows we are relaxed and not anxious to leave. And while the other person is talking, we should not be thinking about what we are going to say next.

2. *Listen without interrupting.* While your husband speaks (we'll use him for the sake of illustration), you can show him you are listening by not interjecting questions or comments such as, "Why didn't you . . ." or "I thought you said you were going to . . ." Though there are times when it's important to speak, Scripture tells us there are also times when it's best to be silent (Ecclesiastes 3:7).

3. *Listen without passing judgment.* Often conversations get heated because we jump to conclusions, like the Red Queen's backward dictum in *Alice in Wonderland:* "Sentence first—verdict afterwards."[2] Passing judgment frustrates our husbands, children, or friends, who end up being defensive, trying desperately to prove their innocence. It would be better to defer to others, giving them the benefit of the doubt.

4. *Listen to what isn't said.* Sometimes we hear only the words but miss the real message. What a person is saying nonverbally often adds a lot to the story or even tells us the real story when words do not. Is there hesitancy in the voice? A sudden change in body position? A tight smile? A tired look on the face? A sudden breaking of eye contact? Swallowing or a licking of the lips? A revealing expression that lasts for only a fraction of a second? These clues can tell us things, especially when they fit a larger picture that includes what a person is saying with his or her words, how he or she is acting, and what you

know of his or her situation in life. Listening to the nonverbal message along with the verbal one can help us uncover exhaustion, pressure, disappointment, lack of honesty, and a myriad of other problems or issues. It can lead us to the real problem.

5. *Listen with God at your side.* As you listen to your husband, child, or friend, ask God to reveal Himself through you. Ask Him to show His love, peace, patience, and discernment.

Anticipate Problems and Prepare Solutions

Anticipating problems is key to controlling circumstances in such a way that they do not become overwhelming. For example, each morning prior to getting one foot out of bed and onto the floor, I pray that God will control my spirit and allow my responses throughout the day to be godly, since I anticipate that many things will affect me negatively. The children may fuss or quarrel, an appliance may break down, or my husband may stay late at the office. This is not being pessimistic but being prepared. It's amazing how much better I can deal with things when I am diligent to place them before the Lord and ask for His resources to handle whatever comes my way.

What about those times when we have anticipated and prepared for problems but still cannot avoid becoming upset? One method is to take a time-out. It does wonders! I once knew an athlete who taught me all about time-outs. Whenever he felt a referee had made a bad call, he would keep his temper in check by removing himself momentarily from the game. He didn't trust what would come out of his own mouth.

If I need a time-out, I try my hardest politely to excuse myself, go into another room, and pray or listen to worshipful music. If I cannot leave the room, I meditate on Scripture, personalizing it by putting my name before the verse:

- Donna, remember, "a gentle answer turns away wrath" (Proverbs 15:1).

- Donna, let your speech be "sweet to the soul and healing to the bones" (Proverbs 16:24).

- Through God's love Donna can be patient, kind, not jealous, and keep from acting unbecomingly (1 Corinthians 13:4-8).

By personalizing Scripture, I remind myself that God speaks to me, comforts me, strengthens me; and it is His Word I want to obey.

Lastly, though none of us wants to excuse wrong behavior, we must consider that sometimes a medical problem, such as a hormonal imbalance, is making things worse.

Overcome Physical or Medical Problems

I am one of those women who struggles with PMS. Medically it stands for premenstrual syndrome, and spiritually it stands for a lack of patience, mercy, and stamina.

All in my head? Not at all. I don't want to excuse unspiritual behavior, but to be fair, according to *The American Medical Association: Family Medical Guide*, PMS is a common problem in many women and can occur when physical or emotional difficulties upset a woman's hormonal balance.

Some physical disorders are evident from changes in the menstrual cycle, such as periods that are absent, infrequent, painful, or heavy. Premenstrual tension, the most common problem, is a combination of physical and emotional changes that often occur approximately seven days before a period. The main symptom is a change in mood, increased irritability, aggressiveness, or depression,[3] and lest we forget—a lack of patience.

Have you ever wondered about the woman who touched the fringe of Christ's garment? She had been bleeding for twelve years. I have often wondered what could have caused her hemorrhaging all those years without causing death. Though it's speculation, my guess is hormones. To confirm this I asked my Christian gynecologist. He, too, believes that the hemorrhaging was most likely a result of a hormone imbalance. How kind of God to put this story in Scripture for us women! What I appreciate most about this account was that Christ, before healing the woman said, "Take heart, daughter" (Matthew 9:22

NIV). Something about those words show so much compassion toward this woman who probably had her hormones "out of whack."

Likewise, the Lord offers this same compassion toward you— even when no one else around you understands. If you think you may have a hormonal imbalance that is disrupting your life, see a doctor who understands this problem. Even if you don't think you have a PMS problem, please be aware that hormonal imbalances aren't due only to that "time of the month." Some can be brought on by emotional stress, such as a quarrel or a stressful change.[4]

For a mild case of PMS (limited to one week out of the month or less), my doctor advised me to:

- exercise on a regular basis.
- stay on a healthy diet.
- stay off caffeine such as in coffee and chocolate for two weeks before my cycle (easier said than done, especially because that's when I crave chocolate most!).

So what about those days when I don't follow those guidelines (tisk, tisk)? Well, I begin to feel and, worse yet, look like Dr. Jekyll and Mr. Hyde.

On down days I try to deal with PMS through prayer, meditation, and song. Prayer comes first thing in the morning—crying out for help for the day. Meditation comes throughout the day as I dwell upon what I learned from the Word. And my singing also occurs throughout the day. Solo? Not me. To be sensitive to those around me, I sing along with uplifting music. It does wonders in keeping tension from surfacing.

This same technique can help those with physical disorders. Difficult? At times, yes. Some of my friends struggle with pain all day— every day. What has made it easier for them (along with prayer, meditation, and song) is finding a prayer partner who is struggling, too.

One church I know has a weekly Bible study for women who are suffering physically. A few friends of mine attend this study, and it has given them great encouragement and strength.

The most important lesson I have learned from my difficult

times is that no matter how lousy I may feel, emotionally or physically, and whether under a doctor's care or not, I cannot use health problems to excuse ungodly conduct in my life. Rather, I must draw on the power of Christ, who promises that "my grace is sufficient for you, for power is perfected in weakness" (2 Corinthians 12:9).

By developing internal restraint through practicing these principles, I have had much more control over my temper, especially during mishaps and disagreements.

And yet in this fast-paced world of demands and pressures, even my strongest internal restraints are severely tested. For example, since the industrial revolution, the pace of life has increased to an incredible clip. We now live in an age of the half-read page, the quick hash, and the mad dash,[5] which simply means we are always in a hurry. This can build up internal tension, which often affects the way we speak and the tone in which our words are communicated. Fortunately, there is a way to please God with our tongue even while living in the fast lane.

CONQUERING RUSH-HOUR LIVING

Have you ever been half-dressed, with hot rollers in your hair and makeup partially on, rushing yourself and everyone else along, trying to get ready for church? As you hurry to get the kids looking presentable and out the door on time, your tone of voice grows more and more impatient. Soon a sense of urgency gives way to frustration and then pure exasperation. You find yourself talking in a way you don't want to.

"Hurry, hurry, Kathy. Put down your dolls and get dressed for church. You can't go looking like that!"

"Michael, you aren't finished with breakfast yet? Hurry up and eat; we don't have all day!"

"Peter, why are you playing outside in your church clothes? I can't believe you would get mud all over them. Think, Peter, think! Now hurry and get changed before we're late!"

By the time you get everyone buckled into the car, with the motor starting, one of the kids inevitably says, "I have to go to the bathroom." By now you are fully frazzled and shout, "We're going to be late!" You arrive at church in no mood to worship, the kids are sulking, and you, too, just want to cry as you silently ask God's forgiveness for blowing it.

We can avoid exploding during the "rush hour" by planning ahead, even preparing the night before. We can lay out clothes and iron them, find the missing socks (I'm convinced the dryer eats them), give the kids a bath, and set the table for the morning.

During the time crunch, I have learned to be more realistic regarding what I can and cannot do. I cannot prepare a fabulous breakfast, get everyone's hair perfect, and have clothing crisp with every wrinkle nuked out. Some things will have to be sacrificed for the major goal of meeting a deadline.

It also helps to see the bigger picture. On Sunday, for example, remembering that we are going to worship the King of kings lets us not be so concerned about the crumbs on the table.

We often blow it under pressure when the trivia of life becomes more important than people. Yet people are ultimately more important than hair, clothes, and where the two hands point on the clock. People mattered in Jesus' life. When the disciples scooted the children out of the way so they wouldn't interfere with His busy schedule, He reproved them and spent time with the children. Do we scoot people aside to maintain our schedule? What should be the priority in my rat-race world? God would tell me that it's people.

We can put people first by embracing three important aspects of godly living. The first aspect is to rise above our circumstances; second, avoid strife with others; and third, replace negative attitudes with virtues.

Rising Above Circumstances

In an old movie, Jimmy Stewart portrayed a young man in love with a beautiful woman. Wanting to impress her in his simple way, he took her to the country to meet his grandmother. The young woman could not help noticing the older woman's peaceful nature, a sharp contrast to her own stormy temperament. Trying to excuse herself, the young woman commented that the grandmother's tranquility must have come from living in the country and escaping life's problems.

But the gentle old woman had seen plenty of troubles. "Out here in the country," she said, "I had a baby die at birth, a young husband die from a falling tree, children to raise on my own, and a flood that had us going hungry for a year." She added thoughtfully, "A woman doesn't amount to anything unless she can rise above it."

No matter what comes our way, rising above it is what gives us a gentle spirit, a controlled tongue, and the ability to think more of others than ourselves. Here are some things to keep in mind:

- *Think calmly.* God tells us to cease striving and know that He is God (Psalm 46:10). We can be calm because God is on the throne. He sovereignly controls all things in our lives, and His providence guides us (Psalm 48:14).
- *Think unselfishly.* When we focus on the needs of others, our own problems seem rather trivial. I have personally known a few people and have read of others who while dying were able to live out their remaining days in peace and joy by concerning themselves with other people's needs. One such person was John Eliot, referred to as "the apostle to the Indians." On his dying day in 1690, Eliot used his final hours to teach an Indian boy how to read. When Eliot's friend urged him to save his strength, he replied that as long as he had life, he would use it to serve others and that the little boy must learn to read.[6]
- *Think humbly.* God gives grace to the humble (James 4:6). Pride paralyzes us by keeping us more concerned about what others think than what God thinks. Instead of empowering us to rise above circumstances, pride motivates us to have a pity party. Humility lets us move beyond past failures and present difficulties to focus on serving God and others.

Avoiding the Beginning of Strife

God's Word tells us that "the beginning of strife is like letting out water" and warns us to "abandon the quarrel before it breaks out"

(Proverbs 17:14). From experience I see the value of this verse, for strife usually has a very small beginning. It may start with just one word that stabs at the heart. That little word, Scripture says, is "like letting out water." First, the hole is small, letting only a trickle of water flow through. The trickle quickly erodes the hole and soon becomes a stream and then gushes out of control.

A piercing word said to your husband, coworker, or friend—a word that was a small drip of water—can lead to more words and quickly become a torrent. Strife between two people usually ends up with an audience of others such as our children, friends, or coworkers.

Proverbs tells us to recognize the trickle and abandon the quarrel before it breaks out. Here are ways you can do that:

Stop and listen to the tone of voice. When the conversation is heating up, you are straying into a hot zone of potential strife.

Change the subject, postpone the discussion until a better time, or agree with the other person as much as possible, and then drop it. Jesus gave advice on settling large-scale strife, the sort that was on its way to court. He said to try to settle with your opponent before you get to court (Matthew 5:25). Whether big strife or small, settle it and abandon it as quickly as you can.

Recognize the issues worth striving for, such as what glorifies God and benefits people, truth, and the Gospel.

Watch your words. If you pause for a moment before you speak, you will avoid letting even a trickle get started. You can pause, bite your tongue, count to ten, pray, and of course recite Scripture to yourself.

Whatever you choose to do, the key is that you can gain control if you let thought rather than words be your first reaction. Reflecting a little before speaking (instead of after) makes for wise words that bring healing (Proverbs 12:18), fruitful words that bring satisfaction (12:14), and good words that make the heart glad (12:25).

OUT OF VIRTUES COME RIGHT WORDS

In a television drama, two friends were competing for the love of the same woman. One scene showed the two men in a parachute competition. After they both jumped out of the plane, one was horrified to see that the other's parachute did not open. He quickly maneuvered into position through free fall, tied himself to his friend's tangled canopy, and opened his own chute. The two landed safely. Then came the real shock. His rescued friend said nothing and just walked away.[7]

Jesus faced a similar situation. On the way to Jerusalem, He came across the most tragic sight in Israel—lepers. There were ten of them; because of their disfiguring disease, they were outcasts. They were required to live outside the city, cover their mouths, wear torn clothes, and shout, "Unclean!" wherever they went (Leviticus 13:45-46). Christ answered their heart-wrenching cries and healed them in an instant. But of the ten, only one returned to thank Him and glorify God (Luke 17:11-19). Where were the other nine?

This illustration shows us how we can do more than just refrain from wrong use of the tongue, such as gossiping, nagging, or arguing. We can express thanks, show graciousness, and be encouraging. It's helpful to remember that just as bad speech originates from wrong attitudes (Matthew 15:18), edifying speech comes out of right attitudes. Once we begin to transform those deeper attitudes, godly speech will follow.

I was impressed with this truth one day while waiting in a long line at the bank. It was a hot, muggy day, and in subtle ways people were making their impatience known to the tellers. While waiting my turn, I prayed for the opportunity to encourage one of the frazzled bank employees. When my turn came, I did my transaction and tried to be encouraging, but I felt as if what I said amounted to little more than small talk. The teller, putting down the paperwork, asked, "Are you a Christian?" Surprised, I asked how she knew. She said, "Talking to you, I can tell you spend time with Jesus."

That episode taught me something very valuable: Our tongue reveals who we are inside. Now when I speak, I frequently ask myself, *What kind of person do others see in me? What about my husband? My children? My friends? What about strangers? Am I kind, thankful, and encouraging—or mean, nagging, and gossipy?* Through pondering over these questions (which can be convicting at times!), I discovered yet another important key in the fight to control my tongue. It's called reflection. Whether we are striving toward increasing our internal restraints or conquering rush-hour living, or both—all that we do to please God with our tongue comes through the channel of reflection.

DISCOVERING THE POWER OF REFLECTION

The bank experience not only reminded me that my tongue reveals who I am inside, but it also showed me that the tongue that pleases God is the fruit of a godly life. Godly speech is the result of godly living, and that godliness is nurtured not by strain but by reflection: "We all, with unveiled face beholding as in a mirror the glory of the Lord, are being transformed into the same image from glory to glory, just as from the Lord, the Spirit" (2 Corinthians 3:18). Godly character is the result of a Spirit-empowered life. It is the Spirit who transforms our character to become more like God's as we continually focus on Him (2 Corinthians 3:18; Galatians 2:12). Beholding His character and keeping His example continually before us is the Spirit's way of changing us to be like Him.

Godliness comes as I set aside time each day to find God as He has revealed Himself in His Word. It means taking time in my busy day to contemplate, to think deeply about the character of God. It means thinking about God as revealed in the life of Christ. As Charles Sheldon put it in his spiritual classic *In His Steps*, we need to approach crucial decisions with the question, "What would Jesus do?" Becoming godly means finding examples of godliness in Scripture and in the lives of people around me as I dwell on whatever is true, honorable, right, pure, lovely, of good reputation, excellent, and worthy of praise (Philippians 4:8).

God Reflected in Our Words

One of the wonders of spiritual growth is that we don't have to sit passively and wait for it. We grow when we dwell on God and actively do what pleases Him (Philippians 2:12). A woman, for example, who depends on God to transform her into a kind person does so by dwelling on the kindness of God, finding examples of kindness in others, and thinking of kind things to say. In doing these things, she will surely become a kind person.

These same principles can be applied to other aspects of sterling character, such as compassion, gratitude, wisdom, and so on. When these principles are applied to our words, our speech will shine. Right attitudes enable us to master the art of choosing our words carefully. The end result? We will truly have tongues that please God.

A Fruitful Harvest

God takes pleasure in those who use their tongues to accomplish good, who can discern what to say and how to say it, and who thereby build up others. But we don't attain these good results just by trying to control our words. Because things like gossip and anger come from the heart, we need God's grace to change our attitudes. The result of these deeper changes will be a full harvest from the seeds of godly speech.

As Proverbs says, the tongue holds the power of life and death (Proverbs 18:21). We can encourage people and build them up, express gratitude and love, help the erring with gentle reproof, and share the Gospel with the lost. To God we can express worship and thanks, share our most intimate thoughts and feelings, and intercede for people and situations.

As we please God with our words and the attitudes in which they are communicated, our lives will reflect more and more of God's character. And God, like the goldsmith testing purified gold, will see a clearer and clearer reflection of Himself—in us.

Thinking It Over

1. How might you increase your internal restraints?

2. What goals will you set to conquer "rush-hour" living?

3. This week what could you do to begin developing the power of reflection?

Chapter 3

FRIENDS THAT
SHARPEN

At eighty-six Evie could no longer enjoy many of life's simplest pleasures, such as seeing in detail and hearing clearly. However, she had a simple pleasure many others, young and old, may never experience—the joy of loving others.

I watched Evie many times as she cheerfully helped those weaker than herself get to the dining room for meals in the retirement home where she lived. Whenever someone started coughing, Evie would get them water. She always had with her a black sweater, but others used it more than she did, because she was constantly putting it around someone else's shoulders. She reached out to the lonely who lived there and even to me as a visitor. Once she commented that I needed to wear jewelry. In spite of pain in her arthritic hands, she made me a necklace out of buttons. I wear it proudly to this day.

One day during a Bible study Evie made a sad but very profound comment: "Many of the people around here complain that their children never call them or visit them, but I am not surprised. Where were they when their kids were growing up? Did they give their children the love they so desperately needed? I believe many of these lonely people are seeing a reflection of themselves in their children."

Evie knew that people are responders: When they are loved, they love back. Evie was free from concerning herself about what she would get out of relationships. We need to remind ourselves that friendships cannot be bought. Certainly there must be mutual esteem, respect, and honor, but that isn't something we should expect, just as Evie's life revealed. Our focus in friendships should be more on giving love than on getting it.

CHOOSING OUR FRIENDS WELL

A very wise man named Aristotle said centuries ago, "Without friends no one would choose to live, though he had all other goods; even rich men and those in possession of office and of dominating power are thought to need friends."[1] Everyone needs friends, whether they admit it or not. Even Jesus needed friends.

Have you ever thought, even for a split second, that Jesus made a mistake when He chose Judas as a disciple and friend? I have. But trusting Christ, I have full confidence that He made the right choice, not only because I know the end of the story, but because of the steps He took in choosing His friends.

Steps in Choosing Friends

Jesus was a man of caution when choosing His disciples—His friends. Taking the high road of prayer, He prayed not just for a few minutes or even for an hour but all night (Luke 6:12-16). Jesus knew Scripture's age-old advice: "A righteous man is cautious in friendship" (Proverbs 12:26 NIV).

We too can be cautious. Prayer will keep us from making bad choices and will help us know the type of friendships to cultivate. God's Word will serve as our protector. We can find out about the best and worst kinds of friendships when we look up the word *friendship* in a concordance. For instance, Scripture cautions us about the risks of making an intimate friend of someone with an uncontrollable temper (Proverbs 22:24). In situations when we cannot find a specific verse to guide us, we can pray for wisdom and seek it from a godly person.

Another step we have to make in relationships requires discerning the influence we have on one another.

Influences

Influence is powerful, especially influence by example. Our impact on others is not something abstract but very real and active in our lives—for better or for worse. Though clearly seen in our small circle of family and friends, influence can travel far and wide. One life is impressed by the life of another. Long after we have left this world, our example can influence our descendants. What example will you leave? In the worst case scenario, we will affect future generations by our sins (Deuteronomy 5:9), or in the most blessed way, our lives will inspire those who come after us toward godliness (Deuteronomy 4:9; 6:5-7).

While we would like to think we can be a godly influence on our family, friends, and those around us, we must not forget their influence on us. Influence, for better or for worse, can change our convictions, our thinking, our actions, and even our beliefs. If being around a person weakens us or tempts us to sin in deed or attitude, we must ask ourselves a humbling question, *Am I strong enough to continue this relationship at this depth, or do I need to back off?*

I have known several women who have had to ask this very question in their friendships. Some have had to end a relationship due to the friend's gossiping, negativity, or worldliness. Some of my single friends have chosen to turn down dates with nonbelievers, even though it seemed that these men were the last available males on earth! No matter how sweet and wonderful the men seemed, these friends knew they could not afford to be dragged down spiritually. For good reason Scripture warns about becoming entangled in such alliances (2 Corinthians 6:14).

I've known other women who thought they were spiritually strong enough for such a dating relationship, believing that they could share the Lord and, if need be, cut the relationship at any time. But rarely does it work out that way. Usually missionary dating leads to missionary marriage, which eventually leads to evangelistic parenting. After a few years of that kind of spiritual drain, the women themselves are in need of—a missionary!

I believe there are two ways in which the Christian community can help women avoid that predicament as well as many others. First, we can utilize one of the greatest untapped resources in the church—the godly older women. Paul said that older women are to help teach younger women (Titus 2:3-4). We need to encourage the older women to share their maturity—the godly wisdom developed through years of joys, sorrows, mistakes, and victories. They may need an encouraging nudge because we live in a culture that devalues age and idolizes youth. Mature women and the rest of the church need to realize the valuable contribution these women can make.

Secondly, the church can emphasize the role that friendships have in Christians' lives. Friendships have a place alongside the husband-wife relationship, the parent-child relationship, and the employer-employee relationship. Some of us seldom think seriously about the role of friendships. Yet Scripture is quite serious about this role. It bids us to have a sharpening effect upon one another (Proverbs 27:17).

SHARPENING OUR FRIENDS

One evening when I was dating Brian he came to my apartment and surprised me with a long, narrow green box. It was decorated with a burgundy bow, and naturally my imagination went wild as I began opening it. Was it something delicate, like a few long-stemmed roses?

Opening the box, I found divinely scented tissue. I reverently took out the paper and put it gently on my lap. Then going back to the box, I looked inside. I just stared. Brian was all smiles, and I was, well, puzzled. "What is it?" I had to finally ask.

Reminding me that a few days earlier I had remarked that my knives needed sharpening, Brian took out a long silver thing by its black handle and went to the kitchen drawer and pulled out all of my dull knives. He carefully sharpened them against what he explained was hardened steel. The knives that had been dulled by cutting soft things could only be sharpened by something very hard.

Relationships with others can help us the same way. When one friend becomes dull, the other can sharpen her by offering encour-

agement and motivation, challenging her with ideas, and even pointing out blind spots.

Encouragement

There are so many ways to encourage a friend. You can send her a note
of appreciation or tell her the things you admire in her life, such as her
character. You can help her in the areas where she realizes she is weak.
One of the best ways I have found to sharpen through encouragement
is by helping a friend discern the area of her spiritual giftedness.

Though we explore "gifts that give" in another chapter, let me
just say that ignorance of our giftedness is not bliss. We stagnate and
fail to become all we could be for the Lord. Therefore, encouraging
our friends in this area not only sharpens them but transforms them
into more vibrant Christians.

We may need to be aware that the topic of spiritual gifts can be
discouraging to our friends in three ways. First, some people believe
they were overlooked when God gave out spiritual gifts, because they
can't see how they are gifted. My friend Anne struggled with this,
admitting that she didn't think she had a spiritual gift. I was shocked
because her giftedness was so obvious to me. She is the most giving
individual I know and loves to help anyone in need. I shared with her
how time and time again God had used her in my life (as well as in
the lives of others) through her gift of helps. The encouragement
brought a new spark to her spiritual life.

Since that time I have made a special effort to encourage my
friends in the area of their gifts. To do this I usually have to take special
notice of that area for a while. Does my friend have special compassion
for the lost? Is she the first to volunteer to help others? Does she show
leadership skills? Is she unusually hospitable? While watching for special strengths, I also ask her how she desires to serve. By combining
what I see with what she tells me, I can make a fairly accurate guess as
to how she is gifted. Then I know how I can encourage her.

Once a person knows her gifts, she can be discouraged in a second way, by comparing her abilities with others. She can feel others
are "better" at using the same gift. Being "better" can sometimes be

a matter of more experience or training. In this way those who are especially skilled and effective with their gift can become a role model rather than a source of discouragement. Being "better" may simply be a matter of greater opportunity—something we can't always control when we have other commitments and priorities. We can point out to our friend that God expects us simply to be faithful with the opportunities He gives us.

Another way a friend can be discouraged is thinking that her gift is somehow less exciting than some other gift. We can help her see the importance of her gift, reminding her that without her giftedness the world and the church could never be what they were meant to be. If you can think of ways she has already made a difference, share those things with her. We can remind her that heaven will be filled with people like her whose contribution may never have gained them one ounce of praise on earth but who gained great glory for God and won His praise.

Motivation

Motivating a friend takes a bit of discernment because people are spurred on by different things. We first need to know their level of motivation.

On the lowest level, people are motivated by potential for personal gain or loss. On the one hand they want to avoid pain, punishment, or loss; on the other hand they want to gain something worthwhile for themselves. A higher level of motivation seeks the good of others. The highest motivation strives to gain something for God, to glorify and please Him for His own sake.

Scripture has a lot to say about motivation. To be effective, we have to motivate people on their level. Paul, for example, recognizing that the Corinthians were still babes in Christ (1 Corinthians 3:1), motivated them on the lowest level, often speaking to them about lost rewards and the possibility of personal gain. He told them that facing Christ someday will be an experience of either personal gain or loss (vv. 15-17). He warned them that continual abuse of the Lord's table had resulted in the severest chastisement from God (1 Corinthians 11:30). He did not try to motivate these abusers with the idea they needed to change in order to glorify God more; they simply were not motivated on that level. He warned them they would face great personal loss if they continued their practices.

In discerning people's motivation, Jesus was especially sensitive to their needs. For instance, the tax-gatherers and sinners were despised by Jewish society, so He drew them to God by appealing to their need for love and acceptance—thus motivating them on a low level. This He did by telling them the parables of the lost sheep, the lost coin, and the prodigal son (Luke 15:1-32).

Paul knew Timothy had a genuine interest in others (Philippians 2:20). Therefore, he motivates Timothy on a higher level by telling him, at great length, how he can help the church with its worship (1 Timothy 2:1-8) and members' roles (2:9–3:16) and avoid spiritual dangers (4:6-16; 6:3-5), and so on.

Paul himself was motivated on the highest level, caring nothing about imprisonment and even death as long as God's message of grace was proclaimed (Philippians 2:17; Acts 20:24).

When we know that a person is motivated on more than one level—and most of us are—we can encourage that person accordingly. Paul, for example, told Timothy that his obedience would do something for himself and those he served; it would "insure salvation both for yourself and for those who hear you" (1 Timothy 4:16). Peter motivated his readers by telling them that God had done something for them, providing everything "pertaining to life and godliness" (2 Peter 1:3). But he went on to encourage them to add various moral qualities that would accomplish something for God and make them fruitful (v. 8).

So what motivates your friend? Is fear of loss primary? Does she live in fear of losing possessions, a job, a child, or a marriage? Here we can help her see these potential losses from an eternal perspective. Challenging her on a higher level, we can help her focus on how she can be a blessing to others in her family or on her job.

Does your friend already have a deep concern for the welfare of others? This would be a great time to motivate her toward putting those concerns to work in some sort of ministry.

Does your friend concern herself with God's glory? This is the time to motivate, sharpen, and strengthen her in her pursuit of godliness through a spiritual friendship (more about this later).

Sharpening with Ideas

Ideas can be one of the most vital sharpening influences we have on a friend. It all starts with tapping into what makes the friend "tick," what she is passionate about.

Peter had trouble in his relationship with Christ in this area. Christ's passion was to die for mankind, yet His friend Peter never seemed very interested, and consequently he never seemed to connect with Christ here. Instead of offering his support, Peter rejected Christ's mention of death (Mark 8:32), and even after Christ rebuked him for dismissing it (v. 33), Peter still tried to keep the inevitable from happening by attacking a soldier coming to arrest his Friend (John 18:10).

Understanding a friend's deeper drives and motivations can help you sharpen her with new ideas regarding the things she is passionate about. If, for example, the pro-life issue interests your friend, you could keep your eye out for developments in the news, go out of your way to read something on it, bring to her attention something she may not have thought about, or give her an idea that stimulates her interest even more. For example, has she ever thought about writing an article about it for a local paper or a Christian magazine? Has she ever thought about starting a pro-life ministry in her area? Has she ever wondered why God has given her such a burden? Is there a role for her to play?

Another way to sharpen with ideas is to let her know what you are passionate about. This helps both of you since she can grow from sharing your interests, and you benefit from new ideas she gives you.

Eliminating Blind Spots

Pointing out another's blind spots requires a lot of sensitivity and tact, but it can be a great help to the friend. Moses, for example, could not see how overloaded with work he had become until his father-in-law, Jethro, brought it to his attention. Jethro got right to the point, asking, "Why do you alone sit as judge and all the people stand about you from morning until evening" (Exodus 18:14)? He pointed out, "The thing that you are doing is not good. You will surely wear out, both yourself and these people who are with you, for the task is too heavy for you; you cannot do it alone" (vv. 17-18). Jethro's godly counsel helped Moses regain his effectiveness.

People can easily develop blind spots, something that keeps them from being effective for the Lord. It could be anything from spreading themselves "too thin" to being overly talkative or unorganized.

HINTING

When pointing out blind spots, we may not be able to be as blunt as Jethro. The tactful way to get the point across can be a subtle hint. Hinting deals with an issue indirectly. We can, for example, mention how we overcame a struggle in hopes someone will see it as a solution to their own problem.

Just recently a woman named Carol wrote an article for a newsletter. At the end she included a Bible verse that warned against complaining (James 5:8-9), adding simply, "Please join me in working on this one." In no time five women individually approached Carol, each thinking she had directed the message specifically toward her—and some of them were quite upset. This completely surprised Carol because she really had no one in mind but herself! That's how deeply indirect mention of something can affect people!

GODLY COUNSEL

Before we try to point out a person's weak spots, directly or indirectly, we should first consider whether it is our place to do so and whether we have earned the right in that person's eyes.

I raise this issue because we all have probably known people who seem to believe it is their divine calling to correct everyone on everything. Christ warns about being overly judgmental (Matthew 7:1).

Peter may have made the same point. After mentioning that obedient Christians are likely to suffer, he describes some things they should never suffer for. One was for being a "troublesome meddler" (*allotriepiskopos*, 1 Peter 4:15).[2] While the meaning of the word isn't clear, by the fourth century it came to mean a busybody, one who interfered in other people's business.[3] This type of person acts as if he or she has been invited into someone's life, oversteps the boundaries, and actually meddles in another's affairs. The meddler suffers strained relationships and rejection.

So before we become overly zealous to point out blind spots, we need to determine if we are overstepping our bounds. It may help to ask ourselves what credibility we have. Does the friend see us as persons who are not trying to gain something? As persons who can overlook a transgression (Proverbs 19:11)? As friends who love unconditionally and will "stick closer than a brother" (Proverbs 18:24)? And as friends who are themselves living spiritual lives (Galatians 6:1)? If so, we are more likely to build up our friend with our advice, especially if we offer it in a spirit of gentleness while looking to our own weaknesses (Galatians 6:1). If our friend is seeking wisdom, and if we use tact, the friend will love us more for gently pointing something out (Proverbs 9:8b).

Now that we have focused on ways we can sharpen others, let's look at a friendship in which we can sharpen one another within a spiritual framework.

SPIRITUAL FRIENDSHIPS

In our day-to-day friendships we are accustomed to sharing in each other's lives and talking about one another's house, hobby, and interests. And there is nothing wrong with that. But how often does God come into our relationships?

Pastor and writer Gary Inrig once made the following confession: "Few things have challenged me so much over the past few years as the examination of my friendships to discover whether I have encouraged my friends in God. To my shame, I must confess that many of my friendships have been alarmingly shallow because they have lacked the specific concern to encourage in God. Oh, we might both have been Christians, but how little we focused on Him."[4]

His confession can be echoed by so many of us. Yet we need to realize that God won't be the focus of all our relationships, not even all the Christian ones. I discovered that fact years ago when I was getting to know a Christian woman who shared a lot in common with me. I thought things were going very well until she startled me with the question, "Do you always have to talk about the Lord?" It caused me to do some serious thinking for several weeks and to evaluate my other relationships.

I came to see that something I desired in a friendship could be found in only a few people—those who also want what I call—a "spiritual friendship." Spiritual friendships encompass the spiritual dimension of life—our relationship with God, our spiritual gifts, encouraging and strengthening each other in God. It is not only a blessing but a protection as we strive to keep each other on track.

Taking a Look Inside

One thing that can keep us from sharpening one another in the Lord is ungodliness (though we may think we are godly). We can take a candid inventory by asking ourselves a few key questions.

Am I a woman of the Word? A woman who daily studies God's word is sensitive about her own walk with the Lord and trusts the Holy Spirit to lead her (1 Corinthians 2:15).

Am I a woman of habitual prayer? Prayer has been called the "Christian's breath."[5] To neglect it is to neglect God. Only a woman who knows God through prayer can be near to the heart and mind of God.

Is my life hidden in Christ? The woman who knows that her life is nothing without God (Galatians 2:20) can stay close to Him and be joyfully submissive. She knows that God can work through her to be a blessing in the lives of others.

If we can answer yes to the above questions, we are ready to develop the spiritual side of friendships.

Developing a Spiritual Friendship

Developing a spiritual friendship starts with the simple goal of sharpening each other in the things of God within the context of everyday life. As Deuteronomy puts it, "when you sit in your house and when you walk by the way and when you lie down and when you rise up" (Deuteronomy 6:7).

Deepening an existing relationship into this area will usually have to take place slowly. You can start by encouraging one another in the Word and prayer naturally as things come up. For example, if your friend is going through a great difficulty, you can let her know you are praying. Then check with her to see how God has answered. (This is important; often we tell others we will pray but then never follow up with an inquiry.) You can also ask what benefits or lessons she has gained during the trial. This will help your friend focus on the spiritual gain that difficulties often bring (Romans 8:28). It will help you learn something, too. In the process you may have an opportunity to share a struggle of your own and invite her spiritual input. The key is that you make the effort to pull each other up.

Digging Deeper—Spiritually

One creative way to start going deeper is to find out your friend's "spiritual birthday." In our family we celebrate the "new birth" because we believe it is just as important as the first birth. If you can't recall the exact date of your spiritual birth, then pick a day that has affected you the most in your spiritual life. Or if you are not sure that you have ever truly sought forgiveness for your sins, trusted in Christ alone for your salvation, and have a personal relationship with Him, then do so today. (For help, turn to "A Decision to Make" at the back of the book and mark today as your spiritual birthday. See 2 Corinthians 6:2.)

Spiritual birthdays are a great time to remember God's goodness and love and the lessons He has taught us. The one having the birthday can perhaps share what it was like before coming to Christ and retrace the bumpy road that brought her where she is today. This can lead naturally to prayer requests for further growth. Then you can end the birthday party with prayer for your friend. (By the way, the time together is even sweeter when we can find a spiritual birthday gift that will enhance and encourage the growth of the friend.)

Here are some other creative ways to move into the spiritual dimension. Lend a book you have been reading and talk about it together. Or better, you can each get a copy of the book and go through it together. Agree to study a portion of the Bible at the same time. Share with each other a praise. Recite memory verses to each other.

You could challenge one another by finding cassette tapes of sermons or testimonies that really help you to grow. This activity can become a great blessing, especially if done on a regular basis. I will never forget one special afternoon when I gathered a small group of spiritual friends into my living room to listen to the Focus on the Family cassette tape titled "I Will Never Leave Thee," the story of Darlene Rose. (For those of you who have never heard Darlene's story, I encourage you to get the tape.)

We all sat quietly as Darlene told how she went to New Guinea as a nineteen-year-old newlywed missionary. Then during World War II, her husband was murdered, and she was confined in a Japanese prison camp.

At the end of the tape we were all wiping our tears and silently reflecting. After a few minutes, we talked about Darlene's message and discussed ways we could develop the same love and devotion to God. We all grew from this special time and challenged each other in the weeks ahead.

There is another sharpening effect that spiritual relationships tend naturally to foster. It is called accountability. When the two of you are women of the Word, praying and striving to follow Christ, you have the credibility to come alongside each other and to keep each other on track spiritually. It can be as basic as asking one another whether you have spent time with the Lord that day. Or you may get into more serious issues, such as sin that may be creeping into your lives.

It is in this kind of growing, committed friendship that we are willing to make sacrifices for each other so that both of us will become all we can be for God.

THE PRAYING HANDS OF A FRIEND

Rarely in our world do we hear true stories of friends that are dedicated to one another, who seek to sharpen each other. Let me share with you one such friendship—between the artist Albrecht (Albert) Dürer (1471-1528) and his roommate.

When Albert was a boy, he had a strong desire to draw and paint, but he resigned himself to assisting his large family by working in his father's trade. As time went on, his father insisted that Albert's life had another purpose and gave his blessing to Albert to leave home and study with a great artist.

While Albert studied art, he worked to support himself. But times were hard, so he eventually found a fellow artist to share his apartment and the expenses. However, the two still could not make ends meet.

When the two realized that the struggle to survive was conquering their dreams, Albert's roommate made an offer: "This way of working and trying to study is intolerable. We are neither making a living, nor are we mastering our art. Let us try another way. One of us could make the living for us both while the other continues to study. Then when the paintings begin to sell, the one who has worked may have his chance."[6]

Albert thought it over and agreed, offering to be the one to work first. But Albert's new friend refused, giving three reasons: He already had a job in a restaurant, was older than Albert, and was not as talented.

So Albert worked diligently to master his art while his devoted friend worked full time washing dishes, scrubbing floors, and doing whatever else was needed at the restaurant. His hours were long, and the work was tiring, but he never complained, knowing that he was enabling Albert to sharpen his skills.

Finally the day came when Albert received a large amount of

money for a wood-carving project. It was enough to buy food and pay their rent for a considerable length of time. Now the friends could trade places.

So Albert's friend exchanged the dishcloth and mop for a brush. But as he began to paint, he discovered that he had worked so hard with his hands that his muscles had stiffened, his joints had enlarged, and his fingers had become twisted. No longer could he hold the brush with skill. He knew that he would have to give up his dream forever.

Albert was grief-stricken over his friend's plight. Though he would always care for his friend financially and give him a friend's love, he knew he could never give him what he had wanted most.

One day when Albert returned home unexpectedly, he heard his friend's voice in another room. He quietly opened the door and found his friend on his knees in prayer with his toil-worn hands folded. Leaving his friend undisturbed, Albert thought to himself, *I can never give back to those hands their lost skill, but I can show the world my gratitude for his noble, unselfish character; I will paint his hands as they are now, folded in prayer.*[7]

Those hands can be seen in the famous painting *Praying Hands*. As dramatic as the painting is, graphically revealing broken finger-nails, enlarged knuckles, and swollen veins, I believe that the magnificence of the painting isn't in the stroke of the brush but in the message of unselfish love toward a friend.

We can show this same unselfish love because of the spiritual bond we have with our friends. With commitment and sacrifice, we can build up one another (1 Thessalonians 5:11), serve one another (Galatians 5:13), bear one another's burdens (Galatians 6:2), admonish one another (Colossians 3:16), care for one another (1 Corinthians 12:25), teach one another (Colossians 3:16), encourage one another (1 Thessalonians 5:11), speak to one another in psalms, hymns, and spiritual songs (Ephesians 5:19), comfort one another in the Word (1 Thessalonians 4:18), and, perhaps with folded hands, pray for one another (James 5:16).

Thinking It Over

1. What steps will help you in choosing the right friends?

2. This week how are you going to sharpen your friends?

3. What does a spiritual friendship entail? Whom might you ask to become a spiritual friend?

Chapter 4

FREE FROM
POSSESSING

Let us take a trip back in time to the year 30 B.C. We are on the streets of Rome, and the outdoor market bustles with merchants and farmers selling corn, cattle, wine, spices, and much more. As we look around, a man with a long white robe beckons us. He introduces himself as Horace, the poet, the earthy critic of Roman society.[1]

He invites us to sit with him and observe his world. He points out a group of gabbing women buying silk dresses from Rome. Others are buying pottery from Arrentine, perfumes from Campania, gems from Parthia and Persia, and cosmetics from India.[2] But when our guide realizes that we wish we could buy some of the exotic things we are seeing, he frowns, shaking his head in disapproval.

Hoping to instruct us, he points out an older couple shuffling through the commotion of the market. "They live in the city, but they long to live in the country," he said. Then he gestures toward a young couple enthusiastically appraising goods. "They live in the country but wish they could live in the city." He shrugs his shoulders and asks, "Can these people ever be happy?" Without waiting for an answer, he emphatically says, "No, they can't! They will never enjoy what they have because they always want something they don't have. They want to live somewhere else; they want more livestock; they want the latest fashions; but above all, they want more money than they have. They think that more money can buy them more life!" Lowering his voice, he mutters, "Money-madness is the epidemic of Rome."[3]

We try to suppress a smile, but he perceives our amusement. "Why do you laugh at Tantalus?" he asks.[4] We remember the fate of

Tantalus, the king whose punishment for eternity was to stand near water that always moved away whenever he tried to drink. While under branches of a fruit tree, he would never be able to reach the fruit, no matter how close it appeared. The perceptive poet bids us to take his musings to heart. "Change the name," he warns, "and the story is about you."[5]

IS THE STORY ABOUT US?

I think we could take some of Horace's insights to heart because, like Tantalus, you and I and the rest of humanity tend to strive for things that are unattainable.

I found this to be true of myself when Brian and I were moving out of our apartment into a house. I was so excited finally to have some real closet space! Wanting the move to go smoothly, I assigned each room in the new house a number, and each box was tagged with the room number it would go into. On the day of our move, I told all our helpers how my system worked and asked them to put the boxes in the closets of their assigned rooms.

But the first helper to enter a room shouted to me downstairs, "Donna, there is no closet in this room!" I went to investigate. He was right. I looked in another room, only to find a very small closet, less than three feet square. We had the house built for a very reasonable price, so I didn't pay much attention to the house plans. I just thought large closets in all rooms was normal for a home, so it never dawned on me that once again I would be stuck with too little closet space.

For the next five years we kept a lot of our things stored in boxes. Not even all of our modest wardrobe could be hung. The day came when we decided to add onto the house. I told my husband, "I don't care how the addition is designed as long as I have lots of closet space." But my dream master bedroom became smaller and smaller as we had to modify the foundation, allow for a stairway, and make room for six-inch interior and exterior walls. The room became too small to put a closet in!

In my frustration I began to lose perspective. Fortunately I came across a Scripture passage that helped me take my focus off things. Christ was rebuking the prosperous farmer, who reasoned with himself: "This is what I will do: I will tear down my barns and build larger ones, and there I will store all my grain and my goods. And I will say to my soul, 'Soul, you have many goods laid up for many years to come; take your ease, eat, drink and be merry'" (Luke 12:17-19).

After reading the verse, I saw the big problem; it hit me between the eyes. The problem wasn't in the farmer being prosperous—God gives the power to gain wealth (Deuteronomy 8:18). Nor was it in his enjoyment of the things he had—God "richly supplies us with all things to enjoy" (1 Timothy 6:17). Nor did there seem to be any indication that he had gained his wealth dishonestly. So what was the problem? The farmer was living for himself without an eternal perspective. He was in a world of his own making. Through my frustration with a lack of closets, I came to realize that not only did my dissatisfaction keep me from appreciating the blessing of a larger home, but worse, I was allowing the things of earth to crowd out spiritual values.

Those We Love

Tantalus forever longed for things out of reach, and of course we can too. We can also cling to things we have, perhaps becoming very controlling in our effort to hold onto them forever.

I saw how tightly I could hold onto my children when Johnathan was having serious health problems. I feared for his life. What mother wouldn't have a similar fear for her own child? But I sensed my fear had become a problem when I realized that I wasn't considering God's will in the situation. I was not submissive to God's plan because, as I saw it, Johnathan was "mine." I was as possessive of him as anything else I "owned." It wasn't until much breaking of my spirit that I could finally admit to God that Johnathan was indeed His and that I would submit to whatever plan He may have for the little boy He has entrusted to me. I saw how my spiritual life would be damaged if I did not learn to "let go" of my children and of everything else.

LETTING GO

After tragically losing his new wife, C. S. Lewis wisely told his grieving stepson, "You can't hold onto things—you have to let them go."[6]

Do you have difficulty letting go?

Are there people you can't leave in the Lord's hands, trusting that He will do what is best with them?

Are you preoccupied with worries that something will happen to your children even after you have taken all reasonable steps to protect them?

Are you afraid to break up with your boyfriend even though deep down you think it may be God's will to do so?

Are you jealous when a close friend develops other friendships? Do you fear that you are losing your friend as a result?

Do you expect your husband and/or children to meet all your needs?

If you can answer yes to any of these questions, then possibly you are holding on too tightly to these people. And what about other things? Throughout the ages, God has tested His people's loyalty. Is it to Him—or to possessions and people? Loyalty is connected with trust because we are loyal to what we believe will sustain us.

I personally have been learning from Scripture that there are two things I need to keep discerning for my life. One is whether I see things as possessions for myself or as part of what I manage for God (along with managing my spiritual gifts, life's opportunities, and so on). And the other is whether my life's priorities focus on God first and then others.

Discerning Our True Allegiance

Scripture's Hall of Shame includes a number of people who put possessions over God. Achan, for example, took forbidden things from a conquered city (Joshua 7:20-21) and brought disaster on himself, his family, and his nation. Ananias and Sapphira lied about how much they had donated (Acts 5:1-10); God made an example of them, taking their lives. Lot's wife (whom we are warned to remember in Luke

17:32) had such a grip on her possessions that she disobediently indulged in one last, longing gaze at the sinful place that meant too much to her. She perished in God's wrath on the spot and "became a pillar of salt" (Genesis 19:26).

These people are like the two daughters in Proverbs. They are called "Give" and "Give." Their names warn us that the human heart never has enough (Proverbs 30:15).

Convicted by this insight, I have often searched my own heart, asking myself, *Am I discontented with what God is fostering in my life? Do I resent it when He has to take something away or cause a delay to accomplish His purposes? Am I content to go without some things for the sake of spiritual growth? Am I more interested in holiness than in the "good life"?*

It is not always wrong to desire certain things—much of what we desire is probably a form of blessing that comes from God. But I am learning that if I do not keep looking to Him as the source of my life, security, and happiness, I can become more preoccupied with His blessings than with Him. When we lose a proper focus, we have confused our priorities.

Life's Priorities

It was a day that David would never forget. After a three-day journey, he and his men were looking forward to coming home. But when they arrived, they were horrified to find the whole city burned, their loved ones taken away into slavery by the barbarous Amalekites. They wept until they could weep no more. Blinded by bitterness and rage, the men talked of stoning David. But what is so amazing in this story is that in the midst of such tragedy and confusion, David was able to keep his priorities straight. Instead of falling apart emotionally, he "strengthened himself in the Lord his God" (1 Samuel 30:1-6). It enabled him to seek counsel from God with a heart ready to do as he was directed. No wonder God told David to chase the enemy and empowered him to recover everything.

Hannah also had a life-changing experience. She gave birth to a son whom she named Samuel. How remarkable this day was! For years she had thought of herself as unable to conceive. Despite her doubts, she still fervently prayed for a child, promising that if she got pregnant, she would keep her priorities in order. What were her priorities? She would give her child "to the Lord all the days of his life" (1 Samuel 1:11).

Both David and Hannah kept God as their highest priority—one while in great distress, the other in great blessing. All else—people and things—were secondary to what God was trying to accomplish in and through their lives.

Putting God first above all other things isn't always that easy. Why? Well, as with David, who had to make a dangerous pursuit, and as with Hannah, who gave her son to the priest to raise, putting God first means we have to leave the familiar.

The Fear of Change

A lot of us are quite comfortable with the known. It's the unknown we hate, so most of us dread change of any kind. Many of us, for example, would not want to sell our house and move. Though it may not be Primrose Lane, we are used to it. We know the schools, our children's friends, and our church. We have made progress getting our house the way we want it, and the thought of starting over on everything isn't appealing at all!

Contemplating a job change may not seem appealing either. For some people, even taking their vacation in a new place is a venture into the unknown. And then there is the really radical change. What if your husband said one day, "I think I am being called into the ministry"?

For some of us, our biggest dread is the day our children move out of the house. How dare they grow up! Or even worse, one day our son might say he wants to be a policeman or a politician, or our daughter says she feels called to a faraway mission field. No! We beg them, "Get a safe job," or "Stay close to home."

Unfortunately God's will for our life or for our child's life can be forfeited by fear of the unknown. A parent's fear of what may happen can suffocate a child's God-given desire, overturning years of training that child to pursue His will.

On the other hand, if there is something we absolutely do not want to do, it is possible that God does not want us to do it either. For example, if you are scared speechless that God might call you to the mission field, you probably aren't called. If you were truly called, you would more likely fear that God would not call you. That is because God often works through our desires, at least through our sanctified desires. To know the difference it is best to check our motives—we can save ourselves a lot of headaches. We should also check our motives before we attempt to steer another person's life, such as our child's.

Whatever we finally conclude that God desires of us, there is one final step. We must be willing to let God bring changes into our lives, our husbands' lives, and even our children's lives. So much of what we have—our homes, spouses, children, churches, and other things—are so important to us. God gave us people, places, and things to enjoy. While we are thankful for these pleasures, I personally must remind myself that part of that thankfulness is learning to let go. The loving God who gave may one day change our plans and take away. And no matter how dreary or even frightening those changes may appear to be, my fear of the unknown must be put to rest in the will of God. Let's for a moment take a look at Abraham.

Our Fear—God's Will

Abraham was quite content in Ur, one of the most advanced cities of the ancient world. But God told him to leave the security of his home and his country and even leave the people who spoke his language. In return, God gave Abraham a promise that in leaving all behind, he would be given land and descendants. It sounds great, but read the fine print: "Know for certain that your descendants will be strangers in a land that is not theirs, where they will be enslaved and oppressed four hundred years" (Genesis 15:13).

Would you would want such a promise? I can't say that I would, but Abraham did. Despite the bleak outlook for some of his descendants, Abraham committed himself to God and His plan. And because of that trust, Abraham was blessed with descendants that would carry the lineage of the Messiah, who would bless millions throughout eternity.

Like Abraham, I can feel threatened by uncertainty about the future, but I have to realize that God's blessing can come in the shadow of insecurity. There may be some grim fine print; yet God is in the business of affecting my life and the lives of all who are touched by me.

Naturally, this is easier said than done, but I have found that letting go is easier when I focus on the "glory that is to be revealed to us" (Romans 8:18), believe that God has my best interests at heart, and use all I have to the glory of God.

FOCUSING ON THE GLORY TO COME

Let me share with you something that has been quite sobering to me. Two elderly women I knew, Molly and Joan, were very preoccupied with their possessions, which they saw as bringing them comfort, pleasure, and even status. (How many of us have ever done the same thing?)

Well, about an hour before Molly died—and knowing full well that she was dying—she lay in bed inquiring of her son, "What is to become of my beautiful *china?*"

The son patted her hand and with an awkward chuckle said, "Mom, forget the china."

In a low tone Molly confessed, "I can't."

In time Joan also lay dying. I jogged over to her house to see how she was doing, and that very day the doctors had told her that she had little time left. Despite the news of her imminent death, she tired herself uselessly yearning after new furnishings (call it denial or a misplaced sense of self-preservation, if you want). She described in detail the style and color of furniture she wanted and where each piece would go.

Looking at her worn-out body, I asked, "Joan, does it really matter? Shouldn't you focus on other things?"

But just as I was about to share one more time God's love for her and His desire that she know Him, she said with disgust, "Just look at this furniture! I can't stand it any longer!" On and on she went. I couldn't get a word in edgewise.

Just four weeks later Joan got her wish. Her new furniture arrived all right—made out of mahogany, with beautiful burgundy cushioning. It was ornate and graceful. Joan lies in it to this day.

There is much truth in the statement, "The way you live is the way you die." What will we focus on toward the end of our lives? It all depends upon what we focus on now.

The Uglies

While things can be ugly, nothing is more ugly than wrongdoing. And when we see the wrongs in ourselves, it is not a pretty sight. As long as our focus is only on the earthly, our discernment is not keen enough to make our own shortcomings very apparent. But once we change that focus to the things above, we can see more clearly where we can grow.

Sometimes when I reflect, what I notice most are my attitudes. There are times when I focus so much on the little things that I get completely frustrated, especially when things around the house need fixing. On one of my better days, my response might be to henpeck my already very busy husband. I have to align my values with the bigger picture. I remind myself that the Lord could take me home today. He could even return today; but even if not, life is short. In light of that, does it really matter so much that the bathroom needs a new coat of paint?

The uglies emerge in our personalities when we overindulge ourselves. Solomon warned of this dead-end road to fulfillment when he said, "I built houses for myself, I planted vineyards for myself; I made gardens and parks for myself, and I planted in them all kinds of fruit trees . . . all that my eyes desired I did not refuse them. I did not withhold my heart from any pleasure . . . behold all was vanity and striving after wind and there was no profit under the sun" (Ecclesiastes 2:4-5, 10-11).

Though we may not have Solomon's resources for indulgence,

we can misuse our more modest income. I never thought much about this possibility until one night the local news ran a story on impulse spending. A reporter stood at the mall and gravitated toward anyone with bulging bags in both hands. Interestingly, they were all women.

One woman gleefully showed the television audience how much she had bought that day, confessing that shopping was not just a hobby—it was her life. When the interviewer probed a little, the woman admitted she had no savings account because she could not control her spending. It was like alcoholism, she admitted, except that it did not hurt anyone. Watching, I said out loud, "Oh, yes, it does!" Irresponsible spending does hurt when legitimate needs go unmet. I knew that firsthand.

When I was single and on a very tight budget, I had (and still have) a love for missions. Knowing missionaries sacrifice much, I thought I could sacrifice also by giving monthly to at least one family. And so I did, until the day I went to the mall. I spent too much on sale items that couldn't be returned. Because of this overspending, I didn't have enough money to send my support that month to under-supported missionaries who depended on my giving. I broke out all over with a case of the uglies.

Failing to control our impulses can keep us from serving the Lord in many ways. Not only can we be kept from supporting individual missionaries, but we can be kept from supporting whole ministries (including our church) or from helping people who may come across our path with real needs.

There is no telling what God can do through our lives just by the way we use our resources. Whatever His plan, I have found I am better off when I am looking upward rather than getting caught in the downward spiral of wanting and spending on things that I don't really need.

GOD HAS OUR BEST INTERESTS IN MIND

Do you ever wonder why some people seem to "have it all" and you don't? I must admit, I have.

I have—when I once struggled with our lack of closet space. I have—when I drive in our only car that has nearly 300,000 miles on the original engine.

I have—when I have felt isolated living in a beautiful but remote place partly because we can't afford to live in the city where my husband works (if only Horace could hear me now!).

Yes, I have sometimes caught myself wondering why I don't have things others seem to have. But I know I'm not alone in this. The psalmist was puzzled over why the righteous seem to lack what the unrighteous have. The unrighteous don't seek after God; they boast about their evil desires; their mouths are full of curses, deceit, oppression, and mischief. Yet they seem to prosper all the time (Psalm 10:3-7). Why?

Though we may not know the specific answer, we can be assured that whatever the details, God has our best interests at heart. He gives an inward peace and strength that are better marks of His love and provision than any material item can communicate. God comforts the righteous with the knowledge that He is the eternal king, the helper of the fatherless, the judge of the oppressed, and that He hears the desires of the humble (Psalm 10:14-18 KJV).

What words of consolation! *We are not forgotten by God!* Keeping that one truth in mind, instead of dwelling upon what we "lack" and what others have, gives us the opportunity to go deeper with God.

Spiritual Depth

Since being hit by a drunk driver some years ago, I've been nervous about driving long distances. I never thought that one day I would have to drive considerable distances to go virtually anywhere—to church, stores, and even my husband's work. At times the hour-and-a-quarter drive each way gets to be a chore. Yet God knows what He's doing. I have had to lean more on Him than ever before. I pray constantly for our safety, for our car to "make it" to our destination, for my spirit not to be anxious about the crazy drivers on the freeway. Such dependence upon the Lord would never have developed in my life had everything come easily to me.

The greater reliance on God has also helped me focus on what I have rather than think about what others have. The result? I can genuinely rejoice in others' prosperity. At times it takes a little effort, but it is the only way to develop spiritually.

I realized the importance of being glad for other people's good fortune while in the hospital recuperating from the miscarriage of our first child. The morning after surgery, while I was still trying to recover emotionally, my nurse briskly walked in the room and announced ecstatically that she just got news she was going to have a baby. While checking my blood pressure, she chattered away about wanting a girl so she could clothe her in pretty dresses with frilly bows in her hair, but of course her husband most likely wanted a boy so he could . . . As the nurse gleefully shared her dreams, I just wanted to sob. I began to wonder, *Lord, why are You putting me through this? Haven't I been through enough? How insensitive this nurse is. I wish she would be quiet and leave me alone.*

Fortunately the Spirit of God put an end to my pity party and brought to my mind the example of the apostle Paul. He rejoiced in the blessings of others. He was thrilled to watch people be blessed—it was his reward. Despite his own trials, he joined his own happiness to that of others, having learned to "rejoice with those who rejoice" (Romans 12:15). This reminder allowed me to rejoice with the nurse, forgetting my own hurts, and strengthened my faith that God will take care of me. After all, He has my best interests in mind.

Where Should Our Focus Be?

All too often we focus on the things of this world. Yet its beauty is so temporary, withering like a flower in summer heat, fading like a sunset. Weeds overgrow our garden, paint dulls, furniture cracks, dishes chip, and wrinkles emerge on a once-young face.

No matter how hard we may try, we cannot preserve earthly beauty. But there is a beauty that God preserves—one that shall never fade. Paul the apostle thought a lot about this beauty. He spoke of it as "glory that is to be revealed to us" (Romans 8:18), but he also regarded it as incomprehensible (2 Corinthians 4:17).

There were others who looked toward this glory. They were the men and women in the Hebrews Hall of Faith. Resisting seduction by the things of this world, they sought after "a better country, that is a heavenly one" (Hebrews 11:16). It meant being strangers and exiles on this earth (Hebrews 11:13). Because these foreigners focused on things above, earthly objects could not crowd out spiritual values. Therefore, "God is not ashamed to be called their God" (Hebrews 11:16).

So where is this glory, this better country? It is a place where each moment is better than the last, reaching to eternity. Because of the Light that outshines the sun, the darkness of evil shall never have a place there.

Until we get to this glory, we are bombarded with temptations to settle for mere earthly, passing beauty. But such a fraudulant trade comes at a price: We lose the assurance of God's promises; His Word becomes less of a priority and thus less of a joy; our security in God gets traded for things of far less value, such as a secure bank account or a retirement fund (Proverbs 18:11); we can build up a false sense of significance connected with passing things, such as friends, wealth, or status (Proverbs 14:20).

The most damaging thing this seduction can do is make us forget our whole reason for living here on planet earth. We were created not to pursue the comfortable life, but to care for people the way God does. Christ showed how much He cared for the human soul when He gladly exchanged the shining courts of glory, not for something better, but for something worse—poverty, suffering, shame, and death—rather than allow us to perish (Philippians 2:6-8). Throughout His life and in His last hours, He chose to put people above earthly things. One of His last acts was to win a soul (Luke 23:42-43). One of His last prayers was for forgiveness for His tormentors (Luke 23:34). His last command before ascending to heaven was to make disciples (Matthew 28:19).

All of this shows us that living with eternal glory as our goal means living our life by helping others, investing in others, praying for others as a priority. The result? Heaven with its lasting beauty shall not be as much a place of beautiful things as a place of beautiful relationships. That is what will make it a place without locked doors, burglar alarms, police, lawyers, judges, psychologists, or even armies. Above all, it will be a place of a relationship with our Lord, His majesty and glory filling all of heaven. That is why despair will be replaced with joy, discouragement with hope, and doubt with trust. It is no wonder that Paul said he preferred to "be absent from the body and to be at home with the Lord" (2 Corinthians 5:8). Paul realized how earthly beauty dims compared to what lies ahead. Infinity isn't large enough to include all that our eyes shall behold. Eternity isn't long enough to thank God for His unfathomable mercy on sinners like us.

TO THE GLORY OF GOD

"Truly I say to you," said Christ, " that one of you will betray Me" (Matthew 26:21). We, of course, know whom Christ meant, but the disciples didn't. They never suspected it was Judas. They were asking, "Surely not I, Lord?" (Matthew 26:22).

Judas did everything the other disciples did. He followed Christ in the heat, walked dusty roads, and sometimes labored far into the night. The tragic difference was in his motives. Anyone can appear to be doing great things for the glory of God and yet be doing the right things for wrong reasons. We need to discern our own motives.

Discerning Our Motives

Discernment enables us to tell the difference between identical acts done for different reasons. Two people can tithe, attend church, share the Gospel, and be kind to others—but for very different reasons. We can do the most spiritual things with the most selfish motives.

How can we discern when we have impure motives? It's not always obvious, but often it has to do with who gets the credit. If we want others to notice us, like us more, respect us, or remember us fondly, then chances are that our motives need changing.

All of us can easily succumb to drawing attention to ourselves. We can gain the outward signs of success, such as degrees, a career, money, and beautiful things. Scripture tells us that the self-glorifying person is likely to say, "My power and the strength of my hand made me this wealth" (Deuteronomy 8:17). God has a different opinion about where blessings come from (Hosea 2:8-9). The more self-centered we are, the more prone we are to praise ourselves, crediting ourselves for everything. Of course it isn't wrong to recognize our achievements or surround ourselves with things we like, but ultimately we have to give credit to God.

There was a family that lived such a God-centered life, giving Him all the glory in all they had—their children, successes, assets, giftedness, and even their losses. They were the Spafford family.

Horatio G. Spafford was a successful attorney and businessman who lived with his wife and five children in Chicago. In 1871 his only son became ill, and with little warning the boy died. A short time later a devastating fire broke out in Chicago, destroying much of the Lake Michigan shoreline property, including most of Mr. Spafford's extensive real estate investments.[7]

On November 21, 1873, Mrs. Spafford and the remaining four children—Tanetta, Maggie, Annie, and Bessie—boarded the French liner *Ville du Havre* to cross the Atlantic to France. In calm waters the steamer collided with a large sailing vessel.

As everyone began to panic, Mrs. Spafford quickly brought her daughters to the deck. They knelt in prayer with one specific request—that God would spare them if it was His will or make them willing to die if that was His will.[8]

Within a few hours, the ship slipped into the icy Atlantic. Only unreserved commitment to God gave Mrs. Spafford the strength to endure as one by one, her children quietly lost their battle with the sea. Then Mrs. Spafford was rescued when a sailor spotted her floating in the water. Nine days later she landed safely in Cardiff, Wales. From there she sent her husband the grim, terse message: "Saved alone."[9]

Mr. Spafford set sail to join his wife in Wales. At a point in the passage, the captain came to his room and told him that they were now passing over the spot where the other ship had gone down. Grieving for his daughters, he went on deck to gaze over the waters that had claimed their lives. While he prayed, he was comforted with an overwhelming sense of God's presence. Looking down at the vast ocean, knowing that his daughters' remains were somewhere hundreds of feet below him, he meditated on the redemptive work of Christ and the promise of His return.[10] He later told a friend that "poetic thoughts began to shape themselves in my mind."[11] Returning to his cabin, he wrote:

> *When peace, like a river, attendeth my way,*
> *When sorrows like sea-billows roll—*
> *Whatever my lot, Thou hast taught me to say,*
> *It is well, it is well with my soul.*
>
> *Tho Satan should buffet, tho trials should come,*
> *Let this blest assurance control,*
> *That Christ hath regarded my helpless estate*
> *And hath shed His own blood for my soul.*
>
> *My sin, O, the bliss of this glorious tho't—*
> *My sin, not in part, but the whole,*
> *Is nailed to the cross, and I bear it no more:*
> *Praise the Lord, praise the Lord, O my soul!*
>
> *And, Lord, haste the day when my faith shall be sight,*
> *The clouds be rolled back as a scroll:*
> *The trump shall resound, and the Lord shall descend,*
> *"Even so"—it is well with my soul.*

This hymn, written over the grave of Spafford's beloved daughters, has comforted millions. Mr. Spafford could gain emotional victory because he never held on tightly to his financial investments nor even to his children. The Spaffords could say with the psalmist, "Whom have I in heaven but Thee? And besides Thee, I desire nothing on earth. My flesh and heart may fail; but God is the strength of my heart and my portion forever" (Psalm 73:25-26).

Not holding things too tightly and remembering the unspeakable glories of the life to come (Romans 5:2; Colossians 1:27) can help us keep a proper perspective on earthly possessions. Christ Himself gave us an additional way to maintain right priorities. "Do not lay up for yourselves treasures upon earth," He said, because that kind of treasure doesn't last. It is liable to disintegrate or be stolen. Instead, "lay up for yourselves treasures in heaven . . ." (Matthew 6:19-20). We simply compare the value—one lasts; the other does not.

Our challenge then is this. We live in a society where people are prone to overvalue earthly things or to cling possessively to people they think can bring them happiness. But we must be willing to forego pursuing things for their own sake and instead use things to do heavenly good—which will mean using them to serve people. In so doing, our lifestyle becomes one in which we turn our eyes on Jesus, "look full in His wonderful face, and the things of earth will grow strangely dim in the light of His glory and grace."[12]

Thinking It Over

1. Read 2 Timothy 2:4. What things entangle you and keep you from putting God first?

2. Reflect and pray about your attitude toward possessions and toward others. Why do you want things, or why do you want a certain relationship?

3. What steps can you take this week to free yourself from possessiveness?

4. How might you focus on the glory to come?

Chapter 5

POSSESSING

ALL THINGS

They had everything vibrant Christians could ever want. Some had earthly wealth, but some did not. Some were popular, but others were despised. Yet all of them had one thing in common—they had learned the secret of "possessing all things." Such was the case, for example, in southern France.

The queens of Navarre, Queen Margaret (1492-1549) and her daughter Jeanne (1528-1572), were passionate about the Reformation. They opened up their palace to the reformers, allowing them to use it as a place from which to preach the Gospel of Jesus Christ throughout France.

When Queen Margaret died, she took her possessions with her to heaven and Jeanne continued the ministry. As the new queen of Navarre, Jeanne established a large grant for a college of theology and financed household chaplains to translate the New Testament into the Basque dialect.[1] Upon her death, she too did not relinquish her possessions.

Lady Armyne (1594-1675) became concerned about the fate of the Indians of New England and gave generously to those who could reach them for Christ. Selina, the Countess of Huntingdon [sic] in England, shortly after her conversion in 1739, used her assets to erect chapels throughout England and build a college for preachers at Trevecca.[2] These women too took their precious possessions to heaven.

Others have been poor and yet have made many rich (2 Corinthians 6:10). Catherine Booth (1829-1890) had little cash, but she used her God-given abilities to raise money in order to start rescue houses and missions throughout the world. Through her efforts many orphans, prostitutes, and alcoholics discovered Christ. The ministry was named The Salvation Army.

Florence Nightingale (1820-1910) desired more than anything in this world to serve in the church. But unfortunately no ministry was open to her.[3] So she took her gifts, talents, and love to the secular world, working as a nurse. Her compassion for the hurting became apparent to all, and she became known as "The Lady with the Lamp."[4]

Then there was Amanda Smith (1837-1915). Born into slavery, her life changed forever with emancipation. Yet being spiritually freed by Christ changed her more. After the death of her husband and youngest child, she used her remaining years to serve the Lord in an evangelistic ministry on four continents. She, like the other bygone saints, took her possessions with her to heaven.

So what were the possessions these women valued over riches, time, or comfort; that motivated them to labor long and sacrifice so much; that outlasted their earthly lives? Their possessions were spiritual treasures gained through knowing the character of God, introducing people to Him, and serving those who know Him. Those bygone saints gained and kept true riches because they valued what God values.

In our day it is so easy to value the wrong things—wealth, prestige, and beautiful possessions. Yet these things have never impressed God. They have yet to bring true happiness, and we can never truly possess them. More likely they possess us.

Valuing what God values is the only route to true wealth. So what are some of these valuables that surpass man's treasure? To name a few, love (Proverbs 15:17), righteousness (Proverbs 16:8), integrity (Proverbs 28:6), and God's Word (Psalm 119:72). To value them is to be discerning.

The ability to choose them over things of lesser value—the ability to distinguish true riches from those we cannot take with us—is called wisdom. When we have wisdom, then we know we are on our way to "possessing all things."

WISDOM

Wisdom! It sounds so . . . mysterious. We all long for it, but it is easily mistaken for other things. I know. I used to think that such things as knowledge, success, or even certain attitudes constituted wisdom.

These days we are awash in knowledge but starved for wisdom. For instance, we can now plug into the Internet and instantly have access to more facts than previous generations could gain in a lifetime! Amazingly, knowledge in some fields doubles every few years. But knowledge, while valuable in its own way, amounts only to raw data about the world (even when it is actually truth and not just disguised opinion). Knowledge can be mistaken for wisdom because, like wisdom, it tells us about the world. Yet knowledge cannot tell us what to do with our time and money, what to work for, whom to spend time with—those daily choices that develop godly character. Knowledge does not discern the relative importance of things, which is what we really need if we are to make good choices.

British playwright Oscar Wilde once told a U. S. customs official, "I have nothing to declare except my genius."[5] Though he probably regarded genius as a great gift, it pales in comparison to the value of wisdom. As Tennyson said, "Knowledge comes, but wisdom lingers."[6] Its effects outlast this life.

When I was a college student, I used to mistake success for wisdom. If I did something well, such as getting good grades or getting a job other people would have wanted, I considered that I did it wisely. People tend to think that a family who gets a suitable house for a good price and a low mortgage has acted wisely. Success seems like wisdom because it reaches goals in the real world. Wisdom, if it is anything, is the ability to understand and act in the real world. But wisdom is more than that. Wisdom knows the right goals in the first place. I have learned that anything—even the wrong things—can be done successfully. The person who has wisdom knows what to aim at in the first place, not just how to hit a target.

Wisdom is sometimes mistaken for certain attitudes. Some people associate it with an otherworldly aloofness. I recently read in a Christian magazine about a woman who prided herself in not "wasting" her time driving her children all around town—as if the truly wise person is somehow above mundane things such as driving kids to soccer or even helping with a church bake sale. The wise person takes only to "spiritual" things, such as reading the Bible, singing hymns, and sharing the Gospel with lost sinners. While wisdom does change our values because it is based in an eternal perspective, wisdom is expressed in the simple, common things of life. So wisdom leads us to the world—but with the right attitudes; it does not take us out of the world.

Sorrow, too, is sometimes mistaken for wisdom. For instance, have you ever noticed people who can't seem to "lighten-up"? They never smile or laugh. Some of them believe that the truly wise person carries the weight of the world on her shoulders, is preoccupied with the world's pains and lostness, and sees the futility behind every passing joy. On this view, wise people rarely smile or laugh, would never tell jokes (except perhaps those that show the extreme folly of sin), and eventually develop heavy, down-turned creases on their faces—from so much . . . wisdom!

It is true that wisdom can bring some sorrow. Solomon himself said, "In much wisdom there is much grief" (Ecclesiastes 1:18). Wisdom brings awareness that so much of the world is out of harmony with God and that so much of what is regarded as good falls so far short of what it could be. And having the wisdom to see that there is a problem does not mean that we have the ability to change it. But on the other hand, a wise person knows that ultimately God is in control and that somehow His purposes are being accomplished (cf. Habakkuk 3:17-19). Truth, justice, and love will win out eventually. Therefore, wisdom can give us that higher perspective that brings joy no matter what the circumstances. Jesus was no doubt the wisest person who ever lived, and He was also joyful. He promised His (sorrowing) disciples that they would have His joy (John 15:11).

Wisdom—the real thing—brings many gifts to those who pursue it. Its value is said to be above precious jewels (Proverbs 3:13-15). While material wealth never seems to be enough and so never satisfies, the spiritual wealth from wisdom is fulfilling. What's more, wisdom makes us teachable and thus able to get more wisdom. And wisdom brings with it peace, security, and sometimes even earthly prosperity.

How do we get this wisdom? Well, we are told that it can't be purchased (Proverbs 17:16) but that it is obtainable (Proverbs 2:2-11). King Solomon, having received from God the wisest and most discerning heart (1 Kings 3:12), gives us his advice (from Proverbs 2) for obtaining wisdom. Let's take a look.

The Attentive Ear (Proverbs 2:2)

I am completely deaf in my right ear. Whisper in it, and I won't hear a thing. When I am in a noisy room, I can't make sense out of anything being said. Once at a church potluck (we all know how noisy those can get!) a man came up to talk to Brian and me. Though he didn't know I couldn't hear him, he stopped mid-sentence and asked, "Why are you reading my lips?" I was embarrassed and felt like I was caught doing something wrong. Hiding my chagrin, I explained how hard it is for me to hear with a lot of background noise. It takes all of my concentration, all my attention, to block out everything else and focus on what is being said.

We are told to put the same effort into listening to the voice of wisdom. To be attentive (*kashav*) means to sharpen.[7] We are to take dull ears and make them keen toward wisdom.

Can you recall a time when you didn't have a sharp ear for godly advice? During such times it's easy to make choices we regret later. I can recall more than a few times over the years when I didn't heed godly advice. I even remember why I wasn't listening. Usually it's pride that defeats me. When I am proud and overconfident, I feel I do not need to seek wisdom from anyone. Sometimes pride makes me hide the fact that I do not "have it all together." If I let on that I need to grow in wisdom, I reveal that I am not already a super-Christian.

I am learning that I must swallow my pride so that I can be teachable and attentive to wisdom, which is found so abundantly throughout Scripture. As Scripture says, "with those who receive counsel is wisdom" (Proverbs 13:10). How can we discern whose counsel we should receive?

DISCERNING THE COUNSEL OF OTHERS

Being attentive to wisdom doesn't mean that we take advice from anyone who wants to give it. It means we must humbly evaluate whether the advice we are seeking is godly or not. We can ask ourselves if this person has a grasp of God's Word.

Years ago I knew a woman who diligently read the Ann Landers column in the newspaper. Though some of the advice was sound, I wondered why she, or anyone else for that matter, would want to get advice from a newspaper counselor. The mixture of homey chat and shrewdness wasn't usually based on Scripture. If advice has no spiritual foundation, we shouldn't feel compelled to act on it.

We must ask also if the advisor has common sense. Wisdom includes a certain amount of common sense. I have known people who can quote plenty of Scripture but could not apply it to practical situations. Their advice, though peppered with verses, led people in an unscriptural direction.

Others cannot necessarily quote Scripture, but they do have common sense. The men whom the Persian King Ahasuerus consulted regarding Queen Vashti were called "wise men who knew the times" (Esther 1:13). It's unlikely they knew any Scripture, but they had insight into practical matters.

Ideally, of course, we want counsel from someone whose common sense is backed up by the Bible. After all, there are times when "common sense" collides with the right thing to do.

Does the counselor have a good reputation? Daniel was a statesman and counselor to heathen kings, and they recognized the value of his great wisdom. There must have been many others of great learning who were more willing to say what the ruler wanted to hear just to gain personal favor. Not surprising, it was Daniel who had the spotless reputation. It was to him they turned for the most crucial counsel. His advice was never self-serving. Of course, a person's wisdom has value only insofar as it is in harmony with Scripture.

THE BOOK OF WISDOM

God's own words provide wisdom. When we are confused, when we need refreshment for the soul, God's Word feeds us and makes us whole. It comforts and cheers us and directs us in the way we should go. What depth we draw from its pages!

The Bible gives us not only principles but a living example, the Word made flesh (John 1:1, 14). Solomon was known as a wise man, but as the Wonderful Counselor Himself (Isaiah 9:6), Christ far surpasses even Solomon. As a child in Nazareth, Jesus "kept increasing in *wisdom* and stature and in favor with God and men" (Luke 2:52; emphasis added). Unlike the wisdom of ordinary men, Christ's wisdom was united with a pure, sacrificial life and complete victory over sin.

God exhorts His children to listen to the whole counsel of His Word. They are told to "remember the law of Moses" (Malachi 4:4), to keep His word in mind continually as they sit in their houses, take walks, lie down, and rise up in the morning (Deuteronomy 6:7). A rich life in the Word will guide us and refresh our hearts, souls, and minds. Such a life amounts to delighting (or indulging) ourselves in the Lord (Psalm 37:4). Like bygone saints we can be shielded (Proverbs 2:7), preserved (Proverbs 2:8), guarded (Proverbs 2:11), discerning (Proverbs 2:9), and delivered from the evil one (Proverbs 2:12).

Inclining Your Heart to Understanding (Proverbs 2:2)

I remember one day in high school algebra I exasperated my teacher. "Donna, when will you understand?" he said. He saw I wasn't putting much effort into understanding. He knew I had the ability and that I just wasn't paying attention because my heart wasn't in the subject.

Inclining our heart to understanding means that we give our whole self to it. It takes that kind of close attention because we have to go beyond merely gathering information. We have to know how to apply it, how to use it.

Pharaoh is an example of a person who failed miserably to grasp and use wisdom. He refused the warnings of Moses and then failed to learn anything from circumstances (Exodus 7:22-23). Though the lessons were obvious, he failed to make use of them. The results were devastating.

Inclining our heart to understanding requires following Solomon's advice by using wisdom to discern our options and choose the best one. In a practical sense, the need to choose applies to only one small area. It does not apply to God's sovereign will—that part of the divine plan that determines everything that will happen in the universe. God has worked that out, and there is nothing for us to decide. And God has already determined what is right and wrong—those moral guidelines that do not change because they are based on His holiness, having to do with lies, murder, adultery, etc. Where we need discernment to choose is in applying these moral guidelines to our own lives. How should we, for example, be loving, sensitive, and responsible, given our priorities and resources? How do we apply God's will and general moral commands to our own daily lives?

Take for example the principle of diligence extolled in a number of verses (Proverbs 12:11, 24, 27; 13:4). If I were a student, for example, I would think about getting to class on time, doing all my homework well and on time, paying my tuition on time, and studying for exams thoroughly and ahead of time. If I had a job, I would ask myself if I were careful to meet and, where possible, exceed all expectations. With my family I would make sure my time with my husband and children was protected from the tyranny of lower priorities. Also I would see that cooking, cleaning, staying within the budget, and my other responsibilities in keeping the house running were done to the fullest and best.

I could also think about specific areas of life rather than principles. At work am I being diligent, sensitive to people (Galatians 5:22), open to reaching others with the Gospel (1 Peter 3:15), submissive to those over me (2 Peter 2:18)? Scripture is a treasure trove of guidance waiting to be applied to our lives. But it takes a little thought and discernment to apply it to our personal situations.

Some of life's bigger questions are a little more complicated. Should I, for example, become a missionary or commit to some office or ministry within our church? Should I marry? Should I have children? If so, how many? These require discernment on a number of issues, such as how God has gifted me. Who benefits from what I do and how? What opportunities are open to me now? What are my deeper longings? Answering these may require a lot of reflection about Scripture and ourselves and input from discerning people.

There are still deeper issues involved in God's will. Discerning God's will really requires that we align our desires with His. Keeping detailed rules or applying guidelines without the heart motivation is akin to legalism. Israel was criticized for its rote obedience (Isaiah 29:13), and so were the Pharisees (Matthew 23:3-5, 23). So in this deeper sense, obedience involves the whole person.

An example of this is delighting in God, which results in God giving us the desires of our hearts (Psalm 37:4). To delight means to find our satisfaction, joy, and comfort in something. Years ago I literally thought that if I delighted myself in God, He would give me anything I wanted. Many others think the same and regard it as a way to get the boyfriend, husband, or children they want. But, as I've been learning, this isn't what delighting myself in God means. Writer Paul Little explains that as we delight ourselves in the Lord, we come "to will with Him one will."[8] He meant that we will only desire those things God wills for us. This is the key toward having an understanding heart. So Pharaoh's spectacular failure was ultimately the result not of missing a few guidelines but of his being so far from God in his heart.

Cry for Discernment; Seek Understanding (Proverbs 2:3)

This plea for understanding is earnest, almost desperate. It shows the intensity and sincerity we should have in our quest for discernment. Halfheartedness is not enough.

Seek Wisdom as Silver (Proverbs 2:4)

My son Johnathan is a true seeker. If he has lost a toy, he will do whatever he must to find it—unload the toy box, take off the bed sheets, empty the closet, unload the dresser drawers, clear off the bookshelf. Nothing can deter him. He persists until he finds his treasure.

I have often thought that I need to be more like him when I seek wisdom. I need to check the chambers of my heart, unload all its toys, search in the prayer closet earnestly, and leave no page of Scripture unturned.

Such spiritual passion will be rewarded with discernment and wisdom. And it will lead us to something else—the fear of the Lord (Proverbs 2:5).

THE FEAR OF THE LORD

When I was a child, I feared God in a very negative way. I always imagined Him sitting on His throne, holding a fly swatter. One false move and . . . zap! I feared Him all right but out of ignorance.

Even as Christians we can lose sight of a healthy fear of God. We can fear that He is angry with us for past sins, waiting to get even. And thinking of Him as unpredictable, we can dread what He will do next.

True Fear

When I fear something, I act a certain way because I respect its power. In that sense I can have a proper fear of speeding cars and lightning. Usually, though, if I act properly, I need not dread what something will do to me. For example, in a thunderstorm, I can come indoors. From there I can admire the power and majesty of the storm, unafraid of harm.

I think of fearing God as a little like that. Having accepted His love and forgiveness, I no longer dread that He will harm me. I appreciate His power and majesty—but of course I still order my life in a way that pleases Him. This kind of fear is more respect and awe than dread; its opposite is indifference rather than bravery.

Those who do not fear God do not care what pleases or displeases Him. They are likely to transgress His will because they don't care about Him. Ironically, those who do not fear God have the most to be afraid of; those who fear Him need not dread what He will do to them—because of His loving nature.

Awhile ago I talked with a Christian woman whose fear of God consisted almost entirely of a dread of what He would do to her. Not surprisingly, it became obvious as she talked that she was more aware of her imperfections than of God's love for her. Knowing our natural tendency to be in dread of God, John wrote, in a context of judgment, "There is no fear in love; but perfect love casts out fear, because fear involves punishment, and the one who fears is not perfected in love" (1 John 4:18). If I have accepted God's loving forgiveness, I need not dread what He will do to me. Understanding that He loves me makes me respect Him more. As the psalmist wrote, "If you, Lord, should mark iniquities, O Lord, who could stand? But there is forgiveness with thee, that thou mayest be feared" (Psalm 130:4 KJV).

One day as the prophet Nehemiah was praying, he used a phrase that shows us how much God's children desire to fear Him. He asked, "O Lord, I pray, please let Your ear be attentive to the prayer of Your servant, and to the prayer of *Your servants who desire to fear Your name* . . ." (Nehemiah 1:11 NKJV).

God's Name

In ancient times names were chosen for their meaning. A name encapsulated the most important feature about someone or perhaps what a parent hoped a child would become. To know someone's name was to know something important about the person.

Knowing God's name means knowing Him. And fearing His name means being in awe of who He really is. So when Nehemiah talked about servants "who desire to fear Your name," he meant people who want to know Him and be in awe of who He really is.

Nehemiah connects knowing God for who He is to the worship of God. The prophet records the praise of the Levites, who said, "Blessed be Your glorious name, which is exalted above all blessing and praise!" (Nehemiah 9:5 NKJV). When we know God truly, awe and worship follow naturally. Elsewhere in Scripture reverence is also linked to obedience (Genesis 22:12; Jeremiah 26:19).

Nehemiah was energized by zeal for God's reputation, and in a sense he led others to fear God. In the opening of the book, he was deeply grieved by the fact that Jerusalem was destroyed and its people were in reproach (1:3). His opening prayer mentions Jerusalem as the place where God had chosen for His name to dwell (1:9). The prophet's tireless and brilliant efforts focused on restoring respect for God by restoring respect for God's people, city, and program.

No wonder Nehemiah's soul was awakened, seeing God's blessing and action everywhere. He excitedly proclaimed, "the good hand of my God was on me" (2:8), "the God of heaven will give us success" (2:20), and "God turned the curse into a blessing" (13:2).

Can you recall a time when your soul was so alive to God and His name? When you wanted people to know Him better and respect Him? I can recall such times in my life. Usually they were after answers to prayer. My confidence is strengthened, and my praises of God become quite reverent as I try to think of every attribute to describe everything about Him and the name behind my awe.

Fearing Nothing Else

When Nehemiah set out to rebuild the walls of Jerusalem, he had no idea he would have to deal with mockery (4:1-3), conspiracy (4:8), usury (5:7), false accusations (6:6-7), and treachery (7:10). What kept him "together" under the onslaught? Again it was the fear of God. It has been said that the person who fears God fears nothing else.

Nehemiah demonstrated his singular fear by praying to God (4:9), remembering that the Lord is "great and awesome" (4:14), and believing without a doubt that "our God will fight for us" (4:20). We can have the same comfort Nehemiah and other people of God had because God is no respecter of persons (Acts 10:34).

A Healthy Spiritual Life

A healthy fear of God was a central part of Nehemiah's rich spiritual life. He feared God but was not afraid of Him. He reverenced God's infinite holiness, justice, lovingkindness, power, and wisdom.

Nehemiah's fear was that of a son for a loving father, not of a slave for a tyrannical master. True fear of God recognizes that He has our best interests at heart, even when He must discipline us for our good (Proverbs 3:11-12).

Scripture links this healthy fear with happiness (Psalm 112:1), goodness (Psalm 31:19), lovingkindness (Psalm 103:11), and fulfilled desires (Psalm 145:19). All these things we can possess on earth and take with us to heaven. Best of all, like the bygone saints, we are and shall be in possession of Jesus.

> *Wherever we turn in the church of God,*
> *there is Jesus.*
> *He is the beginning, middle and end*
> *of everything to us. . . .*
> *There is nothing good, nothing holy,*
> *nothing beautiful, nothing joyous*
> *which He is not to His servants.*
> *No one need be poor, because, if he chooses,*
> *he can have Jesus for his own property and possession.*
> *No one need be downcast, for Jesus is the joy of heaven,*
> *and it is His joy to enter into sorrowful hearts.*
> *We can exaggerate about many things;*
> *but we can never exaggerate our obligation to Jesus,*
> *or the compassionate abundance of the love of Jesus to us.*
> *All our lives long we might talk of Jesus,*
> *and yet we should never come to an end*
> *of the sweet things that might be said of Him.*
> *Eternity will not be long enough to learn all He is*
> *or to praise Him for all He has done,*
> *but then, that matters not;*
> *for we shall be always with Him,*
> *and we desire nothing more.*

—FREDERICK FABER[9]

Thinking It Over

1. Contrast God's wisdom and worldly wisdom.

2. What steps can you take toward becoming a woman of wisdom?

3. What does the "fear of the Lord" have to do with being more discerning?

4. What thoughts, attitudes, or actions must you change in order to have a healthier fear of God?

6. What are the benefits you receive as a result of properly fearing the Lord?

Chapter 6

USING THE
TIME OF YOUR LIFE

This morning, February 19, at 7:30 A.M., I answered the phone. A shaken, fragile voice said, "Debbie is now in the arms of Jesus." All day I have been in tears, and even as I type, I can't stop the stream. *Why now?* is my initial thought. From a human perspective my dear friend Debbie had her entire life before her. She and her husband, Darrell Fisher, had finally completed the long preparation to become missionaries to Africa. How happy they were! After many years of education and four years of training, two of which were in Africa, they could now focus upon the ministry they had been called to do. While home on furlough, they thought about their hopes and dreams of getting back to Africa to spend many years, perhaps a lifetime, serving as Bible translators. But two days before their departure, anticipation dissolved into dread when Debbie was diagnosed with cancer. She would never return to the land and the people she had grown to love.

I know that God could have easily healed Debbie. I prayed so often that He would. And yet, as I sit here, I realize my prayers for her have been answered—though not the way her friends and family desired. Debbie is healed, her battle is now over, and her perishable body has now put on the imperishable; mortality is now immortality. Truly, "death is swallowed up in victory" (1 Corinthians 15:53-54).

Yet even though there is victory, I still struggle. Is it because Debbie was such a godly woman? A mother of three young children? A missionary? My friend? Is it her youth or the vast amount of experience she had in ministry or the years she invested in language training that leaves me with so many unsettling questions?

In the broadest sense, death itself causes me to ask why. In one sense I must resign myself to the fact that God's thoughts are not my thoughts. His ways are not my ways (Isaiah 55:8), and the secrets of His counsel are known to Him alone (Deuteronomy 29:29). But in another sense Debbie's death is forcing me to think about the earthly dimension of this thing called *time*.

Musing about time and God's plan leads us to the stark realization that there is a special day on the calendar for each of us, a day different from any other in our life. It is our last day on this earth. It will pass like any other day. The sun will rise and set again, and the human race will continue to go on its way with its joys and sorrows. The only difference is that for us, there will be no more time to live.

Meanwhile, time, like an unstoppable chariot, races at a steady pace ever and only forward. Realizing this, Moses prayed that he and the rest of God's people might become more discerning by understanding the brevity of life. "So teach us to number our days," he prayed, "that we may present to Thee a heart of wisdom" (Psalm 90:12). David prayed, "Lord, make me to know my end, and what is the extent of my days, let me know how transient I am . . . surely every man at his best is a mere breath" (Psalm 39:4-5c).

Such prayers may seem a bit morbid in our feel-good age. It sounds as though these spiritual giants could not enjoy life, preferring to sit in a mortuary awaiting their turn to be buried. While not suggesting that we be morbid, Solomon implied that the kind of thoughts a person has at a funeral are not at all alien to a wise person (Ecclesiastes 7:4). The preciousness and brevity of life are to have a prominent place in one's heart. A discerning person does not lose sight of the fact that time is very limited. And knowing that helps her value the best things—which is a foundation for discernment.

MAKING THE MOST OF OUR TIME

Christ had but a few years to change the world. With so little time and so much to do, what was His formula for using time wisely?

First, He never stopped thinking about time. He knew its value: "Are there not twelve hours in the day?" He asked (John 11:9). He knew when He had a bit of time left (John 7:6) and when He did not (Matthew 26:18). Most importantly, He lived by the hour (Mark 14:35, 41; John 4:3; 12:23, 27; 13:1; 17:1).

Christ knew the preciousness of time. He knew of the glory that soon awaited Him in heaven, which made His time on earth that much more crucial. Now was the time to plant seed, before "night is coming, when no man can work" (John 9:4). Now was the time to bring words of compassion, truth, and life—to bring kindness and healing.

Life, minute by minute, goes by only once, and I have learned only too well that when I misspend time, I can never get it back. Time moves relentlessly like the hands of a clock. All too quickly will my abilities to serve God and others evaporate into thin air.

The second attitude that enabled Christ to use time wisely was an awareness that the hours had been entrusted to Him. Time wasn't His to spend carelessly. He was to use it according to the will of the Father (Matthew 6:10; John 14:10). Paul emphasizes this point when he tells the Ephesians, "Do not be foolish, but understand what the will of the Lord is" (Ephesians 5:17). In other words, he was telling them not to be careless, thoughtless, or lackadaisical in their use of time. The only way they could avoid misuse of time was to possess a perfect understanding of God's will.

The Master's Will

Because the days in which Paul lived were evil (sound familiar?), he exhorted not only the Ephesians but all Christians to use time wisely by discerning God's will for their lives (Ephesians 5:16-17). Paul says that the way to understand God's will is through renewing the mind (Romans 12:2). Why the mind? Because much of our use of time deals largely with what's going on inside our head. If worldly thoughts consume our time, our actions will show it. The key, Paul tells us, is to let the Word of Christ richly dwell within us (Colossians 3:16).

Up where we live there are hundreds of acres of open pasture for our Siberian Husky to run free off the leash. Hanna loves it. As soon as we stop the car near the meadow, she is eager to get out of the car and race down the trail. She sniffs wildly in all directions, distracted by everything that catches her interest. One time it was a rabbit. If it weren't for the fact that mountain rabbits are faster and smarter than Hanna, I would have been concerned. For the moment I simply watched the chase. The rabbit streaked this way and that with dog in hot pursuit but losing ground. Hanna finally lost sight of her most exciting distraction and sat down to contemplate where in the world she was. After a moment's rest she trotted back to the trail and sniffed—for another distraction.

Sometimes I am like Hanna on the trail. Though desirous to stay on track with the Word of God, I soon find myself on rabbit trails. The phone rings, the breakfast needs to be prepared, hubby needs assistance with some administrative-type thing, and the children need schooling.

Once those things are done, I try to get back on track, but another "rabbit" appears in the form of dishes needing to be washed, ironing to do, or errands that need to get done. Though all these things are important, I find myself straying from my desire to get closer to the Lord through His Word. Does that ever happen to you? Frustrating, isn't it? At the end of many a day, I've sat down wondering how the frenzy got me so far off the trail.

One way I am learning to stay on track and avoid all the rabbit trails is to have a Bible at my bedside. I will not get out of bed until I have had some quality time reading from Scripture. That way I reach one of my goals before any rabbits get a chance to cross my path. I can start the day focusing on one thing—the Lord. I can benefit greatly by meditating throughout the day on the passage I read that morning. I usually function better and enjoy the day much more because I can maintain a more spiritual focus.

Along with being in the Word, I have also learned to depend more upon prayer, which benefits us not only with the use of our tongue and thus helps our relationships, but it also helps us control time.

PRAYER MAKES THINGS HAPPEN

Reformer John Calvin once exhorted all Christians to reckon with God for every moment of their life.[1] But how can we do this, practically speaking? The Word of God gives us the answer. At the start of each day we can pray that we would be able to throw off everything that hinders us and the sin that so easily entangles us (Hebrews 12:1), and we can consider our steps carefully (Proverbs 14:15). So how can we discover where we ought to be more faithful with our time? How can we effectively examine our every step?

Record Keeping

Philipp Schwarzerd, later known as Philipp Melanchthon, was one of the intellectuals of the Reformation. Luther described him as having "almost every virtue known to man," and because of this, Luther humbly sat among 500 to 600 university students to learn from his friend.[2] Even Erasmus, who disagreed with the direction of the Reformation, said that Melanchthon was "a man of gentle nature; even his enemies speak well of him."[3] To hold himself accountable, Philipp kept a record of how he spent his time. And each day he calculated how much time he had wasted and confessed it to the Lord. No doubt Melanchthon's concerted effort to make the most of his time helped make him such a formidable instrument of God.[4]

Inspired by Melanchthon, I have kept records of my own time to see where I could improve. I recorded what I did each hour for one week and then asked myself some simple questions. What could I eliminate? What took too long? How could I save time? Was I giving enough time to the most important tasks, such as studying God's Word and prayer? The exercise revealed two common thieves stealing my time. One was procrastination; the other was interruptions.

PROCRASTINATION

A thief steals what is not his, and procrastination steals what is God's—time. Putting off something can waste time because in trying to avoid an unpleasant but important task, we fill our day with less important things; then when it comes time to do what really matters, either we don't have time to do it, or we don't have time to do it well. Procrastination has at least three disguises: "Mr. Tomorrow," "Sloppy Joe," and "Miss Understanding."

The Thief That Wants Tomorrow

Remember the popular song in the movie *Annie*? Part of it says, "Tomorrow, tomorrow, there's always tomorrow . . . it's only just a day away." I don't know how many times I have used those words when not wanting to deal with things that must get done. But there are consequences. For instance, I hate going to the gynecologist (what woman doesn't?). Because I hate it so much, it's easy to forget.

Is there some task you'd rather put off or "forget"? Think over the last few weeks, months, or this past year, and consider one thing you are putting off. Ask yourself, *Why am I putting this task aside? Is it unpleasant? Is it because I feel inadequate? Do I not know how to do the task and don't know whom to turn to for help? Or do I know what to do but just hate doing it?* If you are like most people, any one of these is plenty of motivation to "forget."

One thing that motivates me to get something done at the proper time is remembering the consequences of leaving it undone. I used to be unmotivated to get my yearly checkup. But after putting it off, my gynecologist told me frankly, "Donna, there are many woman in the grave because they procrastinated on this." That comment got my attention and caused me not only to remember my checkup but to reflect on other problems that come with Mr. Tomorrow. What might be the consequences of putting off other things? Focusing on the consequences instead of the unpleasantness of the task can prevent problems.

The Thief Named "Sloppy Joe"

Occasionally a consequence of my delaying a task has meant that when I finally got around to it, I didn't have enough time to do it well. I ended up doing what I call a "Sloppy-Joe" job. Sloppy Joe likes to hang around my house, trying to get me to do an inadequate job on my housework. From time to time I wait too long before showing him the door.

Writer Anthony Trollope gave the best advice for keeping sloppiness out of the house. He said, "A small daily task, if it really be daily, will beat the labors of a spasmodic Hercules." That applies to any goal. Doing a little bit every day keeps a task from becoming the kind of unmanageable thing we are tempted to run from. We don't have to get it all done today—just some today and some tomorrow.

TIME MANAGEMENT

The other day while cleaning my kitchen counter, I watched an ant trying to pick up a piece of crust. It was double his size and weight and no easy task. But rather than put off the job, he worked at it until he was able to move it. No wonder Proverbs commends his kind saying that "the ants are not a strong folk, but they prepare their food in the summer" (Proverbs 30:25).

Why is the most insignificant critter on earth our scriptural example? We have superior intelligence, whereas the ant hardly has a brain. Yet while we have phones, faxes, computers, and every tool for every conceivable job—the ant has only his industriousness. It is always making the most of its time.

Here are some things I have found that keep Mr. Tomorrow and Sloppy Joe away from my door.

1. *Prioritize.* Make a list of tasks for each day. List them in order from the most to the least important (pray about the order). It's very tempting to put important but unpleasant things (like asking for someone's forgiveness) on the bottom of the list even though we know in our heart they must get done.

2. *Schedule goals.* As my husband has taught in time-management seminars, "Schedules make plans happen." After you have prioritized, write down at what time you will try to accomplish these things. Write the things that don't get done today in a slot for the next day. If possible, try to do the most important things early in the day, so as not to run the risk of putting them off. Try to put each task in its best time. The things that take a lot of concentration should be scheduled when you know you will be the sharpest. For most people, that is a couple of hours after you start your day (not right after lunch). If some things are fun, schedule them between harder tasks to serve as breaks.

3. *Keep a routine.* Having a well-thought-out routine works

wonders. For example, my routine around the house looks something like this:

Monday—laundry and ironing. Tuesdays—sweep, mop, vacuum floors. Wednesdays—clean up kids' room. Thursdays—clean out refrigerator. Friday—clean bathrooms and dust. Saturdays—general pickup.

4. *Don't hesitate to say no to some things.* It's an unfortunate fact of life that we can't do everything and help everyone. An important difference between a well-balanced life in which the important things get done well and a life that is frazzled and spread so thin that little is accomplished is the ability to say that one simple word. Marriages have failed, and children have grown up to be walking disasters because of the inability to say no.

5. *Exercise!* Exercise wakes up the heart, fills the brain with oxygen, and gives us more energy throughout the day. It can even lengthen our life span, which gives us more time to use!

6. *Eat healthy food.* Eating well cannot be underestimated. I have found that when I lack protein and vitamin B, I cannot think quickly, am not as alert, and do not feel like exercising.

7. *Know how much sleep you really need.* Chances are, you are either getting too much sleep or not enough. Understanding how much your body really needs allows you to be much more effective. If I get too much sleep, I become sluggish and find it easier to let Sloppy Joe hang around.

Miss Understanding: The Most Dangerous Thief

"Miss Understanding" has a knack for damaging relationships by making us misread people or delay dealing with them. Have you ever waited too long to make something right with someone else? We would probably act sooner if we realized that a delay in dealing with something can jeopardize a relationship. I think many friendships and marriages are seriously damaged by the failure to deal promptly with irritations and communication breakdowns.

How about with our children? Are we putting off fulfilling a promise simply because Miss Understanding tempted us to use our time on something less important? Children remember broken promises. Think back in your own life. You can probably remember a broken promise for years, perhaps even decades. If we think our children will understand how busy we are, we are probably being fooled by Miss Understanding. To someone else, especially a child, a promise is a promise, no matter what else has to be done.

What about things in ministry that need to be made right? Having been through two church splits in the past ten years, I have seen how years of hard work by dozens of saints can all be ruined because a few key people failed to understand a problem in time and deal with it quickly. It can take years to recover from the damage.

Sometimes the damage wrought by Miss Understanding cannot be reversed. I remember once being in a group and getting a very strong prompting from the Spirit to share the Gospel with one of the young women. However, I thought that it would be awkward to take her aside to talk privately. I figured I would see her again, but she was killed a few days later in a car accident. Because God understands our tendencies to procrastinate, He puts the emphasis on "today."

TODAY IS THE DAY

With some sense of urgency, Jesus said to Zaccheus, "Hurry and come down, for today I must stay at your house" (Luke 19:5). Why couldn't Jesus wait until tomorrow? Perhaps it was because He knew that today Zaccheus and his household would accept Him (Luke 19:9). It can be dangerous to put things off. Scripture says, "Behold, now is 'the acceptable time'; behold now is 'the day of salvation'" (2 Corinthians 6:2). It can be dangerous to delay accepting the Gospel. It can also be dangerous to delay sharing it.

INTERRUPTIONS

There are two types of interruptions. One distracts us from what we should be doing; the other delays us, merely postponing our progress. Distractions jeopardize our chance to reach our goal, while delays merely grant us unexpected opportunities.

Distractions

I remember when I was a college student, I was asked to be involved in an outreach program at my church. My answer was a quick, decisive no. At that time in my life I was both a full-time student and employed full-time, and I couldn't imagine taking on one more thing. But the person who asked me to get involved wouldn't take no for an answer. He offered some advice instead. "Get involved," he said, "and then ask God to weed out other things in your life." I took his advice and got involved, but God didn't weed anything else out of my life! I was still a student, still employed, and now involved in a ministry that took a big chunk of time. I became stressed and miserable. I wasn't able to perform as well for my employer, and my grades began to suffer. Though the outreach program was a good one, I had allowed it to jeopardize what I believed were God-given goals, things I was already committed to. Distractions are like that.

Through it all, I learned a very important lesson. No matter how good things appear to be, the key is to discern between the better and the best thing. And part of that is discerning what you realistically can and can't do. Let's face it, there is no end of good things to do. To decide whether something is a distraction, ask yourself: 1) Will it keep me from my other responsibilities? 2) Will it keep me from being effective at what I am already committed to do? 3) Will my family, employment, grades, or anything else suffer as a result of taking this opportunity? 5) Will I have this opportunity again later after my current obligations and goals are fulfilled?

Delays

As we know, Christ had many interruptions. With each He had to discern which would hinder His purposes and which He could turn into opportunities. The opportunities became temporary delays in His schedule.

For example, He met the Samaritan woman at Jacob's well and allowed her to delay Him. The opportunity brought her and many others in Samaria to the saving knowledge of the Messiah (John 4:7-42). The temporary delay in a city called Nain allowed Christ to bring a young man back from the dead. It resulted in townspeople coming to a saving knowledge of God (Luke 7:16).

Temporary delays are not easy to accept when we have our schedule made out. Personally, I like arriving at places right on schedule, getting things done in a timely matter—even getting the kids to bed on time. People like me sometimes need a divine lesson to see delays as opportunities. I had a lesson one crisp Saturday morning.

Brian, the kids, and I were on our way to an appointment and had to make a quick stop at a grocery store. As we were getting out of the car, I asked Brian, "Please make your conversation short with whomever you run into." I said this because no matter where we are, whether it's the store, the bank, or even another country, Brian always seems to run into someone he knows.

Brian guaranteed that we weren't going to see anyone he knew, especially since it was very early in the morning. In the store he proved to be right; he didn't see anyone he knew. And he reminded me of this as we were walking out the door. But I replied, "Yes, but we haven't made it to the car yet." No sooner had I expressed my skepticism than we heard, "Hey, Dr. Morley!"

For the next fifteen minutes the kids and I waited for Brian in the car while he talked to a few college students. When he got back to the car, he sat there for a moment amazed by God's timing. Apparently one of the students, Jim, had a sister who was seriously doubting her faith. Jim asked my husband if he could help her. The amazing part of the story is that Jim's sister was home from a secular college for just a few days and had agreed to speak with Brian if Jim could somehow reach him before Monday morning, when she had to leave. Had he not bumped into Brian, the opportunity to be of help would have been lost. That sister rededicated her life to the Lord. Obviously, this was a divine interruption. I cringe when I think that my insistence on keeping our schedule could have gotten in the way of God's plan.

Through this episode I discovered three main ways to help me welcome temporary delays when they come. The first is that I must submit the unexpected to God, knowing that "my times are in Thy hand" (Psalm 31:15). The second is having a godward perspective: I must understand that God's glory is more important than my schedule. Thirdly, I leave room in my schedule for unexpected opportunities. Since the grocery store incident, we have made it a practice to leave fifteen minutes early. This allows us to help those who come our way and yet still be on time. Knowing that use of time has to be guided by priorities, we must ask: Are we looking ahead that we may influence others?

PLANNING AHEAD

To use time effectively takes some planning. Start by asking practical questions. Does your husband see himself as a priority? Do you look ahead while he is at work to get your house in order? Do you look ahead and freshen up before he walks through the door? Do you look ahead hours before dinner to ensure that you have the right ingredients to make a nutritious meal? All this takes planning.

What about your children? Do you look ahead to their future? What kind of individuals do you desire them to be? Do you plan each day to do something that will help them to mature into godly individuals? On a more basic level, do your children know you love them? They can easily discern whether or not they are loved by how they fit into your priorities. If they are young, do you find time each day to read to them? Play with them? At any age your children might be, do you find time to just sit and converse with them?

When life seems too busy, I have found that doubling up on activities with my children works well. Because kids can be flexible, it doesn't always matter what you are doing as long as it's with them. So taking them with me while I do errands, help a neighbor, or work out in the garden communicates volumes. Although there is no substitute for undistracted time alone with a child, he or she can still consider activities special if I make it clear that I want to be with them.

What about at work? What do we communicate to those we work with? Does our conduct make coworkers curious about our faith?

What about friends? Do we set time aside for them? Christ made time for His friends even when things got busy.

My friend Debbie made her life worthwhile by investing in the lives of her friends. Though bedridden and in pain, she wrote notes and made phone calls to encourage people. She used her time up to the very last breath.

What about others outside our private world? It's easy to regard "outsiders" as a hindrance to our plans. And yet much of Christ's ministry was to outsiders. Had we followed Him around, we might have hardly noticed them—a blind beggar in a large crowd, a woman with a hemorrhage, children wanting His attention on a busy day. The same seemingly inconsequential faces cross our path—a child knocking at the door selling cookies, a salesman phoning about insurance, a person outside the grocery store wanting a signature on a petition.

These can be temporary delays—opportunities. I learned this one day when a sixteen-year-old girl came to my door selling children's books. I was right in the middle of doing a "million things" and had no desire to be disturbed. I quickly went to the door and was about ready to tell her that I wasn't interested when I sensed the Spirit quickly prompting me to welcome her into my home.

I invited her to sit on the couch. She introduced herself as Ivy and then proceeded to show me all the books from a catalog. After her sales pitch, I asked Ivy if I could share something with her. She gave me permission, and for the next half hour or so I shared with her the good news of Christ's love. She asked a lot of questions about sin and forgiveness, salvation, and eternal life. She didn't sell any books, but she did accept Christ. I later found out that Ivy's parents had been arduously praying with sweat and tears for the daughter they thought they had lost. We have no idea what is in store when we see delays as opportunities rather than distractions!

Let me end by sharing with you something Brian and I found in a dusty bookstore behind the London Museum. At the far corner of the store sat a dilapidated box filled with old comic strips. Weeding through those cartoons, we found to our surprise an original sermon preached at St. James's Church in London on February 6, 1708. The occasion was Her Majesty's birthday, and a Rev. Richard Willis exhorted the congregation to ask God to "teach us to number our days, that we may present to Thee a heart of wisdom" (Psalm 90:12). He closed with these searching words.

> We should frequently call ourselves to account and examine what improvements we have made of that time of life which God has allowed us. I have now lived so many years in the world; what have I been doing all this while? How have I answered the end of my creation? What honour have I brought to God? What good have I done to others? How have I improved my own mind? Do I find myself better than I was some years ago? Am I more temperate, more sober, more chaste, more honest in my dealings, more charitable, and more heavenly-minded than I was before? Have I so spent my time that if God should call me away, I should be able to give a tolerable account of it? . . . How few more days we may have to live. . . .[5]

That 300-year-old sermon has had a sobering effect on me as I consider how to use the time I have remaining. I want to use it to the fullest, as I am sure you do, too.

Thinking It Over

1. Currently how do you prioritize your time?

2. Try record-keeping for one week. Does something need to be eliminated from your schedule? If so, what?

3. Are you a procrastinator? What are you procrastinating about at this moment? How might you change?

4. What steps will you take to be a better manager of the time God has given you?

Chapter 7

GIFTS

THAT GIVE

One warm summer day while I was a college student on a short-term mission in Costa Rica, my friend Vicky and I were walking in one of the outdoor markets. We wore light blouses, skirts, and flats. I was a bit hesitant to go outside that day because the night before we had been "rough-housing," and Vicky accidentally hit me in the right eye. By morning it was swollen and had turned various shades of black, blue, and purple. "Come on, Donna, no one will notice your eye," said jovial Vicky.

So I reluctantly agreed. As we were strolling past the fresh vegetables and taking in the sights and smells of a foreign culture, I felt a pinch on my behind. With a gasp I said, "Vicky, did you see that?"

"What?" she asked.

"That man over there. He came by and pinched me!"

Vicky just laughed and said, "Ah well, he's gone now."

A few minutes later, I felt another pinch. With a quick turn, I saw that it was the same man. My judgment was instantly drowned by the biggest flood of adrenaline I've ever had. For a moment I forgot about my role as a child of God, a guest in Costa Rica, and a representative of the mission board that had sent me. And I also forgot about the swollen, colorful eye that made me look like I had just stepped out of a boxing ring. I tore after "Don Juan" like a cheetah, all 103 pounds of me.

Once I caught up with him, I was able (because he was my size) to grab hold of his collar and slug him quite a few times, all the while ignoring his cries for mercy. When I stopped, Don Juan took a good look at my eye. A look of fright crossed his face. Probably concluding that I fought quite often, he spun around and ran off as fast as he could, disappearing into the crowd.

While I was straightening out my clothes, I noticed for the first time that a large ring of women had encircled me. They began clapping and shouting at the top of their lungs, "Bravo! Bravo! Bravo!" At that moment I wanted to think of my actions as righteous, but deep down I knew I couldn't.

Looking back on this event, I am reminded of words from an early theologian named Photius: "To institute an action against one who has injured us is human; not to take revenge on him is the part of a philosopher; but to compensate him with benefit is Divine, and shows men of earth to be followers of the Father who is in heaven."[1]

After such a display of revenge, how could I show Don Juan or even my "cheerleaders" that I was a follower of Christ? How could I share with them God's love, mercy, and forgiveness? The most regrettable part of the incident was that I could not use the gifts God had entrusted to me to be of service to those people. Why? Because my actions spoke volumes and communicated some wrong things.

The gifts God has given to us for ministry are not used mechanically in isolation from who we are. They depend not only on our abilities but on our character. So here discernment has a dual role. It guides the use of our gifts and, as well, helps us make those thousands of daily choices that formulate our character. The combination shows people that we have something to give and thus opens up opportunities. Let's begin with that part of character that drives our use of gifts.

MOTIVATION:
OUR INCENTIVE TO USE SPIRITUAL GIFTS

Horatius Bonar (1808-1889), Scottish preacher and hymn writer, had a disturbing dream. He dreamed that the angels took his motivation, his zeal, and weighed it. They told him the quantity was excellent, weighing up to 100 pounds. In his dream Horatius was very pleased.

But then the angels went on to examine the quality of his motivation. They concluded that it was made of:

14 parts selfishness
15 parts sectarianism (zeal to see his denomination succeed over others)
22 parts personal ambition
23 parts love for humanity
26 parts only love for God[2]

When Bonar awoke, he was humbled. If our zeal were examined for both quantity and quality, would we be able to say with Paul, "Be imitators of me, just as I also am of Christ" (1 Corinthians 11:1)?

Proper motivation is grounded in selflessness. Service is not always pure sacrifice because it has its own reward, and God blesses us through service. Nevertheless, if that willingness to sacrifice is not there—if our motivation is at root selfish—we will scarcely make it through the rough times. Whom are we really serving, God or ourselves? How do we gain a willingness to sacrifice? By looking to Christ's example.

Sacrifice and Gifts

Sitting here at my desk typing away, I sometimes look up to a cross on the wall that my dear friend Cynthia made for me. It is decorated in a uniquely symbolic way. Clusters of *black* berries represent our sin; *white* roses are for Christ's purity; *crimson* berries are for His shed blood; the *greenery* reminds us of new life in Christ; a *gold* ribbon symbolizes Christ's gift of eternal life in heaven.[3] To me it sums up how Christ's sacrifice rescued us and gave us everything worth having.

My Lord's sacrifice for me does three things for my motivation. First, it can produce in me profound gratitude. Knowing how much God loved me makes me want to love Him back. As John said, "We love [Him], because He first loved us" (1 John 4:19). I don't have to work up the motivation to love and serve Him. It comes as a response for all He has done.

Second, the cross removes my motivation to serve out of desire for gain for myself because through it God gave us everything. Why strive to gain more for ourselves when we have it all? And that is what we are told we have—everything. Paul said, "For all things belong to you, whether Paul or Apollos or Cephas or the world or life or death or things present or things to come; all things belong to you" (1 Corinthians 3:21-22).

Third, the cross means that I am crucified with Christ. My own identity apart from Christ and my old sinful nature have been crucified with Him (Galatians 2:20). My life should now be a living sacrifice (Romans 12:2), placed once and for all on the altar for Him. And the beauty of it is that it all comes full circle: Christ laid down His life for us, and the Father gave Him joy and rewards (Hebrews 12:2); and we lay down our lives for Him and gain joy and rewards (1 Thessalonians 2:19).

Understanding the cross can purify our motives to serve, but what should we be motivated to do? Well, God has equipped us to serve using gifts—gifts that give. In Romans 12 Paul mentions those gifts as prophecy, service, teaching, exhortation, giving, leadership, and mercy (Romans 12:6-8).

We are strongly advised not to be ignorant of gifts (1 Corinthians 12:1) and not to neglect them (1 Timothy 4:14). Rather we are to be good stewards of our gifts (1 Peter 4:10) for the common good of others (1 Corinthians 12:7). As we go through Paul's description of gifts, you might begin discerning how you think God uses you or how He might use you in the future.

Prophecy

Throughout history God used men to prophesy—that is, to speak directly and authoritatively for Him. On a few occasions He used women in that role (though never in an ongoing prophetic ministry—Miriam, Exodus 15:20; Deborah, Judges 4:4; Huldah, 2 Kings 22:14; Anna, Luke 2:36; and the daughters of Philip, Acts 21:9). Prophecy in this sense does not just mean predicting the future; it means speaking for God.

Prophets, as we know, had a special role in the Old Testament. And after a period of silence in the time between the Old and New Testaments, they again had an authoritative role in the founding of the church. Paul said that the church was "built on the foundation of the apostles and prophets" (Ephesians 2:20). This might be thought of as the strong sense of prophecy.

Many also think there is a weaker sense of prophecy, where the prophet is not speaking the very words of God but is simply edifying, exhorting, and comforting (1 Corinthians 14:3).[4] Edification builds someone up by means of God's Word—directing, enlightening, and guiding. Exhortation "addresses itself to the human will and moves people to action by strengthening their determination to attain a goal."[5] Consoling builds up by soothing and comforting the troubled heart.[6] In Acts we see a husband-and-wife team edifying a teacher (Apollos) by explaining "to him the way of God more accurately" (Acts 18:26).

It is said that "the testimony of Jesus is the Spirit of prophecy" (Revelation 19:10). Christ is ultimately the focus of God's message. Since the message can be proclaimed to a nonbeliever, there is no reason why prophecy cannot have an evangelistic sense. Paul, for example, demonstrated "by the Scriptures that Jesus was the Christ" (Acts 18:28).

Service

I will never forget Phillip. He had the gift of service like no other person on earth. He never asked people what their needs were; he just figured them out and met them.

I remember one night I was studying at the church library until quite late. Phillip noticed that I had been there all day. Without asking me if I had eaten, he took his only form of transportation, an old bicycle, and rode down a dangerously busy boulevard to get me a fast-food dinner with what little money he had.

He was an example of practical service (*diakonia*), what we call the gift of "ministering" or "helps." The gift can be used to support church administration, as the first deacons did (Acts 6:1-4), or simply to help any child of God in need. Martha, for example, was hospitable (Luke 10:40); Dorcas made clothes to give away (Acts 9:36-41).

Before coming to Christ, I, like a lot of people, thought of service as a kind of fire insurance policy. If I did good things, I would get into heaven. I based my life on good works just to reserve myself a spot in the better of the two destinies in the next life. Fortunately, I came to see how misguided that attitude is. None of us can come close to being worthy of heaven through our own efforts. No matter how much we serve, salvation is forever a matter of pure grace (Ephesians 2:8-9).

We should all be helpful—and with the right motives—but those with the gift of helps are especially inclined and equipped to be helpful. It is the Holy Spirit who decides how He shall use believers (1 Corinthians 12:7), and He chooses to use some in this special way. The Christian woman who has this gift and who uses it with pure motives helps others even when it isn't convenient, putting aside her own needs and pleasures. She is not motivated by recognition or praise but by God's glory.

Rarely do you hear people saying, "I sure wish I had the gift of helps!" When people want a gift, it is usually one that brings attention, such as teaching. But those who come alongside others to help in practical ways have their own wonderful reward. I have had friends with this gift, and they are a very special blessing to everyone they come in contact with.

Teaching

Years ago while sitting through a university course on textiles, I had a lot of time to consider why some people should definitely not be teachers. At the beginning of class, the teacher's face would disappear into the course textbook. She would read every word without coming up for air until the class was over. Three times a week for an hour and fifteen minutes, she read line by line, chapter by chapter, never stopping, never explaining. It didn't help matters that she read in a monotone voice and was obviously bored with the subject matter herself. Once the class period started, we felt that only a major earthquake could bring us relief. We could have saved ourselves the time and a lot of tuition money if we had been allowed to stay home during class and read the book ourselves.

Teaching is so much more than reciting from a book. It can involve explaining, making the subject vivid, and motivating people to do the right thing. A teacher should be an example of right belief and behavior as she forms a bridge between the subject (in this case, God's Word) and people. Because of their great influence, God holds Christian teachers to a high standard. To emphasize the seriousness of this gift, James warns that teachers will receive "stricter judgment" (James 3:1).

A teacher must be diligent to know the subject, to communicate well, and to be an example herself. And although some gifted teachers are effective despite a monotonous voice, it helps if they, like the great preacher Jonathan Edwards (who by the way, had a monotonous voice), have passion—passion for truth, passion for God, and passionate love for people.

All of this requires sacrifice in order to have enough time to study and to be an example. It requires spiritual discipline and alertness so as not to leave openings for Satan's schemes. But developing the gift of teaching requires much more. A teacher must be a good listener, alert to what God is saying, and she must be a good follower of God. She is to probe, search, compare, apply, and diligently examine the Word of God that she may effectively minister to others around her.

Are there limits to this gift? Paul says yes. He told Timothy, "I do not allow a woman to teach or exercise authority over a man" (1 Timothy 2:12). However, women should teach women (Titus 2:3-4). Pastor John MacArthur affirms the place of women teachers: "God has gifted women in marvelous ways. Many of them have the gifts of teaching and proclaiming God's Word. But they are not to exercise *those particular gifts* in the mixed assembly of the church when it comes together."[7]

Though all women can appreciate part of Pastor MacArthur's comment, some would disagree with him about women teaching Scripture authoritatively to men. What do you think about this emotion-laden topic? There are definitely two sides here, if not more. Some very knowledgeable women believe that they can teach men because they take Paul's prohibition against it as applicable only to the culture of his day, like his requirement that women wear head coverings (1 Corinthians 11:5).

The opposing view is that in the Timothy passage, Paul bases his point on the creation of Adam and Eve—and their creation certainly was not a part of the culture of Paul's day!

Another popular view is that Paul's prohibition against women teaching men applies only to women teachers who are ill-prepared and influenced by false teachers. According to this view, Eve (1 Timothy 2:13-14) is an example of someone who "taught" Adam without adequate preparation. In this view, then, women can teach men as long as they are well-prepared to do so.

The other camp gives a few reasons why this view, too, is inadequate: 1) Paul says nothing about Eve being a teacher of Adam; 2) There is no evidence that women were teaching false doctrines; 3) Paul points out that Eve was deceived because she took the initiative over the man whom God had appointed to be with her and care for her. Women today can make the same mistake as Eve if they try to become independent of those whom God has appointed over them. Paul's comment about Eve does not imply that all women are more susceptible to doctrinal error. Nothing in the Genesis passage suggests that they are. If that were the case, then women would not be able to teach anyone.

Paul appeals to the order of creation. Man was created *first, then* Eve. The point is that the man has headship because he was created first (cf. 1 Corinthians 11:3-10). That headship is violated if women teach doctrine or exercise authority over men. By linking the issue to creation, Paul shows that this view of women's roles is not just for the local situation or for a limited time. The prohibition is an enduring principle.[8]

The last view I will mention (though there are many others) is the belief that Paul's statement, "I do not allow a woman to teach or exercise authority over a man" (1 Timothy 2:12), does not forbid a woman to teach men. She is only forbidden to teach or exercise authority over her *husband*. Opponents of this view ask, if Paul meant "husband," why do translators always use the word *man*? In the Greek, it turns out that the word Paul used, *aner*, can mean either "man as opposed to woman" or "husband."⁹ Therefore, the context must tell us which meaning Paul intended.

Had Paul been referring to a woman's husband, we would expect that he would have said "her" husband. In this verse, there is no possessive pronoun or definite article with *man*. Elsewhere Paul uses such words: "Wives, be subject to *your own* husbands . . ." (Ephesians 5:22; Colossians 3:18).

Looking at the broader context of the Timothy passage, we see that just prior to Paul's saying that he doesn't allow a woman to teach or exercise authority over a man, he said the following: "I want women to adorn themselves with proper clothing, modestly and discreetly, not with braided hair and gold or pearls or costly garments; but rather by means of good works, as befits women making a claim to godliness. Let a woman quietly receive instruction with entire submissiveness. But I do not allow a woman to teach or exercise authority over a man, but to remain quiet" (1 Timothy 2:9-12).

Paul uses the plural "women" as a class—single and married alike. He uses the singular "a woman" to refer to any woman, not just "a wife." Then in the same breath, while speaking to married and single women, he uses the term in question, *aner* (v. 12). Therefore, that term cannot mean "husband." No wonder it is always translated "man" rather than "husband."

Searching the New Testament to find a woman who held anything like the position of a preacher, religious teacher, or leader of men, I came across many women with various gifts who had been instrumental in the cause of the Gospel. Yet I could not find one woman who had an authoritative position over men as a preacher, Bible teacher, or spiritual leader.

Well, you might ask, "What about Priscilla? Both she and her husband Aquila instructed Apollos" (Acts 18:26). Yes, that is true, but it was done in private and not before an entire assembly of men and women.

Then what about the five Old Testament prophetesses—Miriam, Deborah, Huldah, Noadiah, and the wife of Isaiah? Though I don't want to minimize the great role some of these women had, for the sake of the question about women's roles, we have to take a close look at their position in ministry.

Miriam was a prophetess who led the women of Israel in a great hymn of praise to the Lord (Exodus 15:20-21).[10] We know that she had an important role because in the book of Micah, God says He led the children of Israel through Moses, Aaron, and Miriam (6:4). But we don't know how much prophecy was a part of her ministry nor what relationship her prophesying had to the authority of her brothers Moses and Aaron. We do know that God chastened her severely for attempting to usurp Moses' authority as a prophet (Numbers 12:2, 9).

Deborah was a judge and prophetess during a wicked time in Israel (Judges 4:1). The book of Judges shows that God used a variety of people to confront wickedness. Remember how he used Samson's strength (Judges 13-16) and Ehud's treachery (Judges 3)? God used Deborah to confront evil, not with power and might, but with wisdom, acting as a civil judge who decided court cases (Judges 4:4). And Deborah's influence went beyond judging. She spoke for God when she assisted Barak, the military leader (Judges 4:6-14).

Deborah was Barak's "right hand" as she prophesied to him about Israel's coming victory (Judges 4:9), as she encouraged him with God's presence (Judges 4:14), and as she accompanied him in a song of praise (Judges 5:1-31).

If Deborah's unique role was larger, such as having authority over thousands of men or being a priest, we don't know about it. Certainly we can speculate about what she might have done. Yet to be fair to the text, we must look only at what we have been given. In any case, there's no question that Deborah is highly unusual in Scripture.

Huldah, a "keeper of the wardrobe," was held in some regard for her prophetic gift. Scripture reveals a direct revelation Huldah gave to eighteen-year-old King Josiah through his messengers (2 Kings 22:13-14; 2 Chronicles 34:22). The importance of this incident cannot be underestimated. Huldah's prophetic ministry brought spiritual awakening to a king. King Josiah made a new covenant with God, and from that day forward, he was able to lead the nation spiritually (2 Kings 23).

Noadiah's "ministry" was that of a false prophetess (Nehemiah 6:14), so we needn't say much about her. And the only recorded revelation we have of Isaiah's wife was of her prophesying through her son's name (Isaiah 8:3).

In summary, Scripture clearly shows that Miriam, Deborah, Huldah, and Isaiah's wife had spiritual influence. They were prophetesses. God gave them on occasion authority to say, "Thus saith the Lord." What a high honor for these women—the few who were used in a prophetic way. As we know, God used men almost exclusively, and once He used even a donkey (Numbers 22:22-30)!

If you believe you have the gift of teaching, it is up to you to honestly discern what the Scriptures say. For further study here are some resources:

Women at the Crossroads by Kari Torjesen Malcolm

Man and Woman in Christ: An Examination of the Roles of Men and Women in Light of Scripture and the Social Sciences by Stephen B. Clark

Man and Woman in Christian Perspective by Werner Neuer

Women and the Word of God: A Response to Biblical Feminism by Susan T. Foh

Recovering Biblical Manhood and Womanhood: A Response to Evangelical Feminism, edited by John Piper and Wayne Grudem

While to some women the biblical restrictions may seem unfair, God's role for women in the church is anything but insignificant. If it weren't for two women named Lois and Eunice, Timothy wouldn't have had an early knowledge of Scripture (2 Timothy 1:5). If it weren't for godly mothers throughout the ages, the church would have never been blessed with zealous Christians impacting the world. If it weren't for the women of the past, of the present, and of the future—touching lives for Christ as Sunday school teachers, missionaries, evangelists, counselors, educators, writers, musicians, singers, and so on—the church would be greatly weakened or in shambles.

It's unfortunate that the focus of discussion in the church these days is almost entirely on whether women can or can't teach men. Little is said about the need for women to teach women.

When women do teach other women, it must be done from Scripture. Otherwise something else becomes the authority. Illustrations and stories are important, but we cannot fail to use Scripture.

So should a woman speak with authority when teaching women? As I see it, a woman's authority (or a man's) has to come from Scripture. And if I understand what Paul says about women not being in the place of ultimate authority when teaching (1 Timothy 2:12), it means being under the authority of a man in such a position—a pastor, elder, or professor. When I write for women, I feel I am under my pastor's authority as well as my husband's (he is a Bible professor). Also I try to acknowledge in practical ways that I am not in that place of final authority.

In spite of the recent controversy surrounding women teaching men, and in spite of the fact that God scrutinizes teachers, we can receive great encouragement from Paul. Rather than discourage women who have the gift of teaching, he wholeheartedly encourages them to teach "what is good" (Titus 2:3). Teaching is a rewarding and vital ministry.

Exhortation

Remember Barnabas? If ever a person had the gift of exhortation, it was he. Known as the "Son of Encouragement" (Acts 4:36), Barnabas was highly respected by Christian leaders and became a blessing to many. Shortly after Paul's conversion, for instance, the other apostles were quite skeptical about the renowned enemy of the church. While they questioned the validity of his conversion, Barnabas did not.[11]

Ironically, years later Paul became skeptical of young Mark's fitness for a missionary journey (Mark having deserted them during a previous trip, Acts 15:36-39). Again it was Barnabas who had faith in Mark. He so much wanted Mark to have another chance that it led to a parting of ways with Paul. An encourager like Barnabas doesn't quickly give up on others. Later Paul himself became convinced that Mark was fit for service and asked the Colossians to welcome the younger man when he visited them (Colossians 4:10).

Barnabas was also one of the first to welcome gentiles into the church, whereas others were still unconvinced that God was saving gentiles (Acts 11:17-18; 15:12). And it is said of Barnabas that he encouraged "them all with resolute heart to remain true to the Lord; for he was a good man" (Acts 11:23-24).

Those with the gift of exhortation tend to focus on the will. They encourage and comfort; they strengthen—and sometimes they confront. Peter exhorted nonbelievers to "be saved from this perverse generation!" (Acts 2:40). No matter what form the exhortation takes, the exhorter who has pure motives is always concerned about the spiritual welfare of others. Like any gift, exhortation should be used not to impress others but to please God, who examines the heart (1 Thessalonians 2:3-4). Sometimes this gift requires a lot of sensitivity, sacrifice, and flexibility, because the needs an exhorter meets rarely conform to a schedule.

The effects of exhortation can easily go unnoticed, but they are valuable nonetheless. Though Barnabas never wrote Scripture, without his acceptance of Paul the church might have missed the apostle's contribution, which included founding the gentile churches and writing half the New Testament. And without his encouragement of Mark, we might not have his Gospel. Paul contributed thirteen epistles, Mark contributed a Gospel, and Barnabas contributed the exhortation.[12]

Giving

A roommate I had in my single days dated a seminary student who was the first to admit that he did not have the gift of giving. After every date I would observe a somewhat humorous routine. First, instead of telling my roommate what a nice time he had, he would come into the apartment and sit at the kitchen table. He would take out of his coat a little notebook and write down his expenditures on the date, recounting them to the penny. Then he would go to the couch and think out loud which books he would not be able to buy as a result of the evening's financial losses. Sounds like a real charmer, doesn't he?

After many dates and much financial "waste," the seminarian received an inheritance that could have bought him an entire theological library. Instead, to the surprise of those who knew him, he gave it all away to missions. He showed a lot of maturity in over-coming his selfish attitude, but does that mean he then had the gift of giving? Not at all. The Lord impressed upon him to give it away, and he showed the maturity to respond.

All Christians are to give. We have examples in Scripture of giving to needs in a planned and orderly way (1 Corinthians 16:2), of giving to the poor (Galatians 2:10), and of giving to a ministry (Philippians 4:16). Every believer is told that failing to meet the need of another Christian leaves his sanctification in doubt (1 John 3:17). Giving something as insignificant as a glass of water amounts to giving it to the Lord Himself (Matthew 10:42; 25:35; Mark 9:41).

Those with the gift of giving, though, have a special interest and inclination to give. Usually they see it as an investment in the kingdom. They devote a lot of thought to giving and take great delight in it. To have the gift of giving, a person need not have a lot of money; the amount is not the issue. I have known a few wealthy people who were not the least bit interested in giving, but I have known others with little who gave so much that God had to intervene to meet their own needs.

As with any gift, skill in using it and pure motivation do not come with it. We have to grow into them. Paul exhorts those who give to do it with cheerfulness (2 Corinthians 9:7)[13] and generosity (Romans 12:8). The giver with the right motivation will not feel some legalistic obligation to give, will not begrudge how much she gave, nor consider it a loss, and will not give to get praise and appreciation from people. The Bible says that God especially loves people who give in an openhearted way like the "cheerful giver" (2 Corinthians 9:7).

Leadership

One of the best examples of leadership I've seen was in a most unlikely place. I was in the library of a retirement home and was about to begin the weekly Bible study I had been doing for a couple of years. Just before praying, I noticed a new woman in the group I had never seen before. I thought I would introduce myself to her after opening in prayer, but she decided to interrupt my prayer to let me know who she was. In the middle of my praying she began yelling at me in various weird voices, demanding that I stop the praying. It was bizarre and satanic. The demon-possessed woman began throwing chairs, plants, and books all over the place. She then threatened to beat me up. When I didn't back down, it looked like she was trying to attack me but was being held back by some invisible force (angels perhaps?). Frustrated by not being able to get to me, she began scaring off the other women, saying that if they ever came back to the Bible study, she would come to their room in the middle of the night and kill them.

I prayed out loud for the woman, but it only made her more crazed. Finally I asked her to leave, and without opening the sliding doors, she burst completely through them, knocking them to the ground. When she was gone, I turned to the trembling elderly women and said, "Now that is an example of an unclean heart!"

Immediately Margaret, one of my faithful attendees, admitted, "I have an unclean heart, too."

We picked up the scattered chairs and then sat in a circle and watched the miracle of Margaret's new birth. She repented of her sins and asked Christ to enter her life.

Unfortunately the possessed woman continued to make threats. But rather than deal with such a dangerous person by getting her to a special hospital, the manager of the retirement home asked that I stop the Bible study. For a while I was able to meet with the women "one on one" in their rooms, but soon I was forbidden even to do that.

During that dark time, my heart ached for the women. Forbidden to see them, I often wondered what had become of them. So one year later almost to the day of the bizarre incident, I decided to pay my friends a visit unannounced. Walking into the place, I was astounded to hear a loud, cheerful voice going up and down the hallways saying, "Okay, ladies, it's Bible study time!" Guess who had taken over the work? Dear, faithful Margaret!

Watching her, I was in awe of the incredible leadership skills she had. No one was there to teach her from Scripture, so she had taken the initiative to study on her own. She obtained some commentaries and other resources to assist her. Margaret saw the need for a Bible study, and rather than being intimidated by the possessed woman or trying to confront her, she got the woman moved to a hospital. Then she told the management, "We are going to have a Bible study!"

As Margaret learned so early in her Christian walk, most people want to be led. Since no one else was capable of getting the Bible study up and running, Margaret did.

Like all effective people, those with leadership skills get things done. But leaders are unique in that they accomplish much more than one person could, by motivating and guiding others. The Bible tells us of many who showed leadership, including some women. Deborah was an acting judge to the people of Israel (Judges 4:1-10, 12-16, 23-24). Abigail used her discernment and advice to keep David from bloodshed (1 Samuel 25:23-42). Huldah had a part in rebuking an apostate nation (2 Chronicles 34:22-33). God said He led Israel out of bondage using Moses, Aaron, and Miriam (Micah 6:4). Though those were unusual situations during unusual times in history, God still uses women. And under His authority women with leadership skills have the ability to influence other women for God.

Let's look for a moment at the life of Moses, Israel's hero, who knew the Lord face to face and communicated for Him to Israel. Like Moses, a leader must know the Lord personally and grasp His Word in order to communicate the mind of God. As well, a leader must relate God's message to her own life, reflecting on how to apply what He has said and what He has done in her life.

The woman who is gifted for leadership will not necessarily have confidence—at least not in herself. Often even a gifted leader feels inadequate. She may even be tempted, as Moses was, to try to evade such a daunting task by getting someone else to do it (Exodus 4:13). But she must eventually say, "Thy will be done" (Matthew 6:10), realizing that her adequacy is from God. "Not that we are adequate in ourselves to consider anything as coming from ourselves, but our adequacy is from God" (2 Corinthians 3:5).

Showing Mercy

Every Christian should be in the business of showing mercy. (I know I should have shown it when Don Juan cried for it.) Showing mercy reflects the very character of God, the fruit of the Spirit: love, joy, peace, patience, kindness, goodness, faithfulness, gentleness, and self-control (Galatians 5:22). If we are without mercy, how can anyone recognize that we are Christians?

While we should all be merciful, there are those whom God has selected to show it in a special way through a divine gift. With this gift they have an unusual ability to be extraordinarily compassionate and kind. Seeing other people's grief and hardship does not easily overwhelm their own emotions, as it typically does those who are not divinely enabled. Those with the gift are drawn to the hurting.

I knew a man whose son was shot and killed in an armed robbery of a grocery store. When the robber was arrested, he visited him in jail. Rather than seek revenge or express anger, he told his son's killer that he forgave him and that God loved the man enough to allow His own Son to be killed to provide divine forgiveness. That father showed God's special gift of mercy in action.

The woman with the gift of mercy has a special concern for the hurting and forgotten: the prisoner, the addict, the homeless, the ill, the blind, the deaf, the emotionally troubled, and the physically challenged. She can show mercy to both the believer and nonbeliever, knowing both need Christ's love. She doesn't need a seminar on how to be kind. It's been bestowed upon her divinely by God.

DISCERNING OUR GIFTEDNESS

So how can we discern our giftedness? First, by paying attention to our desires. We can begin by asking ourselves what we want to do. Remember, it is God who gives us the desires of our heart, putting the right ones there (Philippians 2:13) and fulfilling them (Psalm 37:4). Yet through immaturity we can have the wrong motives for

wanting to use a gift. Doing things for wrong motives will not produce fruit for the kingdom.

If you think you have a specific gift, ask yourself, *Am I good at this?
Is God using me in that way? Do others confirm that I have abilities in this
area, and are my efforts bearing fruit?* If we covet a gift that really isn't ours,
we miss out on the wonderful blessings and opportunities to serve in
the way in which God has truly gifted us.

Our Attitudes Toward the Gifts

Remember learning the color wheel in elementary school? Were
you confused by it? I was. I thought that primary somehow meant
more important and that secondary was less important. In my
young mind I imagined that blue, yellow, and red were somehow
"snobbish" toward green, purple, and orange. This wasn't right, I
thought, because to me all the colors were equally pretty and
equally needed.

Sometimes we are tempted to think that way about the gifts, that
some are better or more important than others. Yet Scripture says
each is equally necessary (1 Corinthians 12:15-24). Paul had to confront the Corinthians' desire for the more "showy gifts." We are
tempted to do the same today, coveting ministries of the preacher, the
evangelist, and the singer. In some circles the other gifts don't get
much recognition or encouragement.

But as Paul pointed out to the Corinthians, we have to respect
and dignify each gift. And we have to respect and value our own giftedness, even if it does not get much recognition from others. Making
clothing for unwed mothers is just as valid as having a worldwide tape
ministry.

As I'm continually reminded, no matter what gift we are blessed
with, we have to develop a servant's heart to go with it. Instead of trying to make ourselves look good with our gift, we are just to serve
others with it. The gift should never be a tool to exalt ourselves or get
people to like us. Even Christ, who is the focus of our gift, came not
to be served, but to serve (Matthew 20:28).

ETERNITY

Long ago I memorized a quote by Charles Spurgeon that I've kept close to my heart. As I remember it, he said, "May I, oh Lord, live each day with eternity's values in view."

For most of us eternity seems, well, so far ahead. And it seems like we will never get there. So we are tempted to forget the hereafter and just focus on the here and now. But are we doing anything that will affect the future?

Many hold the view that once in heaven, all Christians are at exactly the same level in terms of knowledge of God, of blessedness, of rest, and of happiness. That may be, but there are some weak points in this view of heaven.

Though there will be complete security, and we shall be forever clothed in purity like a white garment, consider for a moment the possibility that there is more of a connection between this life and the next. Suppose that the things we experience and learn about God we take with us. If so, the deeper knowledge of God we gain through sacrifice, service, and faith will enable us to know God better than we would if we had spent our lives just sitting on the beach waiting for His return. So many opportunities to know God are unique to this life. Only in our fallen world with its pain and evil can we know God as a comforter, provider, protector, forgiver of sin, mercy giver, and so on. To be known, those attributes require a background of sin or pain. Yet in the next life sin and pain won't exist. We have a unique opportunity now in this life that won't be repeated.

The apostle Paul had a deep sense that, though salvation is a gift, heavenly rewards depend on this life. His analogy compares two types of people entering heaven:

> Now if any man builds upon the foundation with gold, silver, precious stones, wood, hay, straw, each man's work will become evident; for the day will show it, because it is to be revealed with fire; and the fire itself will test the quality of each man's work. If any man's work which he has built upon it remains, he shall receive a reward. If any man's

work is burned up, he shall suffer loss; but he himself shall be saved, yet so as through fire (1 Corinthians 3:12-15).

The person who built with materials that did not endure was someone who led a shallow life with no eternal focus. She will be saved, of course, but with a sense of loss at her life having amounted to nothing of lasting value. But the person whose life's work endures will have a reward because of using her gifts and opportunities with the right motives. At the end of this life, what lasts will be all that really matters.

Paul is such an example for all of us. He used his giftedness no matter what the cost. For the rest of eternity he will be meeting those who grew from reading his writings, were blessed by the example of his life, and who came to know Christ somehow through his ministry. What a reward he has for eternity! We, too, can have such a reward if we exalt God through diligent use of our own gifts—that give.

Thinking It Over

1. Why is the right use of gifts dependent upon our character?

2. What should be our motivation for using our gifts?

3. Discern how you may be gifted. Ask mature believers who know you well what gifts they detect in you.

4. How will you use your giftedness in the days ahead?

5. What does our giftedness have to do with eternity?

PART TWO

———

CHOICES
IN OUR INNER LIFE

———

Chapter 8

RENEWING THE MIND IN A
MINDLESS WORLD

Years ago I worked at an airfreight office that was filled with skeptics. They would rather believe that aliens visit earth than that God had sent His Son. Despite that, I loved those people, and my fervent prayer was that God would give me an opportunity to share my faith with them.

That prayer was answered one day when the electricity went out. With computers down, lights off, and phones dead, we could do nothing but stare at one another. My boss came out of his office with a break-time attitude, looking for a good laugh. He said sarcastically, "Okay, Donna, tell us why you believe what you believe."

Excited about the opportunity (however backhanded the offer), I shared with him and my coworkers about God's forgiveness through His Son, His love, eternity in heaven or hell, and the radical change in my life since becoming a Christian. Though it had started out as less than serious, it was a wonderful time of sharing.

One question someone asked caught my attention and really made me think afterwards. "What," asked fifty-year-old Roy, "does a Christian think about? If you say Christians are changed, then what goes on in their minds?" He explained that he had known people who claimed to be Christians but didn't seem any different from anyone else. As he put it, "They laughed at all my dirty jokes and then told a few of their own."

After Roy's remark, the electricity came back on. In a way I was glad because I was at a loss to try to explain what Christians think about. As I mulled over an answer, I connected the Christian mind to a Christian worldview and to Christlike character. The Christian mind should be different from the secular mind, which is based on a secular worldview with its worldliness and ungodliness.

Though these two should be in sharp contrast, they can blur together if we are not tending to our thoughts. As G. K. Chesterton said, "If you leave a white post alone it will soon be a black post."[1]

Paul the apostle saw the outcome of a mind allowed to gather dirt and smudges. Left too long without cleaning and fresh paint, it becomes indistinguishable from a secular mind, smudged with unwholesome thoughts and attitudes. The secret of keeping a fresh coat of paint on, according to Paul, is continually renewing our mind (Romans 12:2). The benefits of that renewal is that we will discern what pleases God (Ephesians 5:10-11) and do what pleases Him (Romans 12:2; Ephesians 5:17). We will discern what is excellent and be attracted to those things (Philippians 1:9-10).

Paul understood that renewing our mind is no easy task. First, it requires that we not conform to the world.

THIS WORLD

Whenever you think about the corrupting influences of this world, what comes to mind? Perhaps it is the world's lusts (2 Peter 1:4). That is what comes to my mind. But just as alluring are its wrong thoughts, its foolishness (1 Corinthians 3:19). Throughout Scripture we see the threat of worldly thoughts, opinions, beliefs, and ideals. For that reason, Paul exhorted us to "take every thought captive to the obedience of Christ" (2 Corinthians 10:5) rather than becoming captive to "philosophy and empty deception" (Colossians 2:8). What could have prompted Paul to exhort Christians to guard their minds?

Doing a bit of research, I discovered that in Paul's time society was saturated with secular philosophy. The influence of Plato and Aristotle had largely given way to the teachings of the Epicureans and Stoics, whom Paul encountered in the gathering of philosophers in Athens (Acts 17:18-34).[2]

The Stoics thought that reason pervades everything and is a kind of god. Since reason controls nature, we should live by it rather than by emotion. They promoted a self-sufficient be-tough attitude toward life. Cicero characterized the Stoic man: "The wise man is never moved by favour, never pardons anyone's faults; only the foolish and weak-minded show pity; it is unmanly to allow yourself to be persuaded by prayers and services. . . . The wise man never holds an opinion, never repents, is never mistaken, never changes his mind."[3] The Epicureans also thought that man should conform to nature, but as they saw it, all of nature seeks pleasure and avoids pain; man should do the same.[4]

No wonder Paul exhorted believers not to be captive to philosophy and empty deception (Colossians 2:8). So what does that have to do with today? A lot! Our society is confronted with different views, new challenges to the Christian mind. One view is that only atoms and molecules exist (called naturalism). It leaves no place for the soul or God. It promotes the view that God does not intervene in the world, doesn't do miracles, or answer prayers, and He did not raise Jesus from the dead. Naturalism also promotes a materialistic attitude that sees "things" as the only objects of value in life. Ever see the bumper sticker that says, "He who dies with the most toys wins"?

Perhaps the most common view—or attitude—of our day is mindlessness. And, sad to say, the church is being affected more than it realizes. The end result is that this attitude keeps us from developing a Christian mind. Where did this mindlessness have its beginnings?

The Beginnings of Our Mindless Age

To some extent it started about the time of the American Revolution when German philosopher Immanuel Kant (1724-1804) rocked the West by saying that we do not know truth as it is; we create truth in our minds. Thus knowledge, he said, is subjective, not objective; and we can never understand the way things really are.

Søren Kierkegaard (1813-1855) and the existentialists he inspired in the twentieth century held that subjective things are more important than facts. Our attitudes and convictions are what matter; "facts" don't count for much. Atheistic German philosopher Friedrich Nietzsche (1844-1900) went further and said that there are no facts, only interpretations.

Today it is popular to believe that what is true for me may not be true for you (called relativism). It is also popular to believe that all paths lead to God because there is a little truth in every religion (called pluralism). The latest trend is to believe that there is no objective truth at all. Everything is a like a story—it has meaning without being true (postmodernism).

So everything has come to be a matter of subjectivity and feelings. How is a Christian to respond? Christian philosopher Francis Schaeffer said, "No man can live without a worldview; therefore, there is no man who is not a philosopher."[5] So what is your worldview? Is there a place for subjectivity and emotions? If so, how do they relate to truth?

Feelings: Do They Have a Proper Place?

Christ had just explained to the disciples that He must be killed but that He would rise again (Mark 8:31). But Peter's misplaced sympathy caused him to take Christ aside and rebuke Him (Mark 8:32). Christ, in turn, rebuked Peter: "Get behind me, Satan!" he said. "You do not have in mind the things of God, but the things of men" (Mark 8:33 NIV). It was natural for Peter to feel grieved, but his feelings had overridden what He knew about God's wisdom.

While feelings can make us stumble, they are also a source of great blessing. We can cry for joy at the birth of a child or at the wedding of a dear friend. We can feel a sense of exaltation over a great piece of music.

Feelings can also challenge our faith and willpower. Job battled his emotions, and sometimes losing, he cried in despair, "I loathe my own life" (Job 10:1). David, overcome with the grief of losing his son, mourned, "O my son Absalom, my son, my son Absalom! Would I had died instead of you, O Absalom, my son, my son!" (2 Samuel 18:33).

Because God made us with emotions, He takes great interest in what we are feeling, whether it is depression, grief, hurt, anger, envy, anxiety, or joy and love. And He knows that feelings, if not dealt with properly, can be quite destructive. To keep emotions in their proper place and maintain their constructive force in our lives, we have to submit them to truth.

Feelings Submitted to Truth

The Old Testament prophets and New Testament saints such as Paul confronted the paganism of their day with truth. Their authority was not some voice within nor their inner feelings but the written Word of God (Psalm 119:160). And contrary to the mindlessness and sub-jectivism of our day, we must make our feelings conform to God's standards for truth and character as well.

Anger, for example, is not necessarily a sin. God Himself is said to be angry, and we are exhorted to "be angry, and yet do not sin" (Ephesians 4:26). Yet because we are naturally self-centered, our anger can easily violate God's standards. The rest of that verse, for example, tells us, "do not let the sun go down on your anger." If we let friction between us and another person go unresolved, it can fes-ter and cause problems. It can deny us of sleep and even lead to phys-ical problems such as ulcers.

Crossing the boundary and committing one sin can lead to com-mitting others. King David was supposed to go out with his troops when they were at war (2 Samuel 11:1). Perhaps his feelings got the better of him, and he stayed home instead. We all remember what happened next. While lustfully looking on Bathsheba, David failed to control his feelings for her and committed adultery. That led to a murder to cover it up, and then God took the life of the baby that had been conceived. The whole nation experienced problems as a result.

Because I tend to be an emotional person (most women are), I have to ask myself, *Am I allowing my feelings to run away with me, or am I using my mind to keep them in line with God's standards?*

THE HEART AND MIND

Most people in our society regard the heart and mind as separate or even opposed to each other. If, for example, a woman's common sense or upbringing tells her one thing, but her "heart" tells her another, what would a Hollywood script have her do? The answer, of course, is to "follow her heart"—leave her spouse and run off with a married man, or whatever. It seems that so many people believe that to follow the heart rather than the mind is living fully, sincerely, and "authentically" (whatever that means).

Every little girl sees Disney's version of *Cinderella*, where a common girl and a prince fall in love at first sight while dancing. In true Hollywood form, they marry almost immediately and live happily ever after. This scenario is a perfect example of the heart-over-mind view so popular today. No wonder the divorce rate is so high. Even Christians have not escaped this philosophy. When the mindless feelings go out of a marriage, there is nothing left to do but try to find that feeling with another partner. A friend of mine recently went to a wedding where the couple vowed to be married, not "till death do us part," but only "as long as we both shall love."

Sampson fell in love at first sight. He saw a gentile woman, and, unwilling to submit his feelings to God's command not to marry a pagan, he told his father, "Get her for me, for she looks good to me" (Judges 14:3). His father indulged him; could that be why Sampson grew up to be so impulsive? Unfortunately for Sampson, life doesn't follow popular myths. His heart-over-mind approach to life resulted in a tragedy—a short marriage, moral failure, wasted abilities, and a pitiful death.

In Scripture the heart and mind are not opposed; they are aspects of the same inner person. A person's heart is the center of her being, not the place of mindless romanticized urges.

Scripture represents the heart as having emotions, such as love (Deuteronomy 6:5), gladness (Psalm 104:15), grief (Romans 9:2), and desires (Psalm 37:4). But more than 700 times the word *heart* relates to our thoughts (for example, in Hebrews 4:12; Matthew 15:19). Our heart has convictions (Nehemiah 4:6), and wisdom resides there. The mind (*phroneo*) thinks, judges, discerns, and has insight.[6] Thus the heart is not just the seat of our emotions, nor is the mind opposed to our affections.[7]

What the Bible teaches collides with the popular notion that we ought to act with the heart—that is, on impulse—rather than with the mind or on reflection. We need both. That's why Scripture commands, "Consider your ways!" (Haggai 1:5).

TRANSFORMING THE MIND

Have you ever seen a copy of the painting *The Transfiguration* by Sanzio Raphael? The original hangs in the Vatican gallery. Its dramatic depiction is divided into three levels. The lower third of the canvas shows people in discord, some looking and gesturing toward a boy caught in sin. The middle part of the painting shows Peter, James, and John beholding the heavenly glory shining from above them. As they shield their eyes with their hands, they are as oblivious to the commotion below as the crowd is to the glory above. Yet the blinding light obscures what the upper part of the painting reveals—Christ talking with Moses and Elijah.[8]

The painting graphically portrays levels of spiritual transformation, from the crowd preoccupied with the sin of this world and blinded to God, to the apostles who are able to see something of God's glory, to the glorified saints who can behold the very face of God.

Wouldn't you love to have such inner transformation that your mind could, like those apostles, be focused on the glory of God rather than this passing world? This certainly is possible, but it doesn't come without a struggle.

The Battle for Our Thoughts

One summer day in 1505, a young man named Martin Luther was returning from his father's house when a blinding flash of lightning struck a nearby tree. Petrified, Luther took it as a warning from God that he needed to get his life right. He gave up the company of his drinking friends and entered a monastery. There he thought he could escape the influence of the world, the flesh, and the devil.[9]

In his anxious quest for piety, Luther would recite prayers in hypnotizing repetition, freeze in his unheated cubicle, fast, and scourge himself—all in the hope of finding purity and God's approval.[10] But none of this worked. Though he had escaped society, he could not escape his own worldly mind.

The battle for our thoughts is "not against flesh and blood, but against the rulers, against the powers, against the world forces of this darkness, against the spiritual forces of wickedness" (Ephesians 6:12). See the battle? Apparently the demonic spirits have their own domains. They certainly aren't going to sit by idly as those domains are invaded by Christians who are submitting to God and glorifying Him and getting others to do so as well. How vitally important it is for us women to pray for our pastors, church leaders, and others involved in ministry. They are prime targets of demonic attacks! And so are you as you strive to love the Lord with all your mind (Mark 12:30).

Attacks can take various forms, including temptations to be depressed, discouraged, to doubt, or to commit sin. Sometimes even physical problems are used, as in the case of Job (Job 2:4-5). Of course, not all physical problems are of demonic origin. Jesus said that a man was born blind so that "the works of God might be displayed in him" (John 9:3). Paul referred to Timothy's "frequent ailments" but said nothing about demons being responsible (1 Timothy 5:23). Nor did he blame demons for the illness of Trophimus (2 Timothy 4:20).

Sometimes attacks come from others who are outside the church. Paul said that Satan hindered him from seeing the Thessalonians (1 Thessalonians 2:18). How? He was run out of town. It seems that one or more persons were used by Satan.

Sometimes the actions of others make a person vulnerable to demonic attack. Paul said that when the Corinthians refused to forgive and to receive a sinning believer back into the fellowship, they were opening the situation to satanic schemes (2 Corinthians 2:6-8).

While attacks involving others depend on circumstances, those against our mind can come anytime. Usually they are sudden and surprising. Paul likened them to "flaming missiles" (Ephesians 6:16). But if we are trusting God with our lives, Paul said that faith protects us like a shield (Ephesians 6:16).

The first thought that caused mankind trouble came as a suggestion to Eve from Satan in the Garden of Eden. She was prompted to disobey God and eat the forbidden fruit. At that point she had a choice. She could reject the thought, realizing that a loving Creator would not withhold any good thing from her, or she could mull it over and consider doing it. She began to think it over and make the thought her own. At that point she had already lost the battle in her mind. Then she acted on the thought. In a similar way, Ananias and Sapphira allowed Satan to "fill" their hearts (Acts 5:3), and they fell.

One woman shared with me how guilty she felt over terrible thoughts that seemed to come out of nowhere when she would pray. While she shared this episode with me, I could only nod in agreement. I knew the story all too well and possibly you do, too. So what do you think? Is it a sin to have an evil thought occur to you? Should it be confessed or ignored?

Christ's Victorious Thought Life

Satan put into the mind of Christ the thought of doing about the worst thing ever. "All these things will I give You, if You fall down and worship me" (Matthew 4:9). What did Christ do after such a thought? Did He dwell on it? Did He think over the pleasures of having all those things or how He might be able to worship Satan and avoid the consequences? Or did He think about the steps He might take to actually do it? He did none of these things. He utterly rejected the idea, answering with Scripture. The devil left Him, and Christ did not sin (Matthew 4:10-11)—a very different ending to the same type of mental assault made on Eve and on Ananias and Sapphira.

Christ's example shows us that having an evil thought isn't a sin. It's what you do with the thought that determines whether it becomes a sin. When we get a sinful idea, we can either throw it out or make it our own. And what we keep in our minds has important consequences.

One way to protect our mind is to remember that if we sow a thought, we reap an act; sow an act, we reap a habit; sow a habit, we reap a character; sow a character, we reap a destiny.[11] We need to do what Christ did—*make Scripture a part of our thinking.*

Memorize

While in eastern Poland, minister Michael Billester gave a villager a Bible. Returning a few years later, he learned that 200 people had become believers through reading it. When they gathered to hear him preach, he suggested that each person quote some Scripture. One man rose and asked, "Did you mean verses or chapters?" It turned out that many of them could recite entire chapters and even whole Gospels. One had memorized all the Psalms. Between them they had memorized virtually the entire Bible.[12]

Seems incredible, doesn't it? Can you imagine memorizing dozens of verses or even whole chapters? What's the purpose anyway? Joshua told Israel that the point of memorizing God's Word was so that they could "be careful to do according to all that is written" (Joshua 1:8). The Word, especially when hidden in our heart, can guide us to purity (Psalm 119:9) and wisdom (Psalm 19:7), warn us (Psalm 19:11), comfort us in times of distress (Psalm 119:92), and delight our hearts (Psalm 19:10).

Many of the college courses I have taken required memorizing, and most of it I didn't enjoy. Memorizing a string of dates for a history class or the periodic chart of elements for chemistry seemed to have little relevance. But when I came to Christ, memorizing was no longer drudgery. It seemed to me to be the easy path to growth and discipleship for myself and others.

Everyone has to pick a way of memorizing that works for her. I take a verse that means a lot to me and write it on a 3x5 card. I can look at it occasionally when I am in the kitchen or doing laundry. I go over it, sometimes aloud, until it is easy to recall.

Another way to memorize is to take a short book of the Bible and read it or a part of it every day for a month. You may not have all of it down word for word, but you will know most of it very well.

I heard of one person who memorized much of the Bible by simply starting at the beginning of a book and reading the first verse out loud, including the verse reference. Then he would read that first verse and the second verse; then the first, second, and third verses, and so on through the chapter.

Another person who memorized whole books of the Bible would read the books into a tape recorder and then listen to them half an hour a day while driving or working around the house. After hearing it over so many times, he could remember everything virtually without having to work at it.

Memorizing verses enables us to recall them when the situation requires, and there are other benefits. Scripture says that as we apply our minds to God's knowledge, it will be pleasant, we will have the Word ready on our lips, our trust will be in the Lord, and we will know the certainty of the words of truth (Proverbs 22:18-21). Lastly, we can take those truths we memorize and meditate upon them whenever we want.

Meditation

Meditation isn't understood as well as memorization. The trouble is, meditation is often associated with the Eastern practice that is the opposite of Biblical meditation. Eastern meditation is done by emptying the mind; biblical meditation is done by filling the mind with biblical thoughts, thinking about them in a deep, concentrated way (Psalm 119:148) and personally applying them. Usually Christian meditation is on the Word of God, but it can also be about what God has done (Psalm 77:12). We are to meditate on the Word constantly, day and night (Psalm 1:2).

Pastor Arthur Pink says of meditation, "There can be no true progress in vital and practical godliness without it."[13] He doesn't mince words about the need to make time for it:

> Meditation on Divine things is not optional but obligatory, for it is something which God has commanded us to attend unto. . . . This plea 'I am too busy to engage in regular and spiritual meditation' is an idle excuse; yea it is worse—it is a deceit of your evil heart. It is not because you are short of

time, but because you lack a heart for the things of God! . . .
That which most occupies our heart will most engage the
mind, for our thoughts always follow our affections.[14]

Ouch! Pastor Pink has a point. Can we say we love the Lord and
yet never think of Him or His Word? Whatever we think of most
often, that is what we love the most. I will be the first to admit that
my mind gets preoccupied with many things, but I am learning that
the spiritual life isn't to be lived out haphazardly. It must be lived
from the inside out, beginning with the meditations of my heart
(Psalm 19:14).

Contrary to what I have always believed, meditation is far from
passive. We can dwell upon the meaning of a particular verse by
thinking about the words, the parts of the sentences, and the whole
thought. With that circulating through our minds, we can ask, how
does this affect us personally? For instance, is there an example from
our morning reading of Scripture for us to follow or a truth to
believe? And most importantly, how can we change as a result of what
we have read today?

I have found that meditation greatly increases my understanding of Scripture and deeply affects my inner life.[15] But ironically, I
have discovered as I grow in knowledge, I must beware of another
threat—pride.

The Humility of Christ

Paul warned that "knowledge makes arrogant" (1 Corinthians 8:1),
and he realized that he had received a thorn in the flesh to keep him
humble (2 Corinthians 12:7). As he knew, humility forms an important part of the Christian mind.

The secular mind has no place for humility and selflessness.
C. S. Lewis says, "It [the secular mind] looks at life through a tele-
scope that is turned the wrong way. It magnifies self and makes the
heavens small."[16]

Paul exhorts us to follow the most astounding example of humility, Christ Himself. Having all the privileges and glory of the godhead,

He set aside their use to become like any other man, and a slave at that. Furthermore, He became obedient to the point of death on a cross (Philippians 2:7-8).

As we look to Christ as our example, His life and death rebuke every form of pride we are capable of having:

Pride of birth and rank. "Is not this the carpenter's son?" (Matthew 13:55)

Pride of wealth. "The Son of Man has nowhere to lay His head" (Matthew 8:20).

Pride of respectability. "Can any good thing come out of Nazareth?" (John 1:46)

Pride of personal appearance. "He has no stately form or majesty" (Isaiah 53:2).

Pride of reputation. "Behold, a gluttonous man and a drunkard, a friend of tax gatherers and sinners!" (Matthew 11:19).

Pride of learning. "How has this man become learned, having never been educated?" (John 7:15).

Pride of superiority. "The Son of Man did not come to be served, but to serve" (Matthew 20:28).

Pride of success. "He came to His own, and those who were His own did not receive Him (John 1:11); "Not even His brothers were believing in Him" (John 7:5); "He was despised and forsaken of men" (Isaiah 53:3).

Pride of ability. "By myself I can do nothing" (John 5:30 NIV).

Pride of intellect. "I speak these things as the Father taught Me" (John 8:28).

Pride in death. "He humbled Himself by becoming obedient to the point of death, even death on a cross" (Philippians 2:8).[17]

Christ's type of humility wears a servant attitude like a badge. He said, "I seek not to please myself but him who sent me" (John 5:30 NIV). Paul had this same mind-set when he exhorted the Ephesians to aim at learning "what is pleasing to the Lord" (Ephesians 5:10). Thus the result of having the humility of Christ is doing the will of God (Matthew 6:10).

The will of God may lead us on a winding road that doesn't make sense, even to the most mature mind. But when the way gets puzzling, we can still trust in the omniscience of God. He knows the end from the beginning, and we can trust His character, knowing that His plans are aimed at accomplishing the best goals.

A Lifelong Mind Quest

In this book we have been discussing how we can form a godly character by discerning and doing the will of God in the various areas of life. In a sense, each of these areas connects to the mind. First of all, becoming godly takes a mind that is redeemed. Then the mind must be sanctified by being equipped with knowledge of the truth, by keeping feelings and impulses under control, and by being alert to the schemes of Satan. And, as we have said, it takes humility to maintain a servant's heart.

We have to think through the need and cost of having a godly mind and then be decisive about developing one. When Peter said, "Gird your minds for action" (1 Peter 1:13), he was using the idea of gathering up the bottom of a robe, which people had to do in order to move quickly.[18] Thus we have to decide to get our minds ready for action.

Making an initial decision to have a godly mind is the important first step. As in all areas of character, it takes continual effort to maintain and grow to greater godliness. It can be hard work! When Paul said that he was "taking every thought captive to the obedience of Christ" (2 Corinthians 10:5), he was likening the process to a military struggle.[19] But the serious effort pays off. As we shape our minds, we are shaping our lives, our character, our future.

Victory!

When we last looked at Luther, he was quite miserable in his thought-life. Monastic life and service failed to gain him peace of mind. Then, while preparing for his lectures at Wittenberg University, he was meditating on Romans 1:17, "The just shall live by faith." In a flash of spiritual light he suddenly grasped that salvation is based on grace; good works are done in gratitude. This insight utterly transformed his life and began the Reformation, which eventually transformed the entire Christian world. Imagine. It all started with a renewed mind.

How might you, too, have victory? You can have it . . .

If

If you can keep your faith in God when everyone about you
proclaims worldly beliefs, declaring Him untrue;
If you can discern those things that are excellent
when others say, "'tis not the thing for you to do";

If you can align your feelings with objective truth
despite the inner battle it brings;
If you can dwell upon whatever is lovely and of good repute,
trusting that peace shall be yours—like an endless stream;

If you can cling to right and spurn wrong,
though it may test your faith;
If you can reject temptation, singing God's song,
giving Him glory, honor, and praise;

If you can learn the Word in humility,
shunning a knowledge that makes arrogant,
If you can fight the battle of your thoughts with purity,
never forgetting you are God's servant;

If you can live out a lifelong mind quest,
which from its first steps is a journey toward godliness;
If you can take every thought captive
to the obedience of Christ,
then you, my friend, are shaping
your mind,
your character,
your future.
This is victory!

—D. M.

Thinking It Over

1. What are the benefits of having a renewed mind?

2. How do you go about renewing your mind?

3. How does Scripture represent the heart? How does it represent the mind? How are the heart and mind involved in the scriptural mandate to "consider your ways?" (Haggai 1:5).

4. This week, how will you work at developing a more victorious thought life?

Chapter 9

HOLDING ON
TO A GOOD CONSCIENCE

What's wrong, my friend?" said the Mind to the Conscience.

"Oh, everything," answered Conscience despairingly. "You get a lot of attention, but I feel as if people don't even know I exist."

Puzzled, Mind said, "I don't know what you mean."

"Well, let me put it this way," said Conscience. "Many people try to stretch you and fill you with knowledge. Most of them use you every day of their lives. Some even use you to try to 'show you off!' But it seems they would rather do without me."

"It can't be all that bad," chuckled Mind.

"I'm afraid it is," said Conscience. "I take a lot of abuse. Why, there was a man in North Carolina awhile back who was brought before a judge in traffic court for having parked his car in front of a sign that read No Stoping. Rather than plead guilty, the defendant argued that the missing letter in the sign meant that he had not violated the letter of the law. Having brought with him a dictionary, he noted that *stoping* means 'extracting ore from a stope or, loosely, underground.' He asked that the case be dismissed because he hadn't tried to extract any ore from the site. The judge had to agree and let him go.[1] It bothers me," Conscience went on, "that people try to get away with things. What's worse—some will even blame me!"

"Don't be discouraged," said Mind. "You have a tremendous purpose! You are actually a blessing because you drive people into the arms of the merciful God. What a friend you are to many!"

OUR CONSCIENCE, OUR FRIEND

How many of us have ever thought of our conscience as our friend? Very few, I am sure. We simply don't think much about our conscience. And yet our conscience is "there" all the time for us. It is well acquainted with us and can better judge us than any human being ever could, "for who among men knows the thoughts of a man except the spirit of the man, which is in him?" (1 Corinthians 2:11).

This friend is good at letting us know when we are crossing the line into gossip or coming close to anger, when we are being dishonest, or when we should flee the appearance of evil. Our conscience warns us of what God says in His Word, keeping many of us on the straight and narrow.

Our friend also tells us from time to time what we are loath to hear. Remember the confrontation King David's conscience had with him? His conscience reminded him of his guilt and brought him to repentance (in the Hebrew, conscience is attributed to the heart, *leb*[2], 1 Samuel 24:6; 2 Samuel 24:10; Psalm 51:10).

While we should place a high value on our conscience, there could be a problem. Remember when Jiminy Cricket told Pinocchio to let his conscience be his guide? This advice could be good or bad, depending upon the condition of our conscience. A person with a weak conscience, for example, can get into a lot of trouble! Anyone who thinks her conscience is an infallible guide can also be misled.

Just as the mind depends upon knowledge to develop, so must the conscience. It must be educated and well cared for. When we can use our conscience for more than just a red warning light, we will be able to discern not only moral values and principles, but we will be able to hear and apply the Word of God to our lives. It is then that we can make right choices in our lives. Unfortunately, some of us confuse our conscience with the voice of God.

Conscience and the Voice of God

While it is true that our conscience helps us hear and apply God's Word to our lives, we must keep in mind that the conscience is part of the human spirit, not the Holy Spirit (although, the Holy Spirit can help and use the conscience).

Our conscience is shaped by our upbringing, experiences, and other things. For instance, let's say my friend Linda was told while growing up that she should never wear jewelry. If Linda doesn't understand how the conscience works, she could be at a jewelry counter and think God is telling her not to buy anything. But that is not God speaking; that is just her conscience telling her what it was taught.

Our conscience gives back principles as guides, but that doesn't mean God is constantly whispering, "Do this; don't do that." People who take their conscience for the Holy Spirit are likely to be disillusioned when they think that God told them something, and it turns out to be wrong. So understanding the conscience is critical. Our conscience is not perfect. It needs to develop.

What makes it difficult these days to train the conscience is that each of us is bombarded with inaccurate moral information. The media constantly tell us that anger, jealousy, revenge, and even adultery are okay. How easy it would be for the woman who lacks discernment to get morally confused! The bottom line is—we have to constantly be maturing the conscience that we may be a reflection of God and His image.

But what if we already have a mature conscience? Everyone, including those with a mature conscience, can improve. Even Paul realized that his conscience might not tell him everything he was doing wrong. He said, "I am conscious of nothing against myself, yet I am not by this acquitted; but the one who examines me is the Lord" (1 Corinthians 4:4). The psalmist also believed that he could develop his conscience further, because he prayed, "Search me, O God, and know my heart; try me and know my anxieties; and see if there is any wicked way in me, and lead me in the way everlasting" (Psalm 139:23-24 NKJV).

So how do we improve the input our conscience can give us? By becoming aware of the ways the conscience gets abused. The conscience can be seared, ignored, defiled, left feeling continually guilty, and even weakened over time. But the conscience can also be kept clear, guilt-free, and growing—which produces a more discerning life. Let's go through these many phases.

THE SEARED CONSCIENCE

Years ago in a small English town lived a four-year-old named Tammi. She was active and carefree like any child her age, but in an important way she was different. At first no one knew that she was different. But then things began to happen. For example, one day after playing, Tammi ran into the house, held up her broken wrist, and said in amazement, "Look, Mommy, my hand is bent the wrong way!" Her mother didn't know whether to be more alarmed at the sight of her daughter's wrist or the fact that there were no tears coming from Tammi's eyes.

On another occasion when Tammi was six, her parents noticed that she was walking with a limp. A doctor discovered that she had a fractured thigh. Because once again the little girl felt no pain, her parents had her examined by medical specialists.

It didn't take long to diagnose Tammi's condition. She had ganglineuropathy. Simply put, Tammi had an insensitivity to pain. As she got older, she came to realize how much of a problem her numbness could be. She had to become alert and cautious in every activity she did. Now, as an adult, Tammi realizes that even the simple task of cooking could leave her seriously burned if she is not careful.[3]

Unfortunately, there is another type of insensitivity that is more dangerous than ganglineuropathy. This condition is a spiritual numbness to sin. The apostle Paul said that those who have this disease have seared their conscience as with a hot iron (1 Timothy 4:2).

This insensitivity starts when someone constantly disregards the conscience. And, in turn, the conscience fails to serve its purpose for the owner in major areas.

First, *the conscience fails the owner spiritually* when she falls away from the faith or pays attention to deceitful spirits and doctrines of demons. As much as the conscience would like to lead her to truth, it can't because she has seared her conscience with that branding iron Paul talks about (1 Timothy 4:2).

Secondly, *the conscience fails her in purity.* Purity is, of course, something internal rather than external. When the conscience is seared, purity dies. Paul mentions the extreme case when women exchanged the natural function for that which is unnatural (Romans 1:26).

Third, *the conscience fails her intellectually.* (Romans 1:18-20). Paul explains that in this world, God has made Himself "clearly seen" (Romans 1:20). At the beginning of history, man and woman knew God and knew His truth. Since that day in the Garden, those who have seared their conscience have not only suppressed the truth, but suppressed it in unrighteousness (Romans 1:18). This is not an issue of ignorance, for down deep women know the truth about God but do not allow the truth of His Word to work in their lives. Running away from conviction of sin, they turn the truth into a lie (Romans 1:25).

Lastly, *the conscience fails her because of rebellion.* If the woman refuses to have a personal relationship with God through Jesus Christ and therefore refuses to worship Him, the conscience cannot be of any real use to her. What she is really desiring is another god—self (Romans 1:25).

Self is the real object of worship when a person sins, whether through sexual perversion (Romans 1:24-27) or other sins such as gossip, slander, greed, strife, deceit, malice, or envy. In essence, the woman who sears her conscience concentrates on the pleasures of this life, whereas the woman who clears her conscience concentrates on joy.

For the Christian woman, joy is based on the fact that while she was still an enemy of God, Christ died for her (Romans 5:6). That makes her relationship with God secure because it can't be affected by circumstances or by her performance. The pleasures of sin cannot even compare to the joy of salvation.

Each one of us must choose between life and death, heaven or hell. The right choice is to be "born again" (John 3:3).

Not Works but Grace

The woman with a seared conscience doesn't realize that only the sacrifice of Christ can cleanse her conscience (Hebrews 9:14). Nor does she consider the fact that she has an eternal choice to make—heaven or hell. Rather, she strongly believes that her ticket into the kingdom comes from being "good."

You might be wondering how a woman who lives with a seared conscience can think of herself as a good person. Since she is numb to sin, she doesn't see herself as doing anything wrong. Though she doesn't accept God's standards for her life, she sees herself as a pretty good person because she isn't any worse than the people around her.

Remember the apostle Paul before he came to Christ? He lived as a Pharisee, the strictest sect of Judaism (Acts 26:5). He most assuredly considered himself as a good person, not to mention, quite zealous for his religion. Yet his conscience wasn't clear—not until he accepted God's own righteousness as a free gift (Ephesians 2:8-9).

Like Paul, most of us probably saw ourselves as pretty good people before having a real relationship with Jesus Christ. Now as Christians we can see that our own righteousness was as filthy rags (Isaiah 64:6 NIV).

While it seems "impossible" for a seared conscience to be healed from its bondage, we must remember that "with God all things are possible" (Matthew 19:26). There is hope for even the most severe case of spiritual ganglineuropathy. Look at Mary Magdalene with her seared conscience. Her suffering was severe. She lived deeply in sin while seven demons lived within her (Luke 8:2). Then one day the Eternal One cast out her demons (Mark 16:9) and liberated her soul. From that day forward she received the same eternal hope that others in Christ have.

Mary Magdalene's life is a perfect reminder that Christ didn't come to offer love and die just for the beautiful, the perfect, and the righteous people in the world. If He had, we would all be doomed, for Scripture says, "There is none righteous, not even one; there is none who understands, there is none who seeks for God; all have turned aside, together they have become useless; there is none who does good, there is not even one" (Romans 3:10-12).

How wonderful our Savior is. He came into this world to reach out to all of mankind—even those in the deepest pit—and offer them a new life with a clean slate. They also receive a new name written in gold, "Child of God."

THE IGNORED CONSCIENCE

Mark Twain once gave the following account:

> I was walking along a street and happened to see a cart full of watermelons. I was fond of watermelons, so I sneaked quietly up to the cart and snitched one. Then I ran into a nearby alley and sank my teeth into the melon. No sooner had I done so, however, than a strange feeling came over me. Without a moment's hesitation, I made my decision. I walked back to the cart, replaced the melon-and took a ripe one.[4]

As humorous as Twain's account may be, I am learning in life that it's dangerous to ignore my conscience on little things. I can end up ignoring my conscience on bigger things.

We remember what happened to King David in the affair of Bathsheba and the murder of her husband. Another example is Pilate. He listened too much to public opinion. He started out right, offering at least token obedience to his conscience by telling people he found no guilt in Christ (Luke 23:22). But rather than release Jesus right there on the spot (as he had wanted to in Luke 23:20), Pilate began to weaken. The pressure from the people was getting enormous, and well . . . Pilate must have surmised that it was easier to ignore his conscience than to ignore the people. He ended up releasing a murderer and letting Christ be condemned (Luke 23:22-25).

How can we avoid these slippery slopes? By being more discerning with our thoughts, actions, Scripture, and prayer.

Thoughts

Thinking about our actions beforehand is so important. Often people end up reflecting on their mistake when they should have been discerning about their plan before they took action on it. While it is helpful to look back over mistakes, that is an expensive way to learn. We all remember what happened to Peter. After denying that he knew Christ, he "called to mind" what Christ had said he would do. Then he wept bitterly (Mark 14:72 KJV). Had he thought ahead of time about the grief and shame his denial would bring, he would never have had reason to weep.

Can you recall a time in your life when you ignored your conscience because you weren't thinking of the consequences? I'm sure we all can. I personally have learned that the time to use my memory is before doing something—recall a principle from Scripture or what happened the last time I or someone else was in this kind of situation.

One of the best ways I have found to sniff out trouble is to look for selfish motives. Do I want something out of it? Am I trying to get people to like me or life to be more comfortable? Am I looking for an easy way out rather than the best way? Is there any compromising? Am I watching out for my weaknesses such as impatience or a desire to be a "somebody"?

With those sorts of things in mind, I can think about consequences:

- How would this course of action affect me personally, spiritually, mentally, and physically?

- How would it affect my family, friends, and people I am responsible for?

- How would it affect my testimony to my unsaved family members, neighbors, and coworkers?

- How would it affect my future? What are the lasting consequences?

Action

Thoughts tend to be followed by actions. If we can remember consequences and think through our situation carefully and honestly, then we are more likely to be more discerning in our actions. But there's an even greater motivating factor. That is to consider ourselves as influencers.

Take a marriage, for example. A woman's actions greatly influence her husband. If she is content, supportive, and responsive to his leadership, he will probably feel at peace and secure. He is more likely to be the leader and to be successful at what he does. If her actions contribute to a godly home environment, then she will be more than just a slightly glorified housemaid. She will be building godly character in children who one day will be ready to inspire the next generation. She may have humble surroundings, but her actions may one day be spoken of in heaven.

Scripture and Prayer

As we consider our ways, we also want to give serious thought to what God says. Rather than compromise His will, we can be a part of His will by asking Him to give us His wisdom (James 1:5) and to direct our steps (Proverbs 16:9). Because it isn't always easy to discern the deeper motives of our hearts, we can pray that God will weigh our motives (Proverbs 16:2).

One advantage of giving our situations and circumstances to God is that we can trust that He sovereignly controls every event. We can entrust our decisions and their outcomes to Him (Proverbs 16:33).

So what happens if a woman neglects to do these things and continues to ignore her conscience? Looking at worst-case scenarios, we can talk about Hymenaeus and Alexander. They ignored their consciences and shipwrecked their faith (1 Timothy 1:19-20). Though the details are not recorded, we know that they ended up blaspheming God somehow. As a result, they were "turned over to Satan" (1 Timothy 1:20).

Paul elaborates on this a little, with regard to someone else in serious sin. He told the Corinthians, "I have decided to deliver such a one to Satan for the destruction of his flesh, that his spirit may be saved in the day of the Lord Jesus" (1 Corinthians 5:5). This we could call "severe mercy" on God's part. Ignoring the conscience can lead people down that road even if they don't actually reach the same tragic ending.

While we may think there couldn't be anything sadder than a Christian ignoring the conscience, we may want to think again. Sadder yet is to defile it.

A DEFILED CONSCIENCE

I'll never forget my conversation with a drifter named Sam. He saw me reading my Bible while I was waiting for Brian at the airport and asked me about "that book." Excited about an opportunity to share, I quickly dove right into the topic of Jesus Christ, telling the man that despite our darkest sins, He forgives. Sam asked a lot of questions about God's forgiveness. And then as if the "lights had turned on," Sam shouted, "Wow, man . . . I get it! We can sin, ask for forgiveness, then sin more, ask for more forgiveness, then sin even more, and ask for more forgiveness. It doesn't matter how much we sin because we are forgiven. This Jesus Christ is a real dude!"

Just for the record, that's not what I told Sam. Somehow he got very mixed up. Sometimes we as Christians can get our interpretation of God's forgiveness a bit mixed up as well. I personally knew a woman who told me "flat out" that she didn't mind disobeying her conscience because she knew that Christ would forgive her sin. Paul says something about this attitude: "What shall we say then? Are we to continue in sin that grace might increase? May it never be! How shall we who died to sin still live in it?" (Romans 6:1-2).

Those who abuse the grace of God don't understand that His commands are based on His love. God knows what is best for His children. People who break His commands hurt themselves. Besides, Christians are supposed to be striving to please and glorify God even in the little things such as eating and drinking (1 Corinthians 10:31).

To defile the conscience is to defile the mind. Those guilty of corrupting their minds in this way need to ask themselves if they are truly followers of Jesus Christ (1 John 3:7-8). When the mind isn't filled with pure thoughts, one's actions aren't pure either.

How might the person with a defiled conscience face this issue? First, by admitting the transgression and, as Christ told the woman in adultery, "sin no more" (John. 8:11). A woman with a defiled conscience can take comfort in the fact that Christ knows of the powerful hold sin can have, and, though He did not sin, He "has been tempted in all things as we are" (Hebrews 4:15). Knowing our weakness, He prayed for us believers, that the Father would "sanctify them in the truth; Thy word is truth" (John 17:17).

A sanctified life is simply one that has been set apart for God's purposes.[5] Our example is Christ, who said He sanctified Himself for our sake (John 17:19). "He died for all, that they who live should no longer live for themselves, but for Him who died and rose again on their behalf" (2 Corinthians 5:15). So then we are crucified with Christ. He lives the new life in us (Galatians 2:20).

Being crucified with Christ means that our ego is vanquished, nailed to the cross. While crucifixion may seem a hard fate for a very real aspect of our natures, Galatians 2:20 is liberating because we now can be free from self-centeredness. We can come to know the joys of being sure of the will of God—really knowing the truth through His Word.

Being sanctified in the Word means that we know what God wants for our lives through His Word.[6] Yet all the knowledge we gain from Scripture won't do us a bit of good if we fail to apply it. Fortunately our conscience helps us apply it. That's why Paul said that the goal of instruction is love and a clear conscience (1 Timothy 1:5).

All this and more a woman with a defiled conscience can have. All she must do to receive cleansing is to embrace the love of God, His forgiveness, His Word, and begin to live a sanctified life. Sad to say, I've known some women who can't seem to get out of their defiled rut. It's not because they love their sin—no, they hate it! For the most part, they can't get out of their pit because they hang onto a sense of guilt over past sins.

THE GUILTY CONSCIENCE

For years now Candee has been experiencing a guilty conscience. She cannot forgive herself for the abortion she had before she came to know Christ. Because of her guilt, she doesn't have a deep sense of peace. No matter how hard she works at erasing her guilty feelings, those feelings follow her like a dark shadow.

Pilate too had a hard time with guilt. He tried to wash his hands of what would happen to Christ, but water couldn't remove his guilt or cleanse his conscience (Matthew 27:24).

Victor Hugo once said, "You can no more keep thought from returning to past transgression than you can keep the sea from returning to the shore after it has gone out. In the sea we call it the tide, but the guilty man calls it conscience. Conscience heaves the soul as the tide does the ocean."[7]

While we usually think of the nonbeliever as the one with a guilty conscience, a believer such as Candee can live with guilt for years and as a result lose her joy and intimacy with God.

Look at what happened to Robert Robinson. He lived in the eighteenth century and had been saved through the ministry of George Whitefield in England. At the age of twenty-three, he wrote the hymn "Come, Thou Fount."

> *Come, Thou Fount of ev'ry blessing,*
> *Tune my heart to sing Thy grace;*
> *Streams of mercy, never ceasing,*
> *Call for songs of loudest praise.*

Robinson wandered far from those streams and, like the Prodigal Son, got into carnality. One day when traveling in a stagecoach, he sat next to a young woman engrossed in a book. She ran across a verse she thought was beautiful and asked Robinson's opinion of it: "Prone to wander—Lord, I feel it—/Prone to leave the God I love."

Bursting into tears, Robinson said, "Madam, I am the poor unhappy man who wrote that hymn many years ago, and I would give a thousand worlds, if I had them, to enjoy the feelings I had then."[8]

Robinson's heart was obviously torn apart by guilt. He longed to come back to the Lord, but perhaps he thought his sin was so bad that God wouldn't take him back.

How can we get rid of the burden of guilt?

Getting Rid of the Guilt

If we are carrying guilt, we can dwell on how much God loves us and how eager He is to forgive. We must turn from sin and rely on the Lord to keep us from falling into it again. If we need to make things right with anyone, such as by asking their forgiveness, we should do that.

But what if things have improved in the relationship? Why dredge up the past? What if the offense wasn't even that significant? What if bringing it up makes things worse?[9]

If apologizing will truly help, then we should do it. In some situations it won't help. If guilt continues to plague us, we should give serious thought to trying to make things right. Remember how much the Lord values harmony between people. He said, "If therefore you are presenting your offering at the altar, and there remember that your brother has something against you, leave your offering there before the altar, and go your way; first be reconciled to your brother, and then come and present your offering" (Matthew 5:23-24).

Making things right takes real humility, and in the process we can look forward to the reward of a clear conscience, a better relationship with the offended party—and a better relationship with the Lord.

If you carry guilt from past sins, embrace the tender words of God, who gently says, "Though your sins are as scarlet, they will be as white as snow; Though they are red like crimson, they will be like wool" (Isaiah 1:18). God truly forgives and remembers our sins no more (Jeremiah 31:34). So why should we? Why visit the graves of dead sins. And why continue to plant weeping willows of penitence over them? Instead, let's cling to the Lord's promises. He says that all who call out to Him will receive from Him a steadfast mind and be kept in perfect peace (Isaiah 26:3). This is what the guilty conscience needs most!

Now that we've looked at the seared, the ignored, the defiled, and even the guilty conscience, let's consider a problem that new believers are most likely to have, but an area where mature believers need to be patient and sensitive.

THE WEAK CONSCIENCE

When I was a new believer, I thought a Christian should never listen to music that wasn't "Christian." While I still believe that the best musical themes are Christian, in my early years I was too dogmatic. I simply believed it was wrong for me to listen to any country, instrumental, or classical music just because Christ wasn't mentioned. My weak conscience made me what you could call a "modern-day Corinthian."

A Look at the Corinthians

The Corinthian church in Paul's day consisted of mostly new believers, and some of them had more zeal than knowledge. Like all believers, they were "sprinkled clean from an evil conscience" (Hebrews 10:22), but being young in Christ, many of them had consciences that were still weak in some areas. Their problem wasn't with secular music but with the local shopkeepers' practice of offering meat to idols for spiritual "cleansing" and then selling it (1 Corinthians 8:7).

Some of the new believers who had recently come out of idol worship thought it was wrong to eat the meat, whereas the older ones knew better because they knew the idols had no spiritual significance. The problem was that some who thought eating it was wrong were doing it anyway because they saw the more mature Christians eating the meat. The weak believers were having spiritual problems, or stumbling, because they were violating their consciences.

Paul said, in essence, to the more knowledgeable Christians, "Okay, we know that idols have no power (1 Corinthians 8:4), and we know we have liberty in Christ (1 Corinthians 8:9); as well, we have the freedom to eat or not eat the meat (1 Corinthians 8:8)—it doesn't matter either way. But let's look out for the weaker believer;

he's still growing!" There are two important lessons here, one for the weak believer and the other for the mature.

Messages to the Weak and the Mature

To the weak Christian, the lesson is that if she doesn't outgrow her overly restrictive conscience, she will never mature. Her thinking will tend to be dogmatic and legalistic. In our day the weak believer has her own list of "evils." For some it might have to do with hair length for men or women or the "sinfulness" of wearing bright colors, fancy jewelry, or even makeup. The most radical belief I've heard is that women are not to take pain relievers while giving birth because it supposedly violates God's pronouncement that "in pain you shall bring forth children" (Genesis 3:16). Strange, I've yet to hear anyone say it would be wrong for a man to work in an air-conditioned office because God told Adam he would have to work by the sweat of his brow! (Genesis 3:19).

There is a warning here for the more mature believer. Though we have freedom from such "rules," we need to be very careful that we don't make the more restrictive Christian stumble, wounding her conscience and "ruining" her walk with the Lord (1 Corinthians 8:11).[10]

For instance, during my dogmatic days one night I had dinner at another Christian's house. The mellow instrumental music playing in the background was a secular song, and that bothered my weak conscience. After struggling with it for a while, I asked that the music be turned off. Rather than argue the point that I was limiting my freedom in Christ, the family wisely turned off the music (1 Corinthians 8:13). What sensitivity!

There are so many gray areas that Christians should be careful not to be dogmatic about debatable issues. Each woman should follow her own conscience (Romans 14:5) and let others do the same (Romans 14:13). After all, each one is really accountable to God alone (Romans 14:4, 12). It all goes back to doing everything to the glory of God (1 Corinthians 10:31), and asking ourselves:

1. Is it beneficial? (1 Corinthians 6:12)
2. Is it addictive? (1 Corinthians 6:12)

3. Will it hinder the spiritual growth of another? (1 Corinthians 8:13)
4. Does it edify and build up? (1 Corinthians 10:23)[11]

CLEAR CONSCIENCE

Each one of us has a personal friend named Memory. She works on our character, and, yes, she must deal with fallen egos. You see, whenever Memory runs into Pride, they seem to argue.

Typically, Pride begins by rationalizing sin away, and Memory tries to get Pride to admit the way it really happened. Pride will reply, "Oh, it couldn't have been like that!" And, as much as Memory insists upon the plain facts, Pride ignores them. They argue their opposing sides trying to convince our consciences. Sad to say, there are times when Pride gets Memory so confused that she eventually gives in to the pressure.[12]

We who want to be more discerning must be aware of the battle between Pride and Memory. We must make sure that truth wins out, or we will never grow; we won't even learn from our mistakes because they will be erased from our mind. But Memory will always win if we are truly humble. Humility tells it like it is.

If we can hold firmly to the deep truths of faith and deal straight with our conscience (1 Timothy 3:9; 2 Timothy 1:3), we will be able to say with Paul, "I have lived my life with a perfectly good conscience before God up to this day" (Acts 23:1).

Charles Wesley's mother, Susanna, gave some advice for maintaining a clear conscience: "We avoid anything that weakens our reason, impairs the tenderness of our conscience, obscures our vision of God, or takes away the relish of spiritual things or increases the authority of our body over our mind. . . ."[13]

Doing as Mrs. Wesley suggests will lead any woman to a strong sense of confidence:

*   Confidence before God and man, because her heart does not condemn her (1 John 3:21).

- Confidence at the coming of the Lord, for there shall be no shame (1 John 2:28).
- Confidence at the throne of God. While all the redeemed have access to the throne, she shall go with a special confidence that allows her to freely confess, worship, praise, and petition.

Truly, she is at peace with God!

Thinking It Over

1. Can God use the conscience as His voice to speak to us?

2. How might a woman ignore her conscience? What are the consequences?

3. How does the sanctified life protect one's conscience?

4. What are steps in getting rid of a guilty conscience?

5. How can you be sensitive toward those with a weak conscience?

6. Read over Susanna Wesley's words and decide for the days ahead what steps you will take to maintain a clear conscience.

Chapter 10

DISCERNING THE
NATURE OF OUR PRAYERS

Today is Rebecca's wedding—a day she has looked forward to since she first tried on her mother's wedding dress when she was eight years old. Now she's wearing that same heirloom gown, with baby's breath and tender pink roses crowning her lace veil. Clutching her bouquet while clinging to her father's arm, she waits as the music beckons her to the altar. How excited she is! And yet she feels a deep uneasiness that won't go away.

She silently prays, "Dear God, I can hardly believe this is my wedding day. I haven't been able to spend much time with You lately, with all the rush of getting ready for today, and I'm sorry. I guess, too, that I feel a little guilty when I try to pray about all this, since Joe isn't a Christian. But, oh, Father, I love him so much—what else could I do? I just couldn't give him up. Oh, You must save him somehow, some way. You know how much I've prayed for him and that we've discussed the Gospel. I've tried not to be too religious because I didn't want to scare him off. He isn't antagonistic—I just can't understand why he hasn't responded. Oh, if only he were a Christian! Please bless our marriage anyway. I don't want to disobey You, but I do love him, and I want to be his wife, so please be with us this day. In Jesus' name, amen."[1]

This prayer sounds sincere, but stripped of its pious language, it would sound something like this:

"Dear Father, I don't want to disobey You, but I really do want to marry Joe. Please don't get me wrong. I do love You, but this is so important to me, and I want it my way. Deep down I know You know what is best for me, and I know that You don't like this, but please show Your blessings by not interfering; please bless the decision I've made and help me have a good time today. In Jesus' name, amen."[2]

One of the many things lacking in Rebecca's life—and in many of our lives—is the ability to discern the true nature of our prayers. Discernment encompasses all facets of our life, including prayer. Christ taught the disciples discernment in prayer just before He left this earth. He knew that without His physical presence, they would be dependent on prayer to make right decisions and choices.

PRAYING IN JESUS' NAME

I repeat, names are important. Those of you with children can probably remember going through a few baby books in search of the perfect name. While looking, you may have thought about what the name meant, expecting that someday it would mean something special to your child. We named our daughter Michelle, hoping she would become what her name means, a godly woman. Likewise with our son Johnathan, whose name means a gift from God. We hope he will become a gift to others throughout his life. Names are precious to us. If they weren't, we would probably see children with names like Judas, Delilah, or Jezebel!

Christ recognized the power names have. He made His name the basis for a promise to all believers throughout the ages that "whatever you ask in My name, that will I do, that the Father may be glorified in the Son. If you ask Me anything in My name, I will do it" (John 14:13-14).

"Whatever" has no limits. All God's resources, His strength, and His willingness to intervene are ours under one condition—that we ask in His name. Sad to say, many of us use Jesus' name like a credit card or, worse yet, like a magic incantation such as abracadabra. I must admit, there was a time when I believed that I had to tag Christ's name at the end of every prayer if I wanted it granted. I've since learned that this is not what praying in Christ's name is all about.

The great prayer warrior E. M. Bounds (1835-1913) wrote that praying in Christ's name means to "bear His nature, to stand for all for which He stood, for righteousness, truth, holiness and zeal. It means to be one with God as He was, one in spirit, in will and in purpose. It means that our praying is singly and solely for God's glory through His Son. It means that we abide in Him, that Christ prays through us, lives in us and shines out of us; that we pray by the Holy Spirit according to the will of God."[3] The essence of praying anything in the name of Christ then is to pray as He would pray. So how did Christ pray?

First, He prayed with pure motives. Often we think prayer starts with our words, but Christ taught that it actually begins with our motives. Motives reveal our character.

Discerning Our Motives

Remember Mrs. Zebedee? We don't know much about her except that she had two sons, James and John, who followed Christ (Matthew 4:21; Mark 1:19-20. Some infer that she is Salome, and even that she is Jesus' aunt). Mrs. Zebedee herself was no stranger to Christ, and one day she made it obvious that there was still room for growth in her relationship with Him.

That day, with appropriate reverence no doubt, she approached Christ, asking, "Command that in Your kingdom these two sons of mine may sit, one on Your right and one on Your left" (Matthew 20:21).

Christ gave little thought to her presumptuous request, for He lovingly but firmly said, "You do not know what you are asking for" (Matthew 20:22). That was the end of that "prayer."

The wrong motives behind Mrs. Zebedee's request were exposed. Granting her request would not only have exalted her sons but herself as their mother. She could have reveled in the prestige, and pride would have had its day with her.

Instead, what a humbling lesson for Mrs. Zebedee—and also for us. How many of our prayer requests, if our true motives were exposed, would be as self-serving? Do we realize what we are praying? Before we pray, we can discern our motives by asking ourselves a few questions.

1. *Why am I asking for this?* It seems obvious that we need to ask this question, but most of us don't. We assume that if we want something, it must be right to want it. And we assume that if what we want is good, then we must want it for the right reasons. Not so.

2. *Am I praying for my own pleasure?* We have to be really honest with ourselves here. Some of us may have to discern, for example, whether we are praying for a marriage partner because we see that person as the ultimate fulfillment of our lives—a role that only God can fill. That prayer for a husband's conversion may have no higher motive than to remove the awkwardness of going to church alone so we can be like our other friends or to allow us to become involved in a ministry we think would fulfill us personally. Behind a prayer for God's provision may be merely the desire to lead a comfortable life that makes few demands on us.

James reminds us that "you ask and do not receive, because you ask with wrong motives, so that you may spend it on your pleasures" (James 4:3). If we desire any benefit or blessing, our focus in prayer must be to honor God, not to seek after our comfort or pleasure.

3. *Am I praying "to the glory of God"?* Paul says that everything we do, even routine things such as eating, should be done to glorify God (1 Corinthians 10:31). How much more should our prayers do so. Our prayers for a husband, for example, might include that we be enabled to help him be all he can be for God. Prayer for financial blessing might have the aim of expanding God's kingdom, pleasing Him by making Him known.

One person who understood proper motives in prayer was Samuel Zeller. In 1911 seminary professor Ole Hallesby visited him in Switzerland where Zeller conducted spiritual retreats. Hallesby observed: "I do not believe that I have ever heard anyone expect so much of God and so little of his own prayers as he did. . . . As I listened to these prayers of his, I had to say to myself, ' . . . he prays only one prayer, namely, that the name of God might be glorified.'"[4] Zeller sought to advance God's purposes, not his own.

PRAYERS WITHOUT ACTION

I remember once meeting a Christian woman who said point blank, "I would love to get to know you by talking on the telephone from time to time, but don't expect our families to get together. No offense—it's just that we don't entertain, and we like to keep to ourselves." After this woman's remark, I started to think how much this is becoming the norm in the Christian community. Why? Because we are living in a society that craves privacy and lack of involvement.

Our tendency to be detached even extends to attitudes toward prayer. Prayer can become a way of doing something without getting personally involved. If we don't want to do something, we simply pray about it. Christ told a story that challenges lack of involvement, and that lesson applies to our prayer life.

The story went something like this: In a hot, barren land, a man has been left for dead by robbers. Lying in his own blood, he moans from deep wounds and desperately needs water.

A priest arrives, wearing the white linen garment that symbolizes holiness and glory. His coat, woven in one piece without a seam, represents spiritual integrity, wholeness, and righteousness. A four-cornered cloth proudly symbolizes that he belongs to the kingdom of God. His cap, which resembles the opening of a flower, signifies fresh and vigorous life. His sash symbolizes service.[5] Despite the meaning of the priest's attire, he fails to stop and help and even crosses the road to avoid the victim (Luke 10:31). Perhaps he offered up a prayer that someone would come and help the man.

Next comes a Levite. As a descendant of Levi, this man assists the priests in Israel's worship, preparing the offering and leading people into confession and worship.[6] Despite his holy position, he, too, passes by on the other side of the road.

Next comes a Samaritan. Most likely he is on foreign soil, because priests and Levites would never set foot in Samaria (John 4:9). Samaritans were twice despised. They were the product of intermarriage with gentiles, and they had adopted what amounted to heresies. Yet this Samaritan stops and treats the victim's wounds, taking him to an inn, and paying for his care. He even gives the innkeeper a blank check by saying, "Whatever more you spend, when I return, I will repay you" (Luke 10:35).

It is as if Christ had said in twentieth-century lingo, "The pastor did not stop; the deacon did not stop. But the pot-smoking, tattooed motorcycle gang member stopped and cared for the injured man." Christ tells us, "Go and do the same" (Luke 10:37).

The story reminds me of a late night when Brian and I were driving home. We were miles from a town when we saw two people in the shadows, stranded by the side of the road. Glancing at our newborn daughter and remembering that a friend of mine had gotten into serious trouble helping a motorist, I begged Brian not to stop. But he suggested that we pull over and, if it looked risky, drive away. In those few decision-making seconds, compassion had to pass the test of discernment (there have been other times when we did not stop—that, too, by the Lord's leading, I would like to think).

As our headlights lit up a couple in their twenties, there was something vaguely familiar about the young man. It was the son of a man we had been trying to reach for Christ. Driving the couple home was the perfect opportunity to show that our faith is more than words.

God loves devotion that goes beyond words. For God, it's action that makes a person's words—and life—genuine. Without action, words are hollow and cheap. Christ blasted the Pharisees for being all religious talk and no godly action. Prayers from such a life will get nowhere with God. But He is especially attentive to the prayers of people who show their obedience in action. As James said, "The prayer of a righteous man is powerful and effective" (James 5:16 NIV).

Bringing Mercy into Prayer

When Jesus was traveling through Samaria toward Jerusalem, He sent messengers ahead to make arrangements for His travels. Word came back that the Samaritans (who knew that most Jews disliked them, and they returned the favor) would not receive Him. Perhaps remembering that Elijah had called down fire from heaven to burn up the wicked King Ahaziah's soldiers (2 Kings 1:10, 12), James and John asked Jesus if He wanted them to call down fire on the inhospitable Samaritans (Luke 9:54). Rather than approve the suggestion, Jesus rebuked them. Christ had come on a mission of mercy, whereas the prayer James and John had in mind missed His emphasis completely.

It's easy for those who represent Christ to miss His emphasis on mercy. One Christian woman found that out the hard way. Years ago Cheryl got pregnant out of wedlock. The father wanted no responsibility for the child, and she was left to carry the burden alone. Little did she realize that from the beginning of the pregnancy to the present day, the hardest people to deal with would be fellow Christians. She has been told constantly that her struggles as an unmarried mother stem from her past immorality.

After the baby was born, Cheryl got a job, but as time went on, it became increasingly difficult for her to raise her child with her weekly paycheck. She went to her church for help. Sitting down with the pastor who handles the benevolence fund, Cheryl explained her struggles. His answer was one that had become all too familiar to her: She was bearing the consequences of her sin. He said he would pray and told her to call back in a month to let him know how things were going. Cheryl left without any assistance, thinking, *How long must I hear the same message? God has forgiven me. Why can't others?* In tears she cried, "All I need is help!"

Mercy reaches out to someone in need, and that often means treating them in a way they do not deserve. God gave us examples in the parable of the Prodigal Son and the conversion of the apostle Paul. And, of course, we ourselves did not deserve God's mercy.

Becoming more merciful begins as we open our eyes, our ears, our hearts, and our hands to others in spite of their past sins. It requires finding out their hurts and needs—and helping. If we personally cannot help, we should ask ourselves who can. We cannot rule out that divine providence may have had a part in bringing that person to us. While we can pray for them, we have to beware of using prayer as a substitute for other ways of helping.

Certainly there are times when we can do nothing but pray—and that is doing a lot—but what about times when we can also become part of the answer to that prayer? So much the better if we can pray for the person who is out of work and then provide money or groceries. Many unwed mothers have many needs—housing, clothing, money, and a listening ear.

We may also substitute prayer for our personal responsibility to evangelize others. While we may pray, for example, that God would bring the elderly to Christ, we ourselves can become the messengers. Most of us live within easy driving distance of one of the neediest places in our society—a convalescent or retirement home. Perhaps you can't go, but God may want to use you to find someone who can.

Years ago a woman named Rosie approached me and asked if I would consider starting a Bible study for women at a retirement home where her grandmother lived. Rosie was moving out of state and hated the thought of her grandmother not having any spiritual input. Instead of merely praying for someone to come along, she went a step further and started searching for the person she was praying for.

We pray best when we are willing to become involved. While God is sovereign, His work is usually done through people. We must discern whether we can do nothing more than pray, or whether God is calling us down a dusty road to help.

PRAYERS OF COMPLAINT

"Dear Lord, when are You going to answer my prayer? I have gone over and over my situation with You, but You don't seem to be hearing me! I am sick and tired of my circumstances! I want to move to a nicer city and get a better job. But because You haven't provided any other job opportunity, I'm stuck here! Why are You tormenting me? Haven't I done much for You? I've been serving You in ministries for over fifteen years now. Can't you just answer this one prayer? Well, I've got to go now. I'll be back."

If I were God, I certainly wouldn't want that person to come back to me in prayer! Prayers of complaint are like the clay that questions the wisdom of the potter (Romans 9:19-21). When adversity comes, it is easy to blame God, even if covertly, by complaining about our circumstances. The Israelites did so time and again in their early history. They complained angrily to Moses when the Egyptian chariots were catching up with them at the Red Sea (Exodus 14:10-12), at Marah because the water was bitter (Exodus 15:23-24), in the wilderness of Sin because they remembered better food in Egypt (Exodus 16:2-3, forgetting they were slaves in Egypt), at Rephidim because they lacked water (Exodus 17:3), and at Kadesh-Barnea because the spies had come back with the upsetting report that Israel could never possess the valley of Eshcol due to the great size and strength of its inhabitants (Numbers 13:25-14:3; they also forgot that God is bigger and stronger).

Though the protests of the Israelites were often directed toward Moses and Aaron, Moses revealed their ultimate target, "Your grumblings are not against us but against the Lord" (Exodus 16:8). There is often a connection between our sin and our tendency to blame God. Remember the very first sin in the Garden of Eden. Adam said that he ate of the tree because "the woman *you put here with me*—she gave me some fruit from the tree, and I ate it" (Genesis 3:12 NIV, emphasis added).

I never seriously thought much about how God receives complaints until getting acquainted with a fellow summer missionary in Central America who complained and argued about everything. He was a classic example of a person who could not see good in anything! If it was sunny, he complained about the heat. If it rained, it was too cold. He complained about the food, the people, and fellow missionaries. It wouldn't have surprised me if he had complained out loud about God!

As time went on, I could no longer handle his negativity. I developed a simple plan. Each time he batted out a negative, I would pitch back a positive. On one occasion I, my complaining associate, and another missionary were walking up a steep hill to a nearby village. Of course, he griped all the way up the hill, especially when we had to force our way through high weeds. What he didn't notice were the gorgeous yellow flowers sprinkled throughout the weeds. Trying to bring out the positive, the other missionary and I collected a handful of these exquisite buds and formed them into a bouquet. Opening our friend's clenched fist, we gently gave him a handful of fragrant beauty. He remained silent during the remaining trek up the hill.

I wonder whether God sorrows over our prayers of complaint. I wonder, too, if He doesn't try to help us look beyond our petty complaints to His beauty and higher purposes. When we complain about the weeds, is He trying to get us to see the bouquet?

We pray, "Lord, I don't want this trial!" God replies, "Consider it all joy . . . when you encounter various trials" (James 1:2).

We pray, "Lord, why did You give me such noisy, inconsiderate neighbors?" He replies: "Love your enemies, and do good" (Luke 6:35).

"Lord, my boss intimidates me and mocks my faith; I don't like going to work!" He lovingly says: "If you should suffer for the sake of righteousness, you are blessed. And do not fear their intimidation, and do not be troubled" (1 Peter 3:14).

"But, Lord, I am so unhappy!" My dear child, "Do not be grieved, for the joy of the Lord is your strength" (Nehemiah 8:10).

Above all, God may be reminding us that He loved the world so much that He gave us His Son to die that we might live (John 3:16).

Collecting Our Thoughts

Contemplating God's great gift, Jesus Christ, I am greatly convicted about my own prayer-life, especially as I am reminded by Solomon to be more thoughtful about my prayers: "Do not be hasty in word or impulsive in thought to bring up a matter in the presence of God. For God is in heaven and you are on the earth; therefore let your words be few" (Ecclesiastes 5:2). I am reminded that when I pray, I am not speaking to just anyone. I am approaching the infinitely exalted God, the King of kings, the Lord of lords. Can I carelessly approach Him without collecting my thoughts?

After Paul had been under house arrest in Rome for two full years, he wrote to his prayer warriors in Asia Minor, "I ask you not to lose heart at my tribulations on your behalf, for they are your glory" (Ephesians 3:13). Though Paul was in miserable circumstances, he prayed that *they* would not lose heart!

We never see Paul throwing his arms up in frustration to God asking the "Why me?" or "How long?" questions. Rather, he looked at his situation and had the maturity to realize that his problems ultimately benefited others. Forgetting the opportunities he had missed while sitting in a stinking, stifling prison, he focused on what God wanted to do in other peoples' lives through his circumstances.

When things seem to be going so wrong—a death in the family, sickness, financial struggles—we should take time to focus on what God may be trying to do. When things get hard, nonbelievers watch to see if the faith we've been sharing with them is real. Peter said that while we are in affliction, we need to be able to tell others why we have hope in God (1 Peter 3:14-15).

Afflictions and other difficulties have a way of keeping our eyes away from temptations that surround us and help us keep our eyes on the Lord. They also help us learn obedience through suffering (Hebrews 5:8). Also hard times strengthen our faith (1 Peter 1:6-7) and produce endurance, which results in our being perfect and complete, lacking in nothing (James 1:3-4). Best of all, Christ will perfect, confirm, strengthen, and establish us.

IN ALL THINGS GIVE THANKS

A right attitude starts with giving thanks in everything (1 Thessalonians 5:18). Does this mean I am to be thankful for every tragedy in my life? No, that's not the point of the verse. I am to be thankful "in" the circumstance, not "for" it.

Learning to be thankful doesn't come naturally to most of us. Sometimes it takes seeing someone who is far worse off, such as the man who stopped complaining about having no shoes when he met a man who had no feet.

The Tasteberry

In Africa there is a fruit called the tasteberry. The uniqueness of this fruit changes a person's taste so that everything eaten is relished as sweet and pleasant. Sour fruit, even if eaten several hours after eating the tasteberry, becomes sweet and delicious.[7]

Gratitude is the "tasteberry" of Christianity. When our hearts are filled with gratitude, nothing that God sends us seems unpleasant. A grieving heart can be sweetened with gratitude. A burdened soul can be lightened by singing God's praises. Discouragement and loneliness are dispelled by making others grateful. Feeble and frail? Grow strong in spirit, thanking God for His love.[8]

So how can we express more gratitude in our prayer lives? We can learn from the Puritans. Centuries ago they used to write out their prayers. Those prayers are a model of thoughtfulness and discernment. But the words they used were not the first ones that came to mind; they wrote and rewrote. If they detected ingratitude, they would rewrite until the prayer expressed praise. The process helped them grow spiritually, because as their prayers improved, they changed, too.

Whatever means we find to grow in prayer, let's keep in mind the words of evangelist R. A. Torrey, who once observed that having discernment in prayer will "promote our personal piety, our individual holiness, our individual growth into the likeness of our Lord and Savior Jesus Christ as nothing else."[9]

Thinking It Over

1. As you pray this week, think about the motives behind your requests. Are you praying unselfishly?

2. What are some things you could do to become part of the answer to your own prayer request?

3. Think over some of the things you pray about regularly. Write a prayer for those things. Then like the Puritans, read it over and rewrite it until you are satisfied it represents your best effort.

Chapter 11

TRUE

SPIRITUAL WORSHIP

Let me tell you a tale. One day a woman named Hilda was praying when she saw the door of heaven open and heard a voice speaking like the sound of a trumpet: "Come up here." Slowly, she entered heaven and witnessed the most glorious sight—God, with a countenance like jasper and sardius stone, sitting on the throne. Around the throne, there was a rainbow, like an emerald in appearance.

Hilda stood in awe as the drama of worship unfolded before her very eyes. Angels surrounded the throne, proclaiming, "Holy, holy, holy, is the Lord God, the Almighty, who was and who is and who is to come" (Revelation 4:8).

Hilda was enraptured, but her concentration was interrupted by an earthly interference, the telephone. Rather than ignore it, Hilda began reaching to answer it, but an angel blocked her way. "Oh, Hilda, why not let earthly things fade for the time being?" Gently grabbing her arm, he beckoned her to follow him.

After walking a short distance, the angel stopped and asked Hilda to observe twenty-four elders casting their crowns before the throne. Kneeling before the King of Kings they proclaimed in unison: "Thou art worthy, O Lord, to receive glory and honor and power: for thou hast created all things, and for thy pleasure they are and were created" (Revelation 4:11 KJV).

As the elders became silent, Hilda was prompted by the angel to go to the throne and commune with God. Slowly and reverently she bowed before the Almighty and prayed: "Dear heavenly Father, my car isn't running very well. Please help me get it fixed. And my dentist appointment is today. May there be little pain. Oh! And before I forget, our family has the opportunity to go to Hawaii for a week. Please let my husband's boss grant his request for an early vacation! And please, Lord—"

"No, no, no!" interrupted the angel. "This is not worship! You are focusing more on *presents* from God than on the *presence* of God. True worship is coming before the Almighty with your will in submission to His—not the other way around. Come, I want to take you back to earth and give you a new perspective on worship altogether."

And so, with a gust of wind carrying them along, Hilda found herself inside a crowded church in the city. With excitement, Hilda shouted, "This is my church! There I am sitting in the pew with my family!" The angel directed Hilda to observe the service quietly.

The ceremony started with the organist moving her fingers over the keys, but no music came forth from the pipes. The choir rose to sing, but while their lips moved, not a sound could be heard. An elder stepped into the pulpit and read Scripture, the congregation joined in repeating a prayer, and the pastor preached his sermon. Through it all, Hilda and the angel heard absolutely nothing.[1]

Puzzled she asked, "Why am I not hearing anything?"

The angel replied, "Because there is nothing worth hearing. You are seeing this worship service not as man sees it, but as God sees it.[2] It hurts Him to see that those who are called by His name know so little about true spiritual worship."

After the service, Hilda followed the congregation outside the church. Then she gasped, "The church's sign says Ichabod Community Church! That's not the name of this church!"

"Hilda," said the angel solemnly, "that may not be what man has named it, but that is the name God has inscribed for it. In Hebrew *Ichabod* means "no glory" (1 Samuel 4:21).

Downcast, Hilda had seen enough and asked to leave. "No," the angel said. "You need to see more."

So the angel took her to her home and said, "Observe yourself." Hilda noticed herself doing housework with a sense of unbearable drudgery, complaining inwardly as she changed diapers. "Is this all there is to my life?" she heard herself wonder bitterly. She looked on as she saw herself prepare meals without a servant's heart and wash the dishes in self-pity. Hilda noticed that while dealing with the children, her patience was short, and her discipline was done in anger.

Her television watching showed little discretion, and time with friends produced little spiritual edification. From her heavenly perspective, she saw that her godly example was dim indeed. Beginning to get defensive, Hilda asked, "Why are you showing me this?"

"It is my hope," replied the angel, "that you will notice the attitude in which all of this is done. Is God being exalted?"

Without thinking much, Hilda asked, "What does that have to do with worship?"

The angel simply answered, "You shall see."

He took Hilda to the inner chambers of her heart and mind where choices in life are made. He asked, "What do you see here?"

She replied, "Nothing much; it's quite dark in here."

"Exactly," said the angel. "It is dark in many a believer's heart and mind because they are not immersing themselves in the things that reflect light. Because of this, their worship of God is neglected. In essence they are saying, 'There is no God,' because they choose not to acknowledge Him and worship Him for what He is—God. Remember when you heard the heavenly elders worshiping? What were they doing?"

Not understanding the question fully, Hilda shrugged her shoulders. The angel answered, "They were proclaiming truth about God. Think about what this means in terms of your own worship. Also," he continued, "keep in mind that worship includes practicing the presence of God in your life. It involves giving Him your heart, not just your tongue, for words to Him are meaningless if they do not come from the heart. Therefore, empty your heart of all that competes with God, for He desires to possess it, direct it, and do with it what He pleases."

As the angel was departing, his last words echoed into the distance, "Ask God to give you the discernment to know when you are reflecting His character and when you are not, for true spiritual worship reflects the glory of God in all things."

What would you see if you were given a heavenly perspective on *your* worship?

ICHABOD COMMUNITY CHURCH

In 1797 Samuel Taylor Coleridge wrote a strange poem about an old seaman who sees corpses of dead men rising up to run a ship. In "The Rime of the Ancient Mariner" these dead sailors are pulling the rope, steering the ship, spreading the sails, and "singing spectral carols."[3]

The poem reminds me of those in Ichabod Community Church who were spiritually dead, corpses participating in singing, in prayer, in praise, in thanksgiving, in worship. The apostle Paul gives us this same idea of a corpse when he talks of the woman who is "dead even while she lives" (1 Timothy 5:6).

Worshipers who are spiritually dead have no enthusiasm for the things of God. What can you imagine would cause such numb worship, a worship that portrays only the "form of godliness?" Possibly a number of things, but there's one thing for certain—these people have an imperfect view of the perfect God. Each one of us needs to discern for herself: Is my concept of God accurate?

An Imperfect View of a Perfect God

A high honor was given to court painter William Scrots when he was asked to paint a portrait of Edward VI, future king of England. Getting to work immediately, Scrots worked arduously on the masterpiece, not allowing anyone to see it.

Finally, at the moment of the unveiling, people gasped in shock. The royal portrait appeared to be nothing more than a bad joke. Many believed the painting to be a mockery and a great injustice to the future king. The skull ballooned in back, the forehead bulged, the nose looked like a beak, and the chin undershot the face.[4]

Furious, King Edward wanted an explanation for such blatant disrespect. Without defending himself, Scrots asked the king to squint at the picture through a peephole. Edward saw in the side of the frame a fine representation with no deformities. Scrots's unusual painting is called "anamorphosis art," which allows a distorted image to appear without distortion when viewed from one particular vantage point.[5] How many of us view God from the wrong angle, seeing Him in a distorted way?

VIEWS OF GOD

Years before I gave my life to Christ, I had quite a few distorted views of God. One view I had was of Father Killjoy who was always snooping around to see if people were enjoying themselves, and, if so, He tried to stop them. [6]

Later as a newborn in Christ, my distorted thinking wasn't altogether eliminated. I began to think of God as Father Slot Machine. I could put in a quick prayer, and out would come nickels, dimes, and quarters of pardon, guidance, or healing.

Others view God as Father Santa, who gives us whatever we want, or as Father Pawnbroker, who's willing to make a shrewd deal—offer Him a bit more evangelism or better church attendance, and He'll give you that house or relationship you want.

Father Revenge pays us back with suffering because of sin in our lives. Only the most pious escape a visit from Him. From time to time I have caught myself viewing God from this distorting angle. The disciples saw God that way, too, on occasion. Meeting a blind man on the road, they asked Christ, "Who sinned, this man or his parents?" (John 9:2). Neither one, was the answer.

Job's three friends also saw God as vengeful. Convinced that God had afflicted Job because of sin, they came to visit with confrontation, not comforting, in mind. Eliphaz urged Job to repent (Job 5:8-27). Bildad said the reason that Job's children were killed was because of their sins (8:4). Zophar, even more blunt and harsh, added that God gave Job only a fraction of what he really deserved (11:6).[7]

Job rejected their views of him and of God, saying that it would have been better had they kept silent (13:4-5). He pointed out that the wicked don't always suffer. In fact, quite often they prosper (9:24).[8]

Though Job tried to defend himself and his view of the Almighty, there was a moment when he, too, had a distorted view of God. He fell to thinking of God as somewhat aloof from him in his need (23:3; 9:32-33). How many of us have ever thought of God as aloof and distant, a sort of impersonal scientist we can't get close to? Or we may feel that God works clandestinely, never wanting us to know what He is doing. This type of thinking can deaden our worship.

A. W. Tozer once said that the most important thing about us is what comes into our minds when we think about God.[9] So how can we develop a right concept of God? A careful in-depth look at His attributes will banish the distorted, damaging views.

The Importance of Knowing God

Years ago on my wedding day, I made some promises to Brian before a host of witnesses. Along with the promise of a lifetime commitment, I also vowed to myself something else. I promised that I would think each day about one of Brian's many good qualities. My purpose for doing this was twofold. First, to keep my love, respect, and admiration for my husband alive and growing; and second, to continually discover new things about him. We can do the same sort of thing in our relationship with the Lord—by dwelling upon His attributes.

Jeremiah saw enough affliction and tragedy (Lamentations 3:1) to stupefy most of us. Yet he could still offer praise because he knew God so well. Jeremiah could exalt God's *sovereignty:* "Who is there who speaks and it comes to pass, unless the Lord has commanded it?" (Lamentations 3:37); His *presence:* "Pour out your heart like water before the presence of the Lord" (2:19); His *love:* "The Lord's lovingkindnesses indeed never cease" (3:22); His *compassion:* "His compassions never fail" (3:22); and His *faithfulness:* "Great is Thy faithfulness" (3:23).

The secret to Jeremiah's spiritual success was that he made the knowledge of God His primary pursuit. The knowledge of God is a prize, something to strive for. God told Jeremiah, "Let him who boasts boast of this, that he understands and knows Me" (Jeremiah 9:24).[10]

THE NAMES OF GOD

One way God helps us to understand Him better is through His names. The names of God have given me a whole new perspective on who He is, for they reveal His attributes. An attribute of God is a quality of His, something true of Him. His attributes have direct application to our lives. For example, because He is sovereign, we can rest in His control of all events. Because He's omnipotent, we can trust His power in the face of adversity. Because He's wise, we can have divine guidance in our lives.

Elohim (el-lo-heem'), for example, is translated "God," and it emphasizes supreme power, sovereignty, and glory.[11] He is in control of all things. As we worship, we can be in awe that Elohim is, "My refuge and my fortress, My God (Elohim), in whom I trust!" (Psalm 91:2). Theologian Elmer Martens points out that one name of God made from Elohim (*El Elyon*) emphasizes that He is exalted and has the right to absolute lordship (Psalm 9:1).[12] He is the Most High One.

Another name, *El-Shaddai* (el shad-di'), is translated "Almighty God" (Genesis 17:1-2) and is used in connection with judging, chastening, and purging (Proverbs 3:12).[13] We can rejoice in worship, knowing it is He who says, "Those whom I love, I reprove and discipline; be zealous therefore, and repent" (Revelation 3:19).

Adonai (a-do-ni') means "Lord and Master" and is used in our relationship to Him as His servants.[14] Abraham, Isaac, and Jacob acknowledged themselves as God's servants.[15] What an honor to be servants of Adonai as we humbly come before Him!

God identified Himself to Moses as *Yahweh*, which could be translated "I Am."[16] Jews regarded this name as so sacred they did not even pronounce it. Martens says that the name indicates that God is present to act and to save.[17] He is near us and helps us in our human struggle. He is often called the "Lord of Hosts" because He is a king whose will prevails (Isaiah 14:24), and He has more than enough forces to win every battle. We can rejoice that He is more than adequate to confront anything that opposes us.

There are over 100 descriptive names for God, each of which tells us something to prompt our worship. He is called "The Lord is my Banner" because we can rally under His leadership (Exodus 17:15).

He is also called "The Lord our Righteousness" (Jeremiah 23:5-6), "The Lord is Peace" (Judges 6:24), Holy One, Ruler, and Father.

God also describes Himself in word pictures—a rock (Deuteronomy 32:4), a judge (Isaiah 33:22), a warrior (Exodus 15:3), a shepherd (Psalm 23), and a tender mother (Hosea 11:1-4).[18]

I cannot here go into the richness of the many attributes of God, but I highly recommend several books that do: *Knowing God* by J. I. Packer (InterVarsity); *The Knowledge of the Holy* by A. W. Tozer (Harper & Row); *The Existence and Attributes of God* by Stephen Charnock (Baker); and *Names of God in the Old Testament* by Nathan Stone (Moody Press).[19]

AN ATTRIBUTE A DAY

Puritan writer William Gurnall once said, "God deserves the best service you can give Him in your generation, so start letting His divine attributes manifest themselves in your life now."[20] To help us glorify God by manifesting His attributes, we can:

1.   Choose one attribute for each day. Here is a month's worth (of course, there are a lot more!).

Merciful	Sanctifier (making holy)
Forgiving	All-powerful (omnipotent)
Compassionate	Ever-present (omnipresent)
Faithful	All-knowing (omniscient)
Loving	Perfect in knowledge
Holy	Never changing (immutable)
Righteous	Almighty (powerful
Judge	and glorious)
Eternal	Living Sacrifice
Wise	Victor
Good	Shepherd
Patient	Savior
Selfless	Deliverer
Provider	Wonderful Counselor
Healer	Mighty God
Defender	Prince of Peace

2. Go to Scripture to see your selected attribute in action (a concordance can help).

3. Ponder throughout the day what you have learned about God.

4. Look for ways God has evidenced His attribute to you this day and at other times in your life.

For example, we could start today by dwelling on God's immutability (He never changes). In His Word, He tells us, "I am the Lord, I change not" (Malachi 3:6 KJV), and that He is "the same yesterday and today, yes and forever" (Hebrews 13:8).

Now how can we meditate on His immutability? Something I've thought about a lot is how we are so often forgotten by others; people's attitudes toward us change, and they disappoint us. We can praise God that because He is immutable, He will never change His mind about us. His promises are sure. He is never moody. He will always have time for us. Best of all, His love for us stays the same regardless of how we may disappoint Him.

Reflecting back over the years, I see evidence of God's immutability in spite of the many times I disappointed Him. He never turned away in frustration saying, "That's it, Donna—I give up! You'll never learn!" His unchanging nature undergirding His patience and unconditional love allowed me to grow.

This morning here in central California, we had sunshine and blue skies, and already in the afternoon it is cold and muggy. No matter how hard I try to plan around our weather, especially during fall and winter, it's always changing. Up here in the mountains we can have snow one day and temperatures in the eighties the next. There's only one word to describe it—*flighty*.

I'm thankful that God is not like the weather. He is as stable as a rock fortress. I can deal with a difficult situation because I know He won't change. He always listens and is at my side to help me. While others may fail me, He never will. How grateful I am for God's immutable character!

I find that meditating on God's attributes in a practical way like that helps me to know Him better and worship Him for who He really is.

REFLECTING GOD'S LIGHT

One day at work years ago, I noticed from the conference room window a young woman who looked about twenty putting mail in the mailbox around 3 P.M. each day. I decided to put our office mail in the box at the same time, thinking I might be able to befriend her and share with her the best news in the world.

Within a few days, I was able to introduce myself to her, and we discovered that we took lunch off at the same time. We arranged to meet the next day at the restaurant on the corner.

When we met, I tried to make small talk. Reaching for my water, I asked, "So, Trina, what do you do for entertainment?"

Without much thought she began talking at length about going dancing, listening to hard rock, looking forward to turning old enough to drink, and occasionally getting "high."

About fifteen minutes later she stopped and asked me the same question. Preparing myself for the chilling effect of my answer, I told her that I enjoy being involved at church and attending Bible study, but before I could finish, she interrupted me and asked through the ice in her mouth, "What church do you go to?"

When I told her, she choked out a laugh and said, "Why, that's my church! I've been going there since I was in second grade!"

I will never forget how utterly shocked I was to hear that she had been worshiping at a solid Bible-believing church for so many years of her life. I was confused that she could be exposed to so much light and yet not reflect it herself.

Though Trina is an extreme example, we must take a hard look at ourselves. Is there something in our lives that is keeping the inner chambers of our heart and mind dark in spite of our being exposed to the light of truth? Could we be immersing ourselves needlessly in things that are the opposite of God's character? What is keeping us from being a reflector of light? Discerning those things is important, for a good part of spiritual worship is reflecting God's light.

Is God Exalted in Our Lives?

Let me share with you a person from Scripture who clearly reflected God. And rather than start at the beginning, let me begin at the end. Stephen, the man who waited on tables for the widows, is dead on the open road (Acts 6:3-5; 7:60). How? Why?

Stephen was falsely accused (Acts 6:11), subjected to a phony trial, and then stoned. The tradition of the rabbis called the Mishnah said the accused was to make a confession of his guilt. But despite loud cries from the people (Acts 7:57), we hear no admission of guilt from Stephen (his only admission was of their guilt). Rather, while being stoned he prays confidently, "Lord Jesus, receive my spirit" (Acts 7:59). And while his persecutors were "gnashing their teeth" (Acts 7:54), he prayed, "Lord, do not hold this sin against them!" (Acts 7:60).

How could Stephen have such a God-glorifying response? Luke tells us that he was consistently filled with the Holy Spirit, and consequently his life overflowed with faith, grace, power, and wisdom (Acts 6:3, 5, 8). Stephen was also a person strong in the Word. There is little wonder he could glorify God to the last minute of his life.

We can, too, by building our character and inner life. We can feed our appetite for those things that are honorable, right, pure, lovely, and excellent (Philippians 4:8). And, like Stephen who served tables (Acts 6:2-5), we can do those humble things that will get little if any recognition. Though simple and hidden, these acts are prayerful worship offered up to the Father in golden bowls of incense (Revelation 5:8).

Such fragrance of character can affect others as much as the artist who gives her entire life to manifesting beauty or a teacher who devotes her life to the service of nurturing. Continual upward focus brings God's presence closer to us and others.

PRACTICING THE PRESENCE OF GOD

Recently I heard on the radio a distraught woman telling a Christian counselor that because she can't sense God's presence in her life, He must not really care about her problems. A few days later, I got materials at a Christian convention that explained how I could get into God's almighty and glorious presence—through dancing. Both perspectives, no matter how sincere, wrongly believe that there must be a euphoric encounter in order to have God's presence. Scripture says the opposite.

Job, who had earlier felt that God was distant, recovered his confident faith: "Behold, I go forward but He is not there, and backward, but I cannot perceive Him; When He acts on the left, I cannot behold Him; He turns on the right, I cannot see Him. But He knows the way I take; when He has tried me, I shall come forth as gold" (Job 23:8-10). Job trusted his conviction, not feelings, that God was present. It got him through his nightmarish trial.

Convictions also helped Elisha. This prophet had a pretty calm life as a tree trimmer and was respected as a theologian. Then one day he got the alarming news that the king of Syria was going to make war against Israel (2 Kings 6:8). Though the events could have overwhelmed him, his confidence in God held steady.

But Elisha's servant, his focus more earthward, was frantic. He asked, "Alas, my master! What shall we do?"

Elisha calmly replied, "Do not fear, for those who are with us are more than those who are with them" (2 Kings 6:16). He then prayed that God would open his servant's eyes. In answer to the prayer, the servant saw that the mountain was full of horses and chariots of fire all around them. Elisha was never shaken because he could see by faith what his servant saw supernaturally. The king of Syria, who had no sense that God was involved at all, suffered tremendously.

Many of us don't fully realize that God is present.

God Is with Us

Do we by faith take into account God's unfailing presence, or are we more like Elisha's servant? Do we worry about the loss of health, loss of a job, the loss of a husband's love, or the loss of a boyfriend?

The reality of these concerns can take our eyes off the Lord if we do not strive to see the world in light of His continual presence. A God-glorifying response to circumstances comes more naturally to the person who sees God as faithful to her every day, in big things as well as small. Like Elisha, that person has "no fear of bad news; his heart is steadfast, trusting in the Lord" (Psalm 112:7 NIV).

A sense of God's awesome presence has always been characteristic of those who have done great things for God. Moses never lost a sense of God's presence when he was trapped by the Red Sea in front, an angry Egyptian army behind, and panicked Jews screaming all around him. He did not have to call a meeting to ask what to do. He told the Israelites, "Do not fear . . . the Lord will fight for you while you keep silent" (Exodus 14:13a, 14).

Listen to the response of Jehoshaphat, who stood before a horde of Ammorite invaders: "O our God . . . we do not know what to do, but our eyes are upon you" (2 Chronicles 20:12 NIV).

Shadrach, Meshach, and Abednego were confident that God's presence would be with them in life or death as they stepped into the fiery furnace (Daniel 3:25, 28). An observer indeed saw a mysterious fourth figure there with them in the flames.

Stephen, steadfast to the last, saw the heavens open and Christ at the right hand of God (Acts 7:55-56).

Despite their hardship, those biblical saints never wavered in their trust that God was with them. Their faith glorified God, and it strengthened them to act in a way that revealed His greatness.

A New Perspective on God's Presence

Practicing God's presence activates the Christian perspective on life. It's a way of seeing the world that helps us to act in a godly way.

God instructed the Jewish people to diligently train their children from the start. They were to dwell on God's presence and commands, known through His Word, as they sat in their homes, took walks, slept, and got up in the morning (Deuteronomy 6:7). A sense

190 /🐛/ *Choices That Lead to Godliness*

of God's presence, doing His will, and worshiping Him were all wrapped together and made part of daily life.

When Paul instructed the Thessalonians, he told them to "pray without ceasing" (1 Thessalonians 5:17). He did not mean to pray without a break, but persistently and regularly.[21] As one commentator said, "It is impossible to be always on our bended knees, but we may be in the spirit of prayer when engaged in the duties of our earthly calling. Prayer may be without ceasing in the heart which is full of the presence of God and evermore communing with Him."[22]

The practice of consistent prayer and saturation in the Word are divinely designed ways to cultivate a sense of God's continual presence. These practices are catalysts God uses to fill our heart, soul, and mind.

Is there anything that can hinder our growth process as our lives become more entwined with God's? Yes. It's called:

Sinful Independence

I once heard someone say that the man who bows the lowest in the presence of God stands the straightest in the presence of sin. Intrigued by that statement, I started thinking about those things that can hinder me from bowing to God and make me bow to sin instead.

The most obvious is sinful independence. While there is a godly independence, one that keeps us from being influenced by the world (Ephesians 4:14), there is also a sinful independence. It keeps us from admitting to ourselves that we need God, making us feel self-sufficient—in our knowledge for example.

Have you ever noticed that very mature Christians who have immersed themselves in Scripture for decades will tell you they still have much to learn from the Word? They know God's Word is full of truths they will never fully grasp this side of eternity. They are constantly seeking God's face through His Word. On the other hand, you have probably met younger Christians who pride themselves in their knowledge of Scripture.

When we have too great a confidence in our limited knowledge, we tend to forget about God. We forget to seek Him out in prayer, through His Word, and even by way of godly counsel—all because we believe we have the answers. This is a dangerous place to be in. Since it ignores God's wisdom and denies Him His rightful place, it is the very opposite of worship.

Our society craves the wrong kind of independence, and in our sinful state, sometimes we can, too. Have you ever had to make an important decision and caught yourself rushing to do something before thinking about God's perspective? We've probably all been tempted to do it.

Sinful independence has many disguises. Failing to acknowledge God's presence is one. Another is having a daily routine that leaves no time for listening to His Word and growing in relationship to Him through prayer.

Agur, who contributed to the book of Proverbs, is an example of proper dependence through humbly realizing his limits. "I do not have the understanding of a man," he said, " . . . but I have knowledge of the Holy One" (Proverbs 30:2-3). He encourages us to take refuge in God, who is our shield (v. 5).

What do we do when we realize we still have pockets of independence? We need to pray, like the Psalmist (Psalm 80:18), that God will restore us.

Revive Us

To revive is to flourish again after a decline. All of us can weaken spiritually, and so revival of our soul is vital.

Isaiah's soul revived when he had the fabulous experience of seeing the Lord sitting on His throne. The very sight of God humbled him and caused him to reflect upon his own unworthiness, bringing him to see his impurity before a holy God (Isaiah 6:1-5).

Isaiah's experience shows that the key to revival is humility. God's presence requires it, but His presence also causes it. God told Isaiah that He revives the soul of the humble person, the one who knows better than to trust in herself, who is broken over her sin. He said, "For thus says the high and exalted One who lives forever, whose name is Holy, 'I dwell on a high and holy place, and also with the contrite and lowly of spirit in order to revive the spirit of the lowly and to revive the heart of the contrite" (Isaiah 57:15).

When David came into God's presence, he was completely humbled and said: "But who am I and who are my people that we should be able to offer as generously as this? For all things come from Thee, and from Thy hand we have given Thee" (1 Chronicles 29:14).

In the Old Testament, sacrifices offered up to God were also to symbolize humility. It wasn't the fierce animal, such as the lion or tiger, used in the act of worship, but the meek creature such as the sheep or goat (Leviticus 1:10), turtledoves or young pigeons (v. 14), and even the young bull (v. 5).

For us, revival of the soul and the continual presence of the Lord shall be ours as we, aware of our dependence, humbly offer everything we do as a loving sacrifice to Him. We can exchange the attitude of a stubborn animal for a meek one suitable for the altar as we do the household chores, take care of the children, and deal with the pressures at work.

Paul recognized the need for humility in order to have continual strengthening from God. God told him that His "power is perfected in weakness" (2 Corinthians 12:9). He concluded that having a sense of weakness was necessary: "I am well content with weaknesses . . . for when I am weak, then I am strong" (v. 10).

Praying for renewal and the touch of the Master's hand brings our practice of His presence into a vibrant reality. As we daily train ourselves to be in God's presence and empty our heart of all that competes with Him, then we, too, shall be ready to please Him and reflect Him with our whole lives—the essence of true worship.

PROCLAIMING TRUTH ABOUT GOD

When most people think of worship, the first thing that comes to mind is singing in church. The last thing is evangelism. Yet by telling others about the wonders of God's grace, we are exalting Him. So does that mean we should each become an evangelist? Go door to door? Should we try to become extroverts and outspoken even if we are not naturally that way?

Not at all. We each can proclaim the truth in our own way, in whatever place God has us, without becoming a "Billy Graham." So where do we start?

Ourselves

Evangelism comes from a heart overflowing with love for God. We want to share Christ when we are vibrantly growing in the knowledge of Him, being taught by Him, sitting at His feet, drinking from the deepest waters of spiritual truth. A dynamic spiritual life also forms the foundation of our witness. Without our saying a word, others will be able to see that we know Jesus. Our lives are the only Bible some will ever read.

Others

How many of us feel too timid to share our faith verbally? I did until I was trained in evangelism at my church. That helped me a great deal. If you feel uncomfortable about participating in the evangelism program of your church, there are other ways you can share the good news with others. One way is through an evangelistic tract.[23] Keep a few in your purse to leave, for example, with your tip in a restaurant, or hand one to the checker at the supermarket.

When I was a nonbeliever and working as a supermarket checker, an elderly couple came through my line. After paying for their groceries, they handed me a gospel tract. I still remember their radiant smiles. I kept their tract and one that I found in a telephone booth on my desk for a long time. While studying for college exams or writing an essay, I would often pick them up and read them. They were very powerful tools for planting seed in my own life. They can be for others as well.

Perhaps you are bold enough to share with the average person but feel intimidated about sharing with a member of a cult. You can be encouraged that there are many who have felt the same and despite their feelings have been used by God to lead others to Christ. It can be helpful to find out what major cults are in your community and then get some Christian books that can help you understand and reach out to their members.[24] You can trust God to send some lost, hurting souls to you—maybe to your very door!

Our Homes

We can make our homes places where we and others are led to think more about God—in a mild sense, led to worship. We once had a neighbor who loved to come to our home. His reason? He said, "I come here because there is so much peace." Our neighbor was sensing the peace of God rather than a worldly sort of peace.

When people visit your home, can they tell that Christ reigns there? Do our conversations identify us as Christians? Does our entertainment glorify Him? Do our children consider us a good spiritual influence? Can each one of us say, "I will walk within my house in the integrity of my heart. I will set no worthless thing before my eyes" (Psalm 101:2-3). Exalting God has a lot to do with our daily lives inside the home.

Something I have found that creates an atmosphere of God's presence, especially a sense of His peace, is to give godly music a prominent place. Hymns, for example, are filled with proclamations of God's truth. Sad to say, many churches are eliminating them from their worship in order to be more contemporary. While it is good to be sensitive to others, it is unfortunate that traditional hymns are viewed as outdated instead of being looked at for their content. Who cannot benefit from the lyrics of hymns such as "A Mighty Fortress Is Our God," "Crown Him with Many Crowns," "Great Is Thy Faithfulness," "How Great Thou Art," or "O Worship the King." What words of power, of exaltation, of majesty to the King of kings! What words of peace!

Also, look at the psalms from Scripture. They were the hymns, if you will, of their day. These psalms teach us a great deal about God. They express not only prayer and praise, grief and joy, repentance and victory; but they also communicate pure doctrine and recount history.

The apostle Paul saw the advantages of singing psalms, hymns, and spiritual songs (Ephesians 5:19). Thankfulness grows in our hearts toward God, and we can teach and admonish one another through these songs (Colossians 3:16).

Even if the church we attend doesn't feature hymns or psalms, we can still enjoy them privately. As a creative way of proclaiming the truth of God, I have taken my favorite stanzas from many of the hymns and from the book of Psalms and written them out. I put them on the refrigerator, above the washer and dryer, or in cupboards. I even had two copies enlarged to about two feet by three feet and hung them on the living room wall. They immediately call my attention to worship and praise.

In my quiet times with God at home, I will sometimes take a hymnbook and think about the message of a hymn. Hymns such as "Crown Him with Many Crowns," "O for a Thousand Tongues to Sing," and "Be Thou My Vision" are so rich in devotional content.

I have noticed that on the days when I add hymns to my Bible study, unannounced visitors to my house will see a cheerful woman full of the joy and peace of the Lord. Because my heart stays calm, my children benefit. We are more likely to thank and praise God for the simple things around us, such as snow or flowers in bloom.

Worship takes so many forms. And because there are so many ways to lift up God, you can be creative. Evangelism alone can take on many different forms, including bringing a friend to church or Bible study, visiting the forgotten in hospitals and retirement or convalescent homes, or inviting a neighbor over and sharing something wonderful God did in your life.

It is all part of knowing God and making Him known, and it starts with offering Him ourselves. The end result? Great joy as we:

sit and think of God.
Oh, what a joy it is!
To think the thought,
to breathe the Name;
Earth has no higher bliss.

Father of Jesus, love's reward!
What rapture it will be,
Prostrate before Thy throne to be,
And gaze and gaze on Thee!
　　　　　　　—FREDERICK FABER[25]

Thinking It Over

1. Today find one attribute of God in Scripture and then meditate upon it. Think about how this attribute affects you personally.

2. What does it mean to be a "reflector of light"?

3. How might you practice the presence of God this week?

4. How might God want you to proclaim His truth?

Chapter 12

BLUNTING

THE SWORD

The other day my husband got a catalog in the mail that showed page after page of reproductions of ancient armor, such as the helmets and shields used by the Vikings, Greeks, and Romans. It featured collections of full armor used by seventeenth-century Samurai warriors, fifteenth-century English knights, and many others. As fascinating as the full armor was, the swords captivated me the most.

Looking regal, their long, silver blades flashed with an aura of majesty and power. The exquisitely crafted Sword of the Three Musketeers was the type used by those whose legendary skill defended the French crown. The Sword of Attila the Hun reflected the savage cunning of the barbarian king who scourged the entire Roman Empire. King Arthur's sword, Excalibur, was designed with the simple strength of the good king whose legacy is now shrouded in legend.

But by far the most remarkable sword, with truly supernatural power, was crafted by God Himself. The Word of God is said to be sharper than any sword, able to pierce our innermost being and do what no other blade can—reveal our true self (Hebrews 4:12). It, too, is a weapon, a spiritual one, that we must use for survival and victory in spiritual battles (Ephesians 6:17).

This supernatural sword, which can protect believers and bring light to unbelievers, is being blunted today. Blunting God's Word isn't anything new; it has happened since the Garden of Eden. Satan challenged what God had said, Eve ignored it, and Adam violated it. Over the centuries the blunting—misuses—of Scripture have taken different forms.

After the apostles spread the gospel message, the church gradually added to Scripture, altering its message and confusing it with human wisdom and tradition. By 1536, when William Tyndale tried to make Scripture available to everyone in the common language, he was imprisoned, strangled, and burned at the stake. John Huss suffered a similar fate. Martin Luther in the sixteenth century declared boldly that he could trust "neither in popes nor in councils" and could only be "bound by the texts of the Bible."[1] Others before and after him who tried to keep the Word sharp and useable thought it was worth the loss of their property, freedom, and even their lives.

Some of the attempts to blunt the Word today are as old as the serpent in Eden and as well worn as the statements of medieval church councils. Some people ignore the Word altogether; others ignore its true meaning, attaching one that appears "relevant." Some bring an entirely different meaning to a passage, while others contradict specific biblical teachings or attitudes. Still others confuse the biblical message with New Age philosophies and contemporary attitudes toward prosperity, health, and self-centeredness.

Today you can find virtually anything taught at a Bible study or conference. Widespread lack of discernment not only allows distortions of the Word to go unchallenged, but it also lets these erroneous teachings pass for "insight." A person can listen to message after message without ever hearing basic truths or having to change ungodly attitudes. During some lessons today, the Bible sits uselessly on the listener's lap, unopened.

Without guidance from biblically discerning teachers, we, too, can blunt the Word in our own Bible study (a problem discussed in the following chapter). However the blunting occurs and wherever it occurs, mishandling the Word always deprives us of our only spiritual weapon.

IGNORING SCRIPTURE

Monday morning after a conference for Christian women, Beverly gave me a call. With enthusiasm she asked, "What did you think of the conference?"

"Well," I replied cautiously, "I've been thinking a lot about it. What did you think?"

"Oh, I thought it was just great!" she said. "The speaker was quite entertaining; she made me laugh so much. What did you think?"

I was afraid she was going to ask that question again. Taking a deep breath, I told her that I didn't want to say anything that would burst her bubble.

"No," said Beverly, "please tell me what you think!"

And so I reflected on the weekend. Being at the conference with other women was great. And it was nice to relax for a few days, though as the women sat around chattering away, I admit that my thoughts were of Brian, Michelle, and Johnathan. *Are they all right? Will Brian remember to change Johnathan's diapers, or will he try an "extended wear" experiment?*

My thoughts were interrupted as the chatter settled down and announcements were given. Then I heard, "And, ladies, one last thing—our speaker is offering a question-and-answer time during this conference. If there is a burden or question on your heart, please write it down and put it in the basket up at the front. She will try to answer all your questions." All of us were filled with anticipation.

Evening came—the time for answers to the women's questions. Everyone sat still as they waited for the speaker's insights. She approached the podium, put on her reading glasses, cleared her throat, and reached into the basket. She read the first question: "My husband and I bicker all the time; what should we do?"

The speaker took off her glasses and looked straight at the audience as she replied, "Stop it and take off your clothes! You can't bicker if your clothes are off!" The audience roared.

The speaker read aloud the next question: "What should I do to prepare myself for disaster?" Then she simply answered, "Don't." On and on the questions and answers went.

The answers reminded me of an exchange between a little boy and his father—that would go something like this.

Timmy asks, "Dad, who made God?"

The father, engrossed in the evening paper, responds, "Beats me, son."

Timmy asks another question, "Dad, why is the earth round?"

"I don't know, son," is the only answer.

Timmy thinks for a minute, then asks, "Dad, is there life on other planets?"

"Nobody knows the answer to that."

Finally Timmy asks his father, "Dad, do you mind me asking you all these questions?"

Without putting down his paper, the father says, "Why, not at all, son. How else are you going to learn?"

Like Timmy's father, the conference speaker left just one thing out—the answers. How could the women at the conference grow spiritually without God's answers? Funny as some of the comeback remarks may have been, the speaker ignored a vast amount of biblical teaching that could have provided real answers.

What happens to the bickering woman who follows the speaker's advice? She must put her clothes back on sometime, and when she does, she will still have a problem with bickering. And what about preparation for disaster? Scripture tells us to "be anxious for nothing" (Philippians 4:6), and Proverbs gives us a lot of advice for avoiding financial disaster. Ephesians tells us how to prepare for potential spiritual disaster in "the evil day" (Ephesians 6:10-18). The Gospels give us Christ's example of intense prayer before the cross (Mark 14:32-39). And we are told that in any crisis we should remember that God can use the difficulty to make us mature and God-centered (2 Corinthians 12:9; 2 Timothy 4:16-18).

The following day throughout the sessions, the speaker focused on her many books, often quoting her own written thoughts, supported by quotations from secular figures. No Scripture was mentioned, nor were the women encouraged to look in the Bible for direction.

The last day of the conference was devoted to communion. Clutching her white Bible to her bosom, the speaker began, "This morning we are going to get into the Word of God." Then lifting her

Bible above her head, she proclaimed, "The Bible is truth!" With an air of drama she slowly put it back on the table and left it there, unopened, with scarcely a mention of those precious truths during the rest of that session.

Leave Your Bible at Home

After the conference, some women said they had never laughed so hard in their lives. Others, impressed with the speaker's communication skills, said it was the best conference they had ever attended. But I wondered about some of the others. One friend later told me that she needed something to "flush out" all that the conference put in her mind. Another woman, struggling with depression, never endured to the end; she left the conference early.

When I expressed to a "veteran" of many such conferences some of my concerns about the weekend, she summed up the whole event, "Well, Donna, when you go to a women's retreat, you can leave your Bible at home." I began to ask myself some searching questions: "Why do I go to conferences?" "What do I expect to get out of a conference?"

Doing a Little Homework

If you, like myself, are investing time and money and expect to be spiritually challenged, you can discern whether a particular conference will meet your spiritual needs, but it does call for doing a little homework.

First, find out who is speaking. This may sound a bit elementary, but let's face it—sometimes we'll sign up for anything just to get out of the house.

Second, find out what you can about the speaker other than the fact that she's a "popular" speaker. If she has written any books, try to read one. This, for me, is key. I will then be able to see if she is scripturally based or whether she relies on human insights.

Last, if the speaker hasn't written any books, go to the women who set up the conference and ask them why they selected the speaker. If the answer is the speaker's popularity rather than her biblical insights, I would rather stay home with my Bible. Crowd-pleasing with humor, communication skills, and human insights can never replace biblical content or divine guidance, wisdom, and comfort. Conferences that are biblically focused can be a real source of blessing, but even these gatherings cannot replace personal Bible study as our main source of growth.

Our homework doesn't stop with conferences but must extend to women's ministries, too. At some groups it is assumed that women are too busy with young children and only want a break; therefore, their time together should be relaxing. Calligraphy, crochet, and basket weaving fill up all the time. Then "fellowship" fills the gaps between the classes.

One church I knew of had a vibrant ministry for women. They offered a variety of art classes along with a Bible study. But after a while, the classes continued, but the Bible study withered and disappeared.

Of course, various classes can offer wonderful refreshment. But when the gathering so resembles a secular event that you can't tell the difference, the group has a problem. More than once I have had to ask, "Is it worth attending this group when I am not spiritually challenged or can't challenge others?"

The Spiritual Challenge

Most spiritually weak groups simply lack the leadership and structure that can pull them toward a spiritual focus. You can discern whether a group is weak by visiting it a few times and listening to the conversations. Are they encouraging? Do they somehow relate to God and spiritual things? Do they lift you up?

It helps to talk to the leader a few times and discover her vision for the group. As I've mentioned, some groups have relaxation as their only goal. Relaxation can be refreshing because life gets hectic. Awakened at 2 A.M. by the baby, we run around all day trying to keep up with older children, keep a house clean, and get the shopping done. But a frantic pace only makes it more important that we have spiritual refreshment.

If you find that a group does not have a spiritual focus, do not lose heart. You can help give it one. Let the leadership know of your interest. You can suggest that the meeting include a time for sharing what God has been doing in people's lives, or have a brief Bible study. In conversations with the women in the group, make sure you have brought a listening ear, a sensitive heart, and, where appropriate, a biblical perspective. The group that becomes spiritually awake will want to invite nonbelieving friends and neighbors so they, too, can share the riches of Christ (Colossians 1:27).

DIVINE AUTHORITY REPLACED BY HUMAN AUTHORITY

Nineteenth-century Scottish pastor and writer Thomas Guthrie said, "The Bible is an armory of heavenly weapons, a laboratory of infallible medicines, a mine of exhaustless wealth. It is a guidebook for every road, a chart for every sea, a medicine for every malady, and a balm for every wound. Rob us of our Bible and our sky has lost its sun."[2]

At the risk of sounding like an FBI agent, I truly believe there is a robbery taking place in our churches and other ministries. This crime is similar to the type of robbery that happened a few years ago when an art gallery made the shocking discovery that a painting on its walls was not the original but a clever copy, a fake. The switch had escaped notice until the painting was closely inspected.

Today the switch is on a spiritual level, one with devastating spiritual consequences: The divine authority of the Scriptures has been quietly replaced by human authority, unknown perhaps even to the ones making the switch.

One switch was made on Sunday morning at Ed and Mary's church. Though they were treated to a new pastor that morning, the switch that surprised them wasn't the man but the message. As the pastor walked up to the podium, the eager congregation reached for their Bibles, ready for him to guide them into the Word. But their Bibles stayed shut as he began with a vague reference to 1 Corinthians 13:13, which briefly states, "The greatest of these is love." The next forty-five minutes were filled with quotations from psychologists, some of them secular, on problems that keep us from loving others. He supported their statements with emotionally charged anecdotes. He shared his personal struggles on the difficulty he has with loving others, asking those with similar experiences to raise their hands. The Scriptureless sermon ended with a quotation from a well-known psychologist on the healing properties of love.

The congregation was impressed with his skill as a communicator and got a lot of practical advice about loving one another. But they also got something else—the feeling that the Bible cannot speak with authority to everyday life and that answers to life's common problems must be found elsewhere.

Opening with a casual reference to a verse of the Bible did not make the message biblical, nor was it sufficient to communicate to the audience that God has something to say to us and should be obeyed. By giving only token mention of the Bible, its authority was blunted.

The Bible can accomplish so much in our lives when we acknowledge that it is God's Word and carries His authority. To ignore its divine authority while looking to some other source for truth and guidance reduces the Sword of the Spirit to a mere ceremonial sword—admired as a showpiece but useless as a cutting implement.

So what are we to do if we attend a church where human authority replaces that of Scripture?

Discern Where to Worship

Years ago my husband and I were involved in a church where at the time respect for human authority surpassed that given to Scripture. Though we loved the people and enjoyed serving among them, we knew we had to leave.

If you are in a church where you are sensing a prompting to leave, think it through carefully. I have known people to leave one terrible situation only to jump into another.

The way to find the best church for you is to visit, not just one other church but, if possible, a number of churches. If you find one that interests you, discernment then must come into play. What may look good now may not look so good in a few months. Therefore, make an appointment with the pastor and ask him pertinent questions. Ask, for example, when and how he prepares his sermons. If he does not get around to thinking about it until late Saturday, then most likely he doesn't make his sermons part of his spiritual life, and he probably doesn't put much effort into digging deep in the Scriptures.

Also ask him his views on doctrinal issues such as "Do you believe that Christ rose bodily?" "Do you believe the Bible contains errors?" You might think that someone could have the wrong answers and still be a good pastor, but come Sunday morning in a sermon, what the preacher believes makes an enormous difference!

If you are in a church that doesn't focus on Scripture, and yet you believe this is where you are called to minister, there is hope. While I was attending a spiritually weak church, I found some keys that helped me thrive spiritually.

Thriving Spiritually in a Dead Church

Charles Spurgeon, the great nineteenth-century London preacher, asked, "What is the best way of hearing the Word? Is it not to search and see whether what the preacher says is really according to the Word of God?"[3]

The believers of Berea lived long before Spurgeon, but they certainly did as he suggested. When the apostle Paul visited Berea, the believers in the town welcomed him as a teacher, but they wouldn't accept his message at "face value." Instead, because of their discernment, they were "examining the Scriptures daily, to see whether these things were so" (Acts 17:11). The Bible praises them for it, calling them "noble-minded."

We, too, can be "noble-minded" by not accepting what we hear at face value, but by going with discernment directly to Scripture to search out, in the fullest sense, what God would have us know about the topic preached.

206 /🍏/   *Choices That Lead to Godliness*

Whether I am in a healthy church or a sickly one, I must take responsibility for my own spiritual growth. Really, we all must take that responsibility for ourselves. You alone—not the pastor, nor your husband—are responsible for your growth. You have the basic resources to grow in the Scriptures. As Paul told Timothy, "Be a good servant of Christ Jesus, *constantly nourished* on the words of the faith and of the sound doctrine which you have been following" (1 Timothy 4:6). That means we are to be in the Word daily, disciplining ourselves for the purpose of godliness (1 Timothy 4:7-8).

Unfortunately, one sobering fact still remains. If we do not rely on the Word, we will rely on something else. I have seen it in Christian women who stop reading God's Word. In time, they start relying on emotional experience or erroneous teaching. They eventually begin to share a problem that is common today: They sever the heart from the mind.

SEVERING THE HEART FROM THE MIND

We all crave good feelings and experiences. This is nothing new. But feeling good used to mean feeling good *about* something, whereas now feelings are often an end in themselves. For many religion has become "a search for religious good feelings."[4] Yet good feelings, even good religious feelings, cannot be severed from their natural connection to what we think.

One Sunday morning a televised religious service entirely replaced biblical content with people dancing, hopping, leaping, and running through the aisles. The sermon was interrupted on a few occasions by people who expressed themselves by running up to the pulpit, "praising the Lord," and then running back to their seats again. No one seemed bothered by the pandemonium but added their shouts of "Amen!" The sermon had no scriptural content and merely used emotional jargon to stir up the audience. Often while the preacher was "preachin," drums and other instruments would interrupt him, as if each had to add its own "Amen." After the sermon was over, the preacher enthusiastically shouted, "Now don't you feel gooood?"

It's very easy for us to ignore ideas and scriptural content in our spiritual life and to seek a purely emotional experience. But the Bible never severs emotion from belief. It regards emotion as a response to truth, not something that can exist in a vacuum.

Emotions and Biblical Truth

When the resurrected Christ met the two disciples on the Emmaus road and opened their minds to His true mission, their hearts burned within them (Luke 24). Though it was one of the peak experiences of their lives, their joy was no mindless euphoria. It was a response to what their minds now believed.

One of the greatest moments in Paul's life was his blinding encounter with Christ on the Damascus road. What an experience! It turned him from persecutor to apostle. Yet, as exciting as it was, he based his evangelism on Scripture, not on his experience.

We can do the same as Paul by ensuring that our emotions respond to biblical truth. True joy, for example, is not just "feeling good." It is founded on the assurance that a caring God is in control, has our best interests at heart, and is working all things for the good of those who love Him (Romans 8:28). Biblical hope is not just a vague feeling that the future will turn out okay, but is established on a conviction about the one who controls the future. Peace emanates from our relationship with God through the work of Christ and knowledge that the things that really matter in life are secure forever.

In my own life, I have learned to check my emotions against God's Word. Failing to do so can cause one to end up in disobedience and heartache.

Maturing in the Knowledge of Truth

We all must discern the areas of life where we allow our emotions to be our primary guide. Is it finances? Do we find ourselves buying on impulse? What about romance? Have we allowed an ungodly relationship to take precedence over what we know to be right? The areas of life that are weak must be subjected to evaluation by the Word.

I am learning that to be mature emotionally as well as spiritually,

I have to be mature in my knowledge of truth from the Word. When I review some truth I already know or discover a new one, I ask myself, "Do I know this, really know it so that it affects how I feel?" If not, I must be sure that the view I do hold—the one that dictates my actions and feelings—really agrees with Scripture.

There are times when I run a quick check of my feelings and ask myself, "Is it right to feel this way? Are my feelings based on what I know to be true about God and His Word?" If not, I correct them. Often it takes time to form a new habit.

For example, if I find myself discouraged, I remind myself, "I shouldn't be discouraged; God is going to work this out." He says, "Be strong and courageous! Do not tremble or be dismayed, for the Lord your God is with you wherever you go" (Joshua 1:9).

If I'm frustrated, I tell myself, "I shouldn't be so frustrated; God allowed this for a reason and will work it out for good." Again I am reminded of what He told Isaiah: "For the Lord of hosts has planned, and who can frustrate it? And as for His stretched-out hand, who can turn it back?" (Isaiah 14:27).

The key is to let thought, with God's Word, be our guide—not our emotions. To ignore God's Word in this process can be detrimental to our thought life—indeed to our whole life.

ON A POSITIVE NOTE

There are many more types of bluntings of the Word of God that I could mention, but I shall end here on a positive note. Though our age has a tendency to ignore and change Scripture, it's up to us to become more biblically discerning about what we are being taught—whether that's at church, Bible study, or a women's conference. Discernment plays a large part in evaluating whether extrabiblical or even unbiblical thoughts are replacing Scripture.

Fortunately, the Bible refuses to go away, and it still accomplishes what God intended it to do. As we saw at the beginning of this chapter, people became martyrs because they were more committed to God's Word than to the word of others or even to the word of the institutionalized church. But the Bible does not owe its survival through the ages solely to the martyrs. It has affected others through the power of God.

God's Word alone gave strength to the Pilgrims as they left their native land to start a new nation under God. Scripture's authority governed their very existence, how they lived, worshiped, and eventually ruled themselves in this new land.

Scripture also breathed life into our national anthem, allowed John Bunyan to dream his dream, and inspired Bach, Handel, Beethoven, and Mendelssohn to create their symphonies. Its poetry gave a powerful impulse to Browning, Cowper, Tennyson, and Wordsworth. Its dramatic settings inspired Murillo's *Feeding the Five Thousand*, Raphael's *The Transfiguration*, and Rembrandt's *Christ Blessing the Children*.

Through those it has inspired, the Lord's Word has done more than any other book to help the helpless. Slaves have been emancipated, prisons reformed, orphanages founded, hospitals established, and children rescued from moral dangers.

Scripture has changed lives throughout the ages, and it continues to do so. We can be among those it inspires. But it takes some effort on our part. To be all God wants us to be, we must know how to properly read, understand, and apply His Word. To build upon these skills, let's venture into the classroom of Christ's school of discipleship.

Thinking It Over

1. In what areas have you found it most difficult to be biblically discerning?

2. What do you think about Charles Spurgeon's quote? How does it relate to having a Berean attitude toward what you hear from others—including this author?

3. What can you do to ensure that your emotions correspond to biblical truth?

Chapter 13

GOD'S WORD

OR OURS?

Imagine we are in an art gallery. Among the thousands of pictures, one hangs on a wall all by itself. Framed in black velvet, it is a life-size painting of Christ praying in Gethsemane. Christ, not a man who worried, is portrayed with an anxious face. His hands show earnest struggle in prayer.

We ponder about Christ's thoughts. Perhaps they are of the one who betrayed Him or about His plea to "let this cup pass from" Him (Luke 22:42). But there is another thought that may have hung heavy on Christ's heart, one usually overlooked. He cared about the future of His beloved disciples and the message He had entrusted to them.

All during His ministry, Christ was concerned that the disciples understand His Word. They had to learn not just to parrot the truth, but to grasp it, live it, and communicate it. Once after teaching on the kingdom, He checked the disciples' understanding: "Do you not understand this parable? And how will you understand all the parables?" (Mark 4:13). On another occasion, He asked Peter, "Are you also still without understanding?" (Matthew 15:16). On one occasion the disciples were confused about the Resurrection. Jesus listened carefully as they discussed "with one another what rising from the dead might mean" (Mark 9:10). He could have easily told them the answer. Instead He led them to a deeper understanding of the truth through their own question.

For today's woman in Christ's school of discipleship, the requirements are no different. You and I must be able to discern truth in order to grasp it, live it, and communicate it. This means we must listen to His Word and treat it as God's Word. We must understand it for what it says, without adding to its message or distorting it.

Developing biblical discernment requires that we avoid a number of common abuses of the Word in order to reach the goal of maturity. We've already examined some ways people can stumble when handling Scripture, but now we must get a bit more personal. How are we doing in our own Bible study? Are we reading Scripture as God wrote it, or are we distorting it and communicating error? Are we turning God's Word into *our* word? Some days we may only have five minutes with the Bible, but on those days when we can give it an in-depth look, here are some ways to interpret it more accurately.

SEARCHING FOR THE "HIDDEN MEANING" OF SCRIPTURE

What would you think if someone tried to tell you that Job's friends really represent heretics, that his seven sons represent the twelve apostles, his 7,000 sheep are God's faithful people, and his 3,000 camels depict depraved Gentiles?[1] After suppressing a chuckle, you would probably shake your head and wonder what Bible college or seminary that person came from! As fantastic as this idea sounds, centuries ago many believed it, including Pope Gregory the Great.[2]

What would you think if someone told you the zodiac is part of biblical revelation? Today many very sincere women who desire to eliminate the secular view of the zodiac have incorporated a more spiritual version into their Bible study. They maintain that according to God's plan, the sign of Virgo "reveals the virgin birth."[3] The name of Virgo's brightest star, Spica, means "seed" and is believed to be mentioned in Genesis 3:15.[4]

Libra, "an exciting constellation," are the scales "which could never balance without Jesus having paid the price for our redemption" (Isaiah 40:12).[5] Sagittarius, the archer who is half-man and half-horse, is said to portray Christ's dual nature as human and divine. The two fish of Pisces are held together by Aries, the ram (which is taken to be a lamb), thus representing Christ tying together the Old and New Covenants, the Old and New Testament churches (Matthew 13:52).[6]

Taurus, the bull, represents a unicorn, which—by an allegory of an allegory—represents Christ (Revelation 6:16).[7] The fact that Cancer the crab "is a water-born animal" shows us "that the church is born of water and the Spirit." Its "many legs represent the many members in the body of Christ." As crabs shed their shells, so must the church shed "doctrine and tradition in order to receive the truth of God's Word" (2 Corinthians 5:1).[8]

Actually this approach to Scripture isn't new at all. It's called "allegorizing," a term derived from a Greek word meaning "to speak other than one seems to speak." In an allegorical interpretation, the "real" meaning is not the obvious, literal meaning but one only superficially related to it.

Allegorizing began with some ancient pagan Greeks who no longer believed in their sacred texts but wanted to link their ideas to them so as not to appear irreligious. They passed the practice to Jewish people in Alexandria, who passed it to Christians. The church fathers and others used it in their attempt to Christianize the Old Testament by finding Christ in every book. It was once taught, for example, that the Proverbs 31 woman is the church and that her husband is Christ. One commentary written in 1872 said that to regard the woman in Proverbs as a literal woman was to secularize her.[9]

Whenever we allegorize away the literal meaning of a passage, we lose the meaning God intended. The Song of Solomon has always been a favorite source of allegories (perhaps because some interpreters think romantic love is unspiritual?). Recently the book was being taught in a Bible study that I attended. Many women at the study thought they were going to be challenged toward a deeper relationship with their husbands. Instead we were taught how to have a close relationship with Christ. *There is no question that we all long to have a deeper relationship with the Lord; however, that message comes best from other verses.*

The teacher said that Christ longs for us to know that we have made His "heart beat faster, my sister, my bride; You have made my heart beat faster with a single glance of your eyes" (4:9). Then we broke into discussion groups to talk about the verse, "May he kiss me with the kisses of his mouth" (1:2), and to share how this principle of intimacy could help our relationship to Christ.

Throughout the study, the teacher reminded us that this book is about our Lord and the shepherdess. But I could not help thinking, *What about our fathers, husbands, and sons? Is Christ telling them that His heart beats faster at a single glance of their eyes, too?*

The problem with allegorizing is that once we depart from the literal meaning, any interpretation is possible. If we allow our imagination to rule over the context, we can teach anything. The Bible study taught that the Shulammite woman's skin (1:5) was darkened by the "sun of worldly endeavors." But by the allegorical method, the passage could just as easily mean that the Shulammite was "darkened" by ignorance, or that her beauty was only skin deep.

Allegories remind me of the misadventure of sixteenth-century explorer Martin Frobisher. He sought a water way through America to India. He did not find it but returned twice for shiploads of a metal that he mistook for gold. After all the effort and expense, the metal turned out to be only fool's gold, commonly known as iron pyrites.

When we search the Scriptures for spiritual gold and find only a resemblance of truth reflected in allegories, we bring back the same worthless cargo in our own Bible study. As Shakespeare said, "All that glistens is not gold."[10]

Discerning Between the Real and the Fake

Because allegorizing is so common and most of us (including myself) have been guilty of it, how can we know when we are allegorizing, and how can we keep ourselves from doing it in our personal Bible study? By asking ourselves a few questions.

1. Do I know what the important words mean?

If we take the Song of Solomon to be about the church, we have difficulty explaining the graphic nature of verses such as, "Let his left hand be under my head and his right hand embrace me" (2:6). In the Hebrew the word for embrace (*habaq*) describes "the embrace of lovers."[11] And how do I know this to be the correct meaning of embrace? Through the use of tools—I'll explain later (I can hardly wait to show you!).

2. Do I understand the context of the passage, the customs and events surrounding it?

3. Does my interpretation ignore historical events, such as what was happening when the author wrote the book and the problem he was addressing?

4. Can this passage be interpreted literally?

5. Does it contain known symbols (light, a dove, oil)?

6. Is the passage quoted in the New Testament as symbolic of Christ?

What about allegories in Scripture itself? Christ spoke allegorically of Himself as the Good Shepherd who died for the flock, meaning the church (Luke 10). He also said He was the vine to which believers must remain attached if they are to have life and bear fruit (John 15:1-8).

A rare biblical example of explicit allegorizing appears in Galatians 4:24-26, where Paul links Abraham's two sons with their mothers, saying they represent two spiritual conditions. Sarah and Isaac represent spiritual Jerusalem and freedom; Hagar and her son Ishmael represent Mt. Sinai (where God gave the law to Israel) and bondage to the law. The key is that here Paul does not ignore the historical events and their literal significance, and he tells us that his explanation is an allegory. So he is not interpreting the Scripture allegorically in the sense of changing the author's original meaning; he is only using an allegory to illustrate his point about the contrast between legalism and true Christianity.

HOW TO MAKE A VERSE SAY WHATEVER WE WANT

Abraham Lincoln once asked his audience, "How many legs would a sheep have if you called his tail a leg?"

The people responded, "Five."

"Wrong! The sheep would still have just four legs. Calling something a leg doesn't make it so."[12]

Lincoln's point should guide us as we think about another interpretive trap. It is called "proof-texting," which is just making a verse say whatever we want. I am sure we have all heard others make Scripture say what they want, and we have probably even done it ourselves. I never thought much about this until our friend Doug came over for dinner. While eating he made a startling statement, "Did you know that the prophecy of Acts 4:31 has recently been fulfilled? Preparing for another of his one-liners, I picked up my Bible and checked the verse: "And when they had prayed, the place where they had gathered together was shaken, and they were all filled with the Holy Spirit, and began to speak the word of God with boldness."

Puzzled, I asked, "What do you mean, finally fulfilled?"

Taking a big gulp of milk to hide a smile, Doug replied that he had attended a Bible study a few days after the California earthquake. The group's straight-faced leader had said with great conviction, "God has fulfilled the prophecy of Acts 4:31 through the earthquake: There shall be great revival in the land." According to the teacher, Acts 4:31 was a prophecy (which it is not), and it would be fulfilled because the earthquake had occurred at 4:31 A.M.!

While visiting from New York, our friends Scott and Diane told me and my husband about a Bible study in their area on the topic, "Why a Christian Should Not Dance." In his zeal to prove that dancing is a sin, the Bible study leader gave some Scripture verses a new meaning: Herodias's dance before Herod and her request for the head of John the Baptist (Mark 6:21-28) showed, in the teacher's view, that lust and murder result from dancing. Israel's dancing during its lapse into idolatry after the Exodus (Exodus 32) was supposed to show that wild parties, lewdness, drinking, adultery, murder, and rebellion against God always go with dancing. Therefore, by extension, loose living, prostitution, venereal disease, tumors, paralysis, and insanity all begin with dancing. Galatians 5:21, which says that people who practice sins such as drunkenness and carousing will not inherit the kingdom of God, was then used to show that dancing ultimately leads people to hell.

The difference between proof-texting and allegorizing is that while allegorizing ignores the literal meaning to find a "hidden" one, proof-texting ignores the literal meaning in order to make a verse prove some preconceived point. The true meaning of the verse is lost as the interpreter manipulates it like a ventriloquist's dummy, making it say whatever he wants.

My conversations with Doug and with Scott and Diane made me look for my own ventriloquism in my study of God's Word. It didn't take long for me to find a few misinterpretations.

For years I had regarded Matthew 18:19 as a blank check: "If two of you agree on earth about anything that they may ask, it shall be done for them by My Father who is in heaven." Yet looking at the context carefully, I discovered that this relates to confronting another believer who is in sin. The Father will be in agreement with the witnesses to sin, whether the sinning believer has repented or refused to repent. As well, God gives His confirmation through empowering the witnesses' decisions and actions regarding the sinning saint.

Also I had misinterpreted Matthew 18:20: "For where two or three have gathered together in My name, there I am in their midst." Again the context relates to church discipline. I had believed it was an assurance that Christ would be in our midst where two or three believers gathered. But this ignores His promise to be with me wherever I am, whether I am with others or alone. Jesus promised, "I am with you always, even to the end of the age" (Matthew 28:20).

How can we avoid these errors? My first mistake was in hearing the two verses misinterpreted by someone else and never bothering to check the verses myself. Again, like those in Berea, it's important to go to the Word ourselves "to see if these things are so" (Acts 17:11).

MAGICAL DEVOTION AND OTHER NOTIONS

George Mueller once said,

> The vigor of our spiritual life will be in exact proportion to the place held by the Bible in our life and thoughts. I

solemnly state this from the experience of 54 years. The first three years after conversion I neglected the Word of God. Since I began to search it diligently, the blessing has been wonderful. Great has been the blessing from consecutive, diligent, daily study. I look upon it as a lost day when I have not had a good time over the Word of God.[13]

Where are we in our spiritual journey? Do we neglect the Bible, or do we search the Scriptures daily and diligently? Some of us may be in between, not ignoring Scripture altogether, yet not studying it regularly either. Why? One problem is that we tend to have a pre-conceived idea of what a verse or passage of Scripture already means; therefore, why study?

In *Understanding and Applying the Bible*, J. Robertson McQuilken says that most people come to Scripture with wrong presuppositions. Most of us are either supernaturalistic, naturalistic, or dogmatic.[14] These views have their problems, and we need to discern whether or not we hold any of them. Why? Because our presuppositions shape the way we understand Scripture.

The supernaturalist, for example, looks for hidden meanings in Scripture (an allegorist, then, would be a type of supernaturalist). The naturalist believes Scripture is merely a human book, not written by divine inspiration. The dogmatist uses Scripture for proof texts, making it say something the author did not intend.

To the supernaturalist, the story of the defeat of Jericho (Joshua 6) might mean that because Israel walked around the walls of Jericho in silence, the Christian must witness in silence. One's "walk" will make the walls of the unrepentant heart "tumble down" in conversion.[15] The naturalist might regard the account as fiction but believe it was meant to show the triumph of good over evil.[16] The dogmatist would make the passage fit whatever doctrinal view she already held—that the people of Jericho were created solely for such judgment or perhaps that the event never happened because a loving God would never order the killing of a group of people.[17]

Those who do not let the Bible say what its divine Author

intended reminds me of the two boys walking home from Sunday school after a lesson about the Devil. "What do you think of this devil business?" one asked. The other replied, "Well, you know how Santa Claus turned out—it's either your mother or your dad."[18]

McQuilken also points out another wrong presupposition. The Bible can erroneously be viewed as a magical book that speaks directly to us whenever we randomly open it. Suppose I wanted to know where God would have me live. I come across the verses, "You have circled this mountain long enough" (Deuteronomy 2:3), and another verse, "And the coastlands will wait expectantly for His law" (Isaiah 42:4). Though I wanted to live in the mountains, I conclude from those verses that God wants me to live on the coast.[19]

By using the Bible as an oracle, I lose all opportunity of allowing God to work through my desires, prayers, the wisdom and counsel of others, and my husband's leading. It short-circuits the growth process since I do not have to discern the will of God, but only obey a supposed divine voice. The oracle approach to God's will does not help me mold my thoughts, be discerning, nor align my desires with God's. It depends only on raw submission, which is good as far as it goes, but can be mindless, leaving the rest of my character untouched.

Opening our Bible and blindly applying a verse to our lives may give us a sense of "blessing," but we can easily mistake our subjective thoughts for God's Word and will. For example, in my early years as a believer, I was diagnosed with a brain tumor. I was shocked by the news, and, after coming home from the doctor's office, I darted toward my Bible. I wanted anything, just anything. So opening my Bible and looking down at the page, I caught sight of only one verse—a verse I had never read before: "Precious in the sight of the Lord is the death of His godly ones" (Psalm 116:15).

I immediately took that verse to mean that I was going to be with the Lord soon. I told only a few people of my diagnosis, and I didn't even ask them to pray for healing since I was convinced that I was going to die. Well, here I am many years later, tumor-free.

What I did is exactly like the woman who, looking for guidance, flopped open her Bible and saw the verse about Judas that says, "And he went away and hanged himself" (Matthew 27:5). She opened it again and saw Luke 10:37 (NIV): "Go and do likewise." The third time she read, "If anyone loves Me, he will keep My word" (John 14:23).

Although God can certainly communicate to us in mysterious ways, the Bible should be understood the way the Author intended it. Let's look at some ways we can pull our Bible study together in a way that will give us an accurate understanding of Scripture.

Discover the Meaning of Scripture

Discovering what Scripture says isn't difficult. The main requirement is a bit of determination and discipline. These two ingredients were what helped the people at the dawn of the English Reformation.

The Bible had just been translated and written out (all by hand!). Because there was only one copy of it, it was chained to a pillar in a great cathedral. Each day those interested in hearing God's Word would go to the cathedral. Gathered on the stone floor around the Bible, they would listen to someone read for hours. They were so attentive that if the reader paused for even a moment, the listeners would cry out, "Read on! Read on!" Zeal such as this can only come from a heart that truly believes God is speaking through His Word.

When I was dating Brian, he used to write me letters all the time. Some told of his care for me; others talked about his desires and goals in life. Letters are important; they expose the heart. What if I ignored his letters, neglecting to read them? Or what if I read them without giving any thought to what he said? Most likely we wouldn't have had much of a relationship. We certainly would not be married today!

Likewise, if I ignored God's letters to me, I wouldn't have much of a relationship with Him either. God wants me to cherish His Word and have a desire to learn every little detail written in it. He wants to tell me so much about Himself—what He likes and dislikes. He wants to tell me about some special people, such as the Old Testament patriarchs and prophets and the New Testament apostles and disciples. He wants to tell me about godly and ungodly examples so that I can learn from both. And He continually reminds me of His everlasting love so that I never doubt it for a moment. The most exciting parts of His letter tell about the home He designed for me. He wonders if I am even a bit excited about it and the prospect of living with Him there. Am I?

I guess this is where the rubber meets the road. The true believer desires to know what is written in the Book, God's love letters to us. We are exhorted to let those letters dwell in us richly (Colossian 3:16). Do we?

How can we allow those letters to dwell in us richly?

By being alert. As you come to God's Word, wake up your soul, leave your anxieties behind, and enter into His presence through His Word.

By being prayerful. Just as you pray before each meal, pray before you read Scripture—your scriptural meal. Ask the Lord to penetrate your soul, guide the meditations of your mind, and grant you conviction of heart. Then expect God to answer your earnest prayer.

By being systematic. In other words, have a plan, a regular and orderly fashion of studying the Bible. When I was a new believer, I didn't study systematically. Instead I would flip around in the Scriptures and zealously write down every verse that fascinated me. This was okay for the time being, but if I had kept on doing this, I would never have developed an understanding of God's Word.

Find the Meat

This past spring Brian, the kids, and I went to a Civil War reenactment. As interesting as the battle was, I was even more fascinated with the paraphernalia at the booths. Going from table to table, I examined genuine artifacts such as the guns used, medical equipment, and even Confederate money. I also noticed a Civil War era cookbook. Thumbing through it, I found a recipe for rabbit soup. The first line of the directions said simply, "Catch the rabbit."

The recipe writer, no doubt with tongue in cheek, stated the obvious: You've got to have the meat. But what is so obvious in cooking isn't so obvious spiritually. The Corinthians, for example, had a diet entirely of spiritual milk (1 Corinthians 3:2). So what's wrong with milk? Nothing at all, but a glass of milk is far from a full meal. Paul was concerned about this limited diet. Yes, the milk the Corinthians were receiving gave them the same spiritual truths found in the meat of the Word. The only difference, and a very important one, is that the meat provides truth in depth and detail.

So just as we need the rabbit to have rabbit soup, we need a Bible to get the spiritual meat. Some prefer the King James above all other versions, and others have a difficult time with it because of the seventeenth-century English. If you prefer a version other than the King James, don't hesitate to get the *New King James Version* or another modern translation. It is still the infallible Word of God.

Second, have a dictionary on hand. We can miss the meaning of a passage if we do not know a word's definition. How many people know the meaning of *offal, spikenard, timbrel*, and *vassal* without looking them up? The meanings of words change. A dictionary is especially important if you use the King James version. The English word *enthusiasm*, for example, used to mean "possessed by a god." *Nice* (from the Latin *nescius*) originally meant "ignorant."[20]

Third, get familiar with the concordance in the back of your Bible (if your Bible has one). It will help you find a Bible passage on a particular subject (faith, anger, love). Of course, if your Bible doesn't have a concordance or you need one more in-depth, get one that matches the Bible version you are using.

Fourth, you will find a Bible atlas very helpful for understanding where things took place. It also can help you understand the passage. When, for example, Elijah fled for his life from Jezebel, it was not just around the corner. He ran from Mount Carmel (1 Kings 18:42) to Beersheba (1 Kings 19:3). On checking the atlas, I discovered he ran roughly 100 miles. Then I better understood how exhausted and how vulnerable to discouragement and depression Elijah was (1 Kings 19:4).

Fifth, if you want more insight on a passage, you can use a commentary. They are as different as their authors, so you will want to find one with which you feel comfortable. And we have to remember that Bible commentators are fallible, like the rest of us, so reading a commentary is no substitute for reading the Bible itself.

Go Back to the Original Languages

Because the Bible wasn't originally written in English, it can be helpful to discover the depth and meaning from the original languages without doing a formal study of them. Each of us can buy a few sources that will bring a dozen Hebrew and Greek scholars into our home.

The most basic source is *Strong's Exhaustive Concordance of the Bible*. You can look up a brief description of a word using the numbers to the right of the verse. Some of the work is done for you if you use *Young's Concordance*. The descriptions in *Vine's Expository Dictionary* are much more sophisticated, discussing how the word is used in specific contexts. My favorite is *Dictionary of New Testament Theology* (three volumes) by Colin Brown. It gives very in-depth studies of specific words such as *mind, heart,* or *conscience* and is a lifetime investment in your study of the Bible. Somewhat more technical is Harris, Archer, and Waltke's *Theological Wordbook of the Old Testament* (two volumes). Let me explain how easy (and fun!) it is to get more out of your study of words.

Strong's Exhaustive Concordance of the Bible allows me to get to the root of a Hebrew or Greek word quite easily. Let's go back to our verse in the Song of Solomon: "Let His left hand be under my head and His right hand embrace me" (2:6).

After reading the verse, I first ask myself, *What is the Hebrew word for embrace?* In *Strong's* main concordance I look up the word *embrace* and find several root words with many Scripture verses offered. This means that I could possibly get several meanings.

In order to narrow it down, I simply find Song of Solomon 2:6, which will be on the left column (all verses will be on the left of the page, and Song of Solomon will be referred to as Ca, for Canticles). Now to the right of the word *embrace* is the number 2263. I look in the back of *Strong's* for the Hebrew and Chaldee dictionaries (also provided is the Greek Dictionary of the New Testament). Finding 2263 in the Hebrew Dictionary, I look for a brief description of the word. *Strong's* tells me that the Hebrew word for *embrace* means "to clasp." Because *Strong's* definitions are so brief, we usually will want to know much more.

For further explanation, I can now go to the *Theological Wordbook of the Old Testament*. The two volumes of this work, in my opinion, are worth every cent you pay for them. Going to the index (found in the back pages of volume two), I see columns of numbers. The column on the left says, "STRONG"; the column to the right has "TWOT" (short for *Theological Wordbook of the Old Testament*). Going down the STRONG column, I locate the original number—2263. On the right (under the TWOT column) is the number showing where I can find the word *embrace* in the *Theological Wordbook*. The new number I am given is 597.1 (597 is the number; .1 is the volume). So going to volume one, I look for number 597.

Under 597 is a discussion of the Hebrew word *habaq*. There I find that *embrace* in Hebrew means an expression of love shown by "the position or action of the hands or arms." Reading further, I find that in the verse in the Song of Solomon, it means "the embrace of lovers."[21]

This process may seem quite technical, but once you use any tool such as these books, it becomes easy and a lot of fun! Besides being enjoyable, you get a much more in-depth understanding of the Bible.

If *Strong's* is too technical for you, consider Colin Brown's three-volume work. You can do everything in English and won't even need to look up *Strong's* number. Go to a bookstore and take a look at these books before you buy them.

Don't forget that you can also use your Bible dictionary or Bible encyclopedia to get more information about important words and ideas too!

Now, with tools in hand, let's dig into the meat. In so doing, we will avoid bringing our presuppositions or magical theories into our Bible study. Most of all, we will become more discerning as to what the Word really says.

TRY IT; YOU'LL LIKE IT!

At every meal, even before we pray, my children sit at the table and examine their food. It's something of a dinnertime ritual. While they are usually anxious to dig in, if I serve something unfamiliar, they want to make some observations. Their doubts are usually erased as soon as they taste the new food, and it's likely they will even want more.

Sometimes people have the same attitude toward Scripture. A book of the Bible or a passage might not look very interesting at first glance. But once they start using simple tools to dig in, they will find that, sure enough—they like it!

Observing What Is Before You

Michelle and Johnathan absolutely will not take big bites of something unfamiliar to them. With fork in hand, they move the "stuff" around on the plate, carefully checking out its texture, color, and especially its smell. They want to understand as much as possible about what they are about to eat.

We should have something of this attitude when we come to the Word. We can, with fork in hand, prick away at the passages, observing what is before us on the page. We should ask first what the author is saying. I answer that question by looking initially at the literary context.

LITERARY CONTEXT

To discern the point of the passage, I look closely at the words, sentences, and paragraphs that come before and after the verse I am reading. If I don't consider the context, I can easily misunderstand what the author is saying. Cults fall into this error, and it is no wonder they come up with twisted ideas about what the Bible teaches.

SUMMARIZE THE PASSAGE, NOTING KEY WORDS

The other day while homeschooling Michelle and Johnathan, I gave them the fun assignment of making our own version of Playdoh (of course, with Mom's help). As we began, I told Michelle to pay attention to what we did, because later I would ask her to summarize the procedure. When it was all over and the kids' hands were stained with bright colors, I asked for a summary. Michelle didn't mince words. She condensed the whole activity into one word for each step: 1) flour, 2) salad oil, 3) water, 3) salt, 4) cream of tartar, 5) mix, 6) cook, 7) stir, 8) color.

She beautifully illustrated what I can do in my personal Bible study. I can write down what I have observed and then summarize or condense the meaning of those facts into key words or ideas. I then can refer to a theological word book, Bible encyclopedia, or even a Bible dictionary for more information.

And whatever I come up with, I need to make sure I reflect accurately what I read. Those of us with children know the familiar experience of telling our kids something, and then we overhear them telling Dad a somewhat different version of what we had just said. The children's interpretation was so close and yet so far from what we actually said.

In our personal Bible study we must make sure we accurately reflect what we have learned—not changing it into what we want nor making it say what we have always thought. This will certainly keep us from having a "magical" approach to our devotional time.

Interpret What Is Before Us

One evening at dinner Michelle and Johnathan were pricking around with their forks with sour faces, most likely trying to buy time to avoid eating what was on their plates. In exasperation my then four-year-old son said, "Mom, I just don't understand why you have to put this food on our plates!" I did my best to explain that it was a nutritious meal, full of vitamins and minerals.

Sometimes, when coming to portions of Scripture, I am like my children, questioning, "Lord, why did You put this here?" As I delve deeper, I start to understand why. I start by asking what the author's purpose is. What was going on at the time he made his statements (the historical context)? What was happening in the culture that would prompt this message (cultural context)?

HISTORICAL AND CULTURAL CONTEXT

The quickest way I have found to understand the basic historical and cultural context of a particular book of the Bible is to read the introductory material in my study Bible. If you don't have a study Bible, I highly recommend that you get one. It can greatly enrich your personal Bible study.

Along with my study Bible, I like to refer to a Bible dictionary and even a Bible encyclopedia. These books help me find information about the times, customs, and people.

Use the Meat of the Word for Your Benefit

My heart goes out to those with eating disorders. This problem is very painful for them, emotionally and physically. Until they can assimilate the food they eat, they will remain physically unhealthy.

Likewise, until we allow the meat of the Word to digest in our heart, soul, and mind, we will remain spiritually weak. Application is the fruit of our personal Bible study. We must allow the food of observation, interpretation, and evaluation to change us as we become "doers of the word, and not merely hearers" (James 1:22).

For me personally, success in Christ's school of discipleship hinges on treating the Bible for what it is—the Word of God. This perspective motivates me to get the meaning God intended—not my own ideas, the ideas of others, or popular notions from the world around me. By acknowledging God's Word as the source of wisdom, that it is He who instructs me to make the right choices in life, I can obtain the true treasure, which is: "wisdom and discipline; for understanding words of insight; for acquiring a disciplined and prudent life, doing what is right and just and fair; for giving prudence to the simple, knowledge and discretion to the young—let the wise listen and add to their learning, and let the discerning get guidance.... The fear of the Lord is the beginning of knowledge" (Proverbs 1:2-5, 7 NIV).

Thinking It Over

1. How can we make a verse say whatever we want?

2. What is the difference between an allegory and proof-texting? How does each fail to explain the true meaning of Scripture?

3. In your Bible study do you ever lean toward a supernaturalistic, naturalistic, or dogmatic view? How do these views fail to explain Scripture?

4. Starting this week, how are you going to be more systematic in the study of God's Word?

5. What tools can help you in your Bible study?

6. Read Proverbs 1:2-5, 7 and write down the practical benefits we receive by being students of God's Word.

A DECISION TO MAKE

IF YOU HAVEN'T MADE IT ALREADY

Let's go into a warm, cozy church and sit down for a moment to listen to Pastor George Parker. Though he is speaking to a congregation, imagine that he is speaking directly to you, to your heart. Listen carefully to his words.

"[My dear friend] the Bible is a book of decision. Whether we read the Old Testament or the New Testament, it confronts men with the inescapable necessity to make up their minds. It unashamedly competes for men's minds. Such a book of decision fits squarely into our day and age. The biblical theme is set there in the book of Joshua: 'Choose you this day whom you will serve; whether the gods which your fathers served or the gods of the Amorites. But as for me and my house, we will serve the Lord.' That's decision.

"Elijah puts the theme in all his derisive satire: 'How long will you halt between two opinions? If the Lord be God, follow him; if Baal, then follow him. But the people answered not a word.' That's indecision.

"The parable of the Prodigal has it: 'And when he came to himself, he said: "I will arise and go to my father."' That's decision.

"Paul's preaching pronounces the theme as he stood in chains before Festus and Agrippa, and Agrippa said: 'Paul, almost thou persuadest me to be a Christian.' 'Almost,' 'maybe,' but not quite. That's indecision.

"The Christian faith demands of us something far more than Agrippa-like indecision. It demands decision. The Bible says that

God has something for us; God has acted in Jesus Christ; the Lord God Himself was directly involved in the most cataclysmic, the most miraculous event in all history—the life and death and resurrection of Jesus Christ.

"And you can't ignore God. This is mankind's great delusion—that God can be ignored if we choose. But you can't get away from God. We can no more ignore Him than we can ignore atomic power . . . or the sun in the heavens. . . . This is God's world. In this world He directly and unequivocally acted in the drama of human history through Jesus Christ. Ignore Him? Indeed, life would be much more simple if we could, but we can't. The theme set by Joshua persists to this very moment and this very place, but now that decision is personified in Christ: 'Choose you this day whom you will serve.' Amidst the battle for men's minds, to answer, 'Almost thou persuadest me to be a Christian,' is no sufficient answer. The Bible is a book of decision. Christian faith demands decision."[1]

Pastor Parker has finished his sermon, and now *you* are confronted with a decision to make. The book of decision—the Bible—says that the witness is this: "That God has given us eternal life, and this life is in His Son. He who has the Son has the life; he who does not have the Son of God does not have the life" (1 John 5:11-12). Simply put, a person gets to heaven by trusting in Jesus Christ and goes to hell by not trusting in Christ. Which destiny shall be yours—glory or despair?

My friend, if you have a softened heart toward Christ, then take this moment to repent of your sins and receive Him into your heart.

> *How far may we go on in sin? How long will God forbear?*
> *Where does hope end and where begin? The confines of despair?*
> *An answer from the skies is sent—"Ye that from God depart,*
> *While it is called today, repent! And harden not your heart."*
> —C. H. SPURGEON[2]

No sin is too great for the one who died for murderers, thieves, prostitutes, adulterers, and liars. All sin can be pardoned. Because "all have sinned and fall short of the glory of God" (Romans 3:23), it's impossible to earn brownie points to get into heaven. Heaven is a free gift (Ephesians 2:8-9), but that gift must be accepted by the person who needs it.

If you remain disbelieving, search the Scriptures and ask God to help you accept His gift of love. Also think about these things:

Receiving Eternal Life

You receive eternal life by genuinely receiving the living, resurrected Christ into your heart and life. It is promised that "as many as received Him, to them He gave the right to become children of God" (John 1:12).

Accepting Christ's Lordship

Jesus wants to come into your life to do many wonderful things—to be your personal Savior, to give you eternal life, to remove the load of guilt for past sins, to be a friend to lean on in time of trouble.

Jesus is Lord and Master. Why not acknowledge Him as Lord and Master of your life now? There's a throne room in your heart. You've been sitting on that throne and doing your own thing. Jesus says that that throne is rightfully His. But in order for you to get off the throne and put Christ on, you must be willing to let Christ be at the center of your life.

Some people say, "There is no way I can live a Christian life!" And I would have to agree with them. None of us can, but God will supply the power to live for Him, through the Holy Spirit.

The Bible says that when you receive Christ as Lord and Master of your life, His Holy Spirit comes to live in you (1 Corinthians 3:16), and your life changes. And this is key: *You* don't change your life. When you begin to dive into the Word of God and talk to Him in prayer, He will reveal what He wants you to do, through His Word, through His Spirit. All you do is yield.

Transfer Trust

You know by now that there is nothing you can do to earn eternal life. It's only through Christ and what He has done on the cross. But you have to be willing to transfer your trust from whatever you are leaning on to make you right with God and admit you to heaven. You have to stop trusting your own efforts and start trusting what Christ has done for you.

Have a Repentant Heart

God is concerned that you have a repentant heart. By nature, mankind desires to walk away from God. Repentance changes that tendency in people, causing a 180-degree change of heart. Repentance gives people the desire to go toward God and do the things that please Him, while at the same time repentance gives us a distaste for those things we used to do.

Invite Christ In

Jesus won't force His way into your life. You may have seen the picture of Jesus knocking on a heavy door. If you look closely, there is no handle on the outside of the door. Speaking to the church in the city of Laodicea, Jesus said, "Behold, I stand at the door and knock; if anyone hears My voice and opens the door, I will come in to him, and will dine with him, and he with Me" (Revelation 3:20). Even though this message is to those already in the Christian church, ask yourself, "Would I like to open the door of my heart and let Christ in? Would I like to receive the eternal life that Christ died to gain for me?"[3]

If so, pray right now. If you are at a loss for words, then pray something like this:

> *Dear Jesus, You know me so well. You know every sin I have ever committed, and yet You died for me, in my place. I know that if I were the only living person on earth, You would still come and die on my behalf—and I would be the only one around to hammer You to the rugged cross. Thank You for forgiving me and cleansing me of my sin. I now place my faith in You as my Lord and Savior. Please come into my life and make me the kind of person You want me to be. Amen.*

A Closing Note

If you just prayed asking God to forgive you, to cleanse you and come into your life, then these promises are for you:

- You are forgiven! "In Him we have redemption through His blood, the forgiveness of our trespasses, according to the riches of His grace" (Ephesians 1:7).
- You are a child of God! "But as many as received Him, to them He gave the right to become children of God" (John 1:12).
- You shall be at peace with God! "Therefore having been justified by faith, we have peace with God through our Lord Jesus Christ" (Romans 5:1).
- You are an heir of God! "Blessed be the God and Father of our Lord Jesus Christ, who according to His great mercy has caused us to be born again to a living hope through the resurrection of Jesus Christ from the dead, to obtain an inheritance which is imperishable and undefiled and will not fade away, reserved in heaven for you" (1 Peter 1:3-4; also see Romans 8:17).
- The Holy Spirit lives in you! "Do you not know that you are a temple of God, and that the Spirit of God dwells in you?" (1 Corinthians 3:16).

Welcome to the family, my dear sister in Christ!

If you have given your life to the Lord, please let those of us at Tyndale Ministries know. We would count it a pleasure to share in your joy. Also if we can offer assistance in sending materials that will help you in your spiritual growth, please let us know.

Tyndale Ministries
Drawer N-N,
Pine Mountain, California, 93222

NOTES

CHAPTER ONE: AVOIDING WORDS THAT WOUND

1. Adapted from the software *Bible Illustrator* (Hiawatha, Iowa: Parsons Technology, 1990-1992).
2. Ibid.
3. Marlowe, Shakespeare, *Harvard Classics: Elizabethan Drama* (New York: P. F. Collier & Son, 1938), 317.
4. Ralph Gower, *The New Manners and Customs of Bible Times* (Chicago: Moody Press, 1987), 248-9.
5. Adapted from Eleanor Doan, *Speaker's Sourcebook* (Grand Rapids, Mich.: Zondervan Publishing House, 1960), 117.
6. Ibid.
7. Adapted, Ibid.
8. Colin Brown, ed., *Dictionary of New Testament Theology,* Vol. 3 (Grand Rapids, Mich.: 1971), 346.
9. Doan, *Speaker's Sourcebook*, 117.
10. Brown, *Dictionary,* 345.
11. Ibid., 347.
12. Ronald F. Youngblood, ed., *New Illustrated Bible Dictionary* (Nashville, Tenn.: Thomas Nelson, 1995), 556.
13. Sherwood Eliot Wirt, ed., *Spiritual Power* (Wheaton, Ill.: Crossway, 1989), 194 (taken from a sermon given by T.DeWitt Talmage).
14. Walter B. Knight, *Knight's Treasury of 2,000 Illustrations* (Grand Rapids, Mich.: Wm. B. Eerdmans Publishing Company, 1963), 411.
15. Ibid., 413 (originally from *Lectures on Acts* by H. A. Ironside, Litt.D.).
16. Michael Hodgin, *1001 Humorous Illustrations for Public Speaking* (Grand Rapids, Mich.: Zondervan Publishing House, 1994), 244 (taken from *Parables, Etc.,* Saratoga Press, March 1990).
17. Charles Haddon Spurgeon, *The Treasury of David* (Nashville, Tenn.: Thomas Nelson, 1984 reprint) 1:220.
18. Knight, *Treasury of 2,000 Illustrations*, 412.
19. John MacArthur Jr., *Perfect Love,* John MacArthur's Bible Study Series (Panorama City, Calif.: Word of Grace Communications, 1985), 51.
20. Ibid.
21. Charles Wallace French, *Abraham Lincoln the Liberator: A Biographical Sketch*, American Reformers Series, ed. Carlos Martyn (New York: Funk & Wagnalls, 1891), 127-8.
22. MacArthur, *Perfect Love,* 51.
23. William E. Barton, *The Life of Abraham Lincoln* (Indianapolis: Bobbs-Merrill, 1925), 1:111.
24. MacArthur, *Perfect Love,* 51.

CHAPTER TWO: TAMING THE TEMPER

1. *Bible Illustrator* (Hiawatha, Iowa: Parsons Technology, 1990-1992).
2. Lewis Carroll, *The Complete Illustrated Works of Lewis Carroll* (London, England: Chancellor Press, 1982), 111.
3. Jeffrey Kunz and Asher Finkel, eds., *The American Medical Association: Family Medical Guide* (New York: Random House, 1987), 595-598.

4. Ibid., 595.
5. Michael Hodgin, *1001 Humorous Illustrations* (Grand Rapids, Mich.: Zondervan Publishing House, 1994), 14 (also found in *Parables, Etc.*, March 1984, submitted by Joe Schmitt).
6. C. H. Spurgeon, *C. H. Spurgeon Autobiography: The Early Years* (Carlisle, Penn.: Banner of Truth, 1962), 29.
7. *Bible Illustrator.*

CHAPTER THREE: FRIENDS THAT SHARPEN

1. Richard McKeon, *Introduction to Aristotle*, (New York: Random House, 1947), 471.
2. Daniel C. Arichea and Eugene A. Nida, *A Translator's Handbook on the First Letter from Peter* (New York: United Bible Societies), 149-150. Apparently Peter coined the word *allotriepisko-pos*, which is used nowhere else in the New Testament nor in fact in the whole of Greek literature before the second century A.D. Because the word is not found anywhere else in Scripture, it is not easy to determine what he really meant. The KJV translates it as "busybody," RSV "mischief-maker," PHILLIPS "revolutionist," NIV "meddler."
3. Ibid., 150.
4. Gary Inrig, *Quality Friendships* (Chicago: Moody Press, 1981), 25.
5. Gardiner Spring, D.D., *The Distinguishing Traits of Christian Character* (Phillipsburg, N.J.: Presbyterian and Reformed Publishing), 53. Reprint of 1829 version titled, *Essays on the Distinguishing Traits of Christian Character.*
6. Cynthia Pearl Maus, *Christ and the Fine Arts* (New York: Harper & Brothers, 1959), 707 (adapted from *Pictures That Preach*, by Charles Nelson Page, Abingdon Press).
7. Ibid., 707.

CHAPTER FOUR: FREE FROM POSSESSING

1. Will Durant, *Caesar and Christ*, Vol. 3 of *The Story of Civilization* (New York: Simon and Schuster, 1972), 245.
2. Ibid., 328-329.
3. Ibid., 245.
4. Ibid.
5. *The Oxford Dictionary of Quotations* (Oxford: Oxford University Press, 1979), 261 (can also be found in Durant, 245).
6. From the movie *Shadowlands*, British Broadcasting Corp., 1985.
7. Kenneth W. Osbeck, *52 Hymn Stories Dramatized* (Grand Rapids, Mich.: Kregel Publications, 1992), 76.
8. Lindsay I. Terry, *Devotionals from Famous Hymn Stories* (Grand Rapids, Mich.: Baker Book House, 1974), 12.
9. Ibid.
10. Osbeck, *52 Hymn Stories,* 77.
11. Ibid., 77.
12. Helen Lemmel, "Turn Your Eyes Upon Jesus," *Great Hymns of the Faith* (Grand Rapids, Mich.: Zondervan Publishing House Publishing House), 204.

CHAPTER FIVE: POSSESSING ALL THINGS

1. David Neff, ed., *The Midas Trap* (Wheaton, Ill.: Victor Books, 1990), 76.
2. Ibid.

3. Ruth A. Tucker, *From Jerusalem to Irian Jaya* (Grand Rapids, Mich.: Zondervan Publishing House, 1983), 233.

4. William Rose Benet, ed., *The Reader's Encyclopedia* (New York: Thomas Y. Crowell Company, 1948), 3:773.

5. Herbert V. Prochnow, *1800 Quips & Illustrations for All Occasions* (Grand Rapids, Mich.: Baker, 1969), 292.

6. Tennyson, *Locksley Hall*, in *Pocket Book of Quotations*, ed. Henry Davidoff (New York: Pocket Books, 1952), 437.

7. H. D. Spence and Joseph S. Exell, eds., *The Pulpit Commentary: Proverbs, Ecclesiastes, Song of Solomon* (Grand Rapids, Mich.: Wm. B. Eerdmans, 1950), 34.

8. Paul E. Little, *Affirming the Will of God* (Madison, Wis.: InterVarsity Press, 1971), 24.

9. A. W. Tozer, *The Pursuit of God* (Camp Hill, Penn.: Christian Publications, Inc., 1982), 41.

CHAPTER SIX: USING THE TIME OF YOUR LIFE

1. John Calvin, *Golden Booklet of the True Christian Life* (Grand Rapids, Mich.: Baker, 1952), 23 (first published in 1550 in Latin and French under the title *De Vita Hominis Christiani*—that is, *On the Life of the Christian Man*).

2. Will Durant, *The Reformation*, Vol. 6 of *The Story of Civilization* (New York: Simon and Schuster, 1957), 349.

3. Ibid.

4. John MacArthur, *The Walk of the New Man* (Panorama City, Calif.: Word of Grace Communications, 1982), 96.

5. Richard Willis, D.D., "A Sermon Preach'd Before the Queen at St. James's" (London: printed for Mat. Wotton, at the Three Daggers in Fleet Street, 1709), 13-14.

CHAPTER SEVEN: GIFTS THAT GIVE

1. John Eadie, LL.D., *Commentary on the Epistle to the Ephesians* (Minneapolis, Minn.: James and Klock Christian Publishing Co., 1977), 363 (originally published by T. and T. Clark, Edinburgh, 1883).

2. Ken Shingledecker and James E. Berney, eds., *Let Every Tongue Confess: A Mission Reader* (Downers Grove, Ill.: InterVarsity Press, 1981), 55 (revised from 1979 edition by Isabelo Magalit under the title *The Messenger's Qualifications*).

3. My thanks to Pat Posthumus, who suggested the design for the decorations and their meaning.

4. Walter Kaiser, Jr., explains these two views and discusses them in "Prophet, Prophetess, Prophecy," *Evangelical Dictionary of Biblical Theology*, ed. Walter Elwell (Grand Rapids, Mich.: Baker, 1996), 646-7.

5. Robert L. Thomas, *Understanding Spiritual Gifts: The Christian's Special Gifts in the Light of 1 Corinthians 12-14* (Chicago: Moody Press, 1978), 121.

6. Ibid.

7. John MacArthur, *Speaking in Tongues* (Panorama City, Calif.: Word of Grace Communications, 1988), 160.

8. Douglas Moo, "What Does It Mean Not to Teach or Have Authority over Men?" in *Recovering Biblical Manhood and Womanhood: A Response to Evangelical Feminism,* ed. John Piper and Wayne Grudem (Wheaton, Ill.: Crossway Books, 1991), 179-193. I am indebted to Moo for his insights and conclusions.

9. G. Abbot-Smith, *A Manual Greek Lexicon of the New Testament*, 3rd ed. (Edinburgh: T. & T. Clark, 1937), 37; W. E. Vine, *An Expository Dictionary of New Testament Words* (Old Tappan,

N. J.: Fleming H. Revell, 1940), 34. Both consider the word in 2 Timothy 2:12 to mean "man as distinct from woman," not "husband."

10. C. F. Keil and F. Delitzsche, *Commentary on the Old Testament in Ten Volumes*, Vol. 1, *The Pentateuch* (Grand Rapids, Mich.: Wm. B. Eerdmans, 1991, reprint), 2:57.

11. C. Peter Wagner, *Your Spiritual Gifts* (Ventura, Calif.: Regal Books, 1994), 143.

12. Ibid.

13. Here Paul is addressing all believers, not just those with the gift of giving.

CHAPTER EIGHT: RENEWING THE MIND IN A MINDLESS WORLD

1. C. S. Lewis, *The Best of C. S. Lewis* (Grand Rapids, Mich.: Baker, 1969), 362, quoted from *Orthodoxy*.

2. M. L. Clarke, *The Roman Mind: Studies in the History of Thought from Cicero to Marcus Aurelius* (New York: W. W. Norton, 1968), 20.

3. Ibid., 33.

4. Ibid., 35.

5. Francis A. Schaeffer, *The Complete Works of Francis A. Schaeffer: A Christian Worldview*, Vol. 1, *He Is There and He Is Not Silent* (Wheaton, Ill.: Crossway Books, 1982), 279-280.

6. Colin Brown, *Dictionary of New Testament Theology*, Vol. 2 (Grand Rapids, Mich.: Zondervan Publishing House, 1971), 616. Philip H. Towner, "Mind/Reason," *Evangelical Dictionary of Biblical Theology*, ed. Walter Elwell (Grand Rapids, Mich.: Baker, 1996), 527-30.

7. Bruce K. Waltke, "Heart," *Evangelical Dictionary of Biblical Theology*, ed. Walter Elwell (Grand Rapids, Mich.: Baker, 1996), 331-32.

8. Adapted from Cynthia Pearl Maus, *Christ and the Fine Arts* (New York: Harper & Brothers, 1959), 250-53.

9. Adapted from Will Durant, *The Reformation,* Vol. 6 of *The Story of Civilization* (New York: Simon & Schuster, 1957) 342-343.

10. Ibid., 343.

11. John R. W. Stott, *Baptism & Fullness* (Downers Grove, Ill.: InterVarsity Press, 1977), 81.

12. *Bible Illustrator* (Hiawatha, Iowa: Parsons Technology, 1990-1992).

13. Thomas McCormick and Sharon Fish, *Meditation: A Practical Guide to a Spiritual Discipline* (Downers Grove, Ill.: InterVarsity Press, 1983), 81.

14. Ibid.

15. Another resource I recommend is the booklet, *Meditations in the Psalms*. It would work well for individual study, a small-group Bible study, or follow-up for a new believer. You can order a free copy from World Missionary Press, Inc., Box 120, New Paris, Indiana 46553.

16. *Bible Illustrator.*

17. Walter B. Knight, *Knight's Master Book of 4,000 Illustrations* (Grand Rapids, Mich.: Wm. B. Eerdmans, 1956), 516 (taken from *Gospel Message*).

18. 1 Peter 1:13, in *MacArthur Study Bible* (Nashville, Tenn.: Word, 1997), 1940.

19. Gene Edward Veith, Jr., *Loving God with All Your Mind* (Wheaton, Ill.: Crossway, 1987), 88.

CHAPTER NINE: HOLDING ON TO A GOOD CONSCIENCE

1. *The Durham Sun*, October 13, 1944.

2. Colin Brown, ed., *Dictionary of New Testament Theology*, Vol. 2 (Grand Rapids, Mich.: Zondervan Publishing House, 1971), 182.

3. Adapted from *Bible Illustrator* (Hiawatha, Iowa: Parsons Technology, 1990-1992).

4. Michael Hodgin, *1001 Humorous Illustrations for Public Speaking* (Grand Rapids, Mich.:

Zondervan Publishing House, 1994), 88; Also found in *Sunday Sermons Treasury of Illustrations*, Vol. 1, Parables, Etc. (Saratoga Press, Nov. 84), 232 (no. 438).

5. John 17:17 in *MacArthur Study Bible* (Nashville, Tenn.: Word, 1997), 1619.

6. Ibid.

7. Walter B. Knight, *Knight's Treasury of 2,000 Illustrations* (Grand Rapids, Mich.: Wm. B. Eerdmans, 1963), 69.

8. Kenneth W. Osbeck, *101 Hymn Stories* (Grand Rapids, Mich.: Kregel Publications, 1992), 52. There is a slight variation of this quote in *52 Hymn Stories Dramatized* (Grand Rapids, Mich.: Kregel Publications, 1992), 39.

9. Joe Aldrich, *Secrets to Inner Beauty* (Santa Ana, Calif.: Vision House Publishers, 1977), 44.

10. Charles Caldwell Ryrie, *The Ryrie Study Bible* (Chicago: Moody Press, 1978), 1737. Theologian Charles Ryrie explains that the word *ruined* does not refer to eternal salvation but to a person's spiritual life.

11. Ibid., 1740.

12. Adapted from *Bible Illustrator*.

13. Knight, *Knight's Treasury*, 360.

CHAPTER TEN: DISCERNING THE NATURE OF OUR PRAYERS

1. Adapted from *Bible Illustrator* (Hiawatha, Iowa: Parsons Technology, 1990-1992).

2. Ibid.

3. E. M. Bounds, *The Complete Works of E. M. Bounds on Prayer* (Grand Rapids, Mich.: Baker, 1990), 252.

4. O. Hallesby, *Prayer* (Minneapolis, Minn.: Augsburg Publishing, 1975), 126.

5. Ronald F. Youngblood, ed., *Nelson's New Illustrated Bible Dictionary* (Nashville, Tenn.: Thomas Nelson, 1995), 1029.

6. Ibid., 762.

7. *Bible Illustrator.*

8. Ibid., adapted.

9. R. A. Torrey, *The Power of Prayer, and the Prayer of Power* (Grand Rapids, Mich.: Zondervan Publishing House, 1975), 17.

CHAPTER ELEVEN: TRUE SPIRITUAL WORSHIP

1. Adapted from Walter B. Knight, *Knight's Treasury of 2,000 Illustrations* (Grand Rapids, Mich.: Wm. B. Eerdmans, 1963), 447-448.

2. Ibid.

3. Samuel Taylor Coleridge, "The Rime of the Ancient Mariner" (Chicago: Scott, Foresman and Co., 1898), 21.

4. *Bible Illustrator* (Hiawatha, Iowa: Parsons Technology, 1990-1992).

5. Ibid.

6. Adapted from C. S. Lewis, *Christian Behavior*, in *The Best of C. S. Lewis* (Grand Rapids, Mich.: Baker, 1969), 457.

7. Charles Ryrie, *The Ryrie Study Bible* (Chicago: Moody Press, 1978), 760.

8. Ibid., 758.

9. A. W. Tozer, *The Knowledge of the Holy* (New York: Harper & Row, 1961), 9.

10. This verse was especially significant to Paul; he quoted it twice (1 Corinthians 1:31 and 2 Corinthians 10:17).

11. Nathan J. Stone, *Names of God* (Chicago: Moody Press, 1944), 14, 17.
12. Elmer A. Martens, "God, names of," *Evangelical Dictionary of Biblical Theology*, ed. Walter Elwell (Grand Rapids, Mich.: Baker, 1996), 297-298.
13. Stone, *Names of God*, 40.
14. Ibid., 51.
15. Ibid., 50.
16. This name appears as "LORD," small capitals in some English Bibles.
17. Martens, *Evangelical Dictionary*, 298.
18. Ibid., 300.
19. *Knowing God* gives a deeper understanding of the knowledge of God and helps us worship Him for who He is. I highly recommend this book to any woman who desires to have a more God-centered faith.

    The Knowledge of the Holy is a devotional. Each chapter begins with prayer and then discusses divine aspects of God. This was the first book I ever read on God's attributes, and I grew immensely from it. The book is written in laymen's terms, so it's very easy to grasp what could have been difficult concepts.

    The Existence and Attributes of God was written back in 1682. I have yet to find another book that compares to Charnock's depth and insight. This book is a must for the serious student.

    The Names of God in the Old Testament defines twelve of God's descriptive names. This valuable resource will enhance your own time in worship.
20. William Gurnall, *The Christian in Complete Armour*, Vol. 1 (Carlisle, Penn.: The Banner of Truth Trust, 1986), 81.
21. 1 Thessalonians 5:17, in *MacArthur Study Bible* (Nashville, Tenn.: Word, 1997), 1850.
22. P. J. Gloag, *1 Thessalonians*, vol. 21 of *The Pulpit Commentary*, ed. H. D. M. Spence and Joseph S. Exell (Peabody, Mass.: Hendrickson, n.d.), 105.
23. Here are some ministries that provide Christian tracts for a small fee: Good News Publishers, 1300 Crescent St., Wheaton, Ill. 60187; American Tract Society, P. O. Box 462008, 1624 N. First St., Garland, Texas 75046-2008.
24. Two books I highly recommend are both by Ron Rhodes (and from Harvest House): *Reasoning from the Scriptures with the Jehovah's Witnesses*, and *Reasoning from the Scriptures with the Mormons*.
25. Quoted in A. W. Tozer, *The Pursuit of God* (Camp Hill, Penn.: Christian Publications, Inc., 1982), 40-41.

CHAPTER TWELVE: BLUNTING THE SWORD

1. *The Life and Letters of Martin Luther*, trans. Preserved Smith (New York: Houghton Mifflin, 1911); quoted from Clyde L. Manshreck, ed., *A History of Christianity: Readings in the History of the Church*, Vol. 2 (Prentice-Hall, 1981; repr. Grand Rapids, Mich.: Baker, 1981), 31.
2. *Bible Illustrator* (Hiawatha, Iowa: Parsons Technology, 1990-1992).
3. Charles Haddon Spurgeon, *Spurgeon's Expository Encyclopedia* (Grand Rapids, Mich.: Baker, reprint, 1985), 5:498. Sermon entitled, "Twelve Covenant Mercies," June 30, 1889.
4. David F. Wells, *No Place for Truth* (Grand Rapids, Mich.: Wm. B. Eerdmans, 1993), 177.

CHAPTER THIRTEEN: GOD'S WORD OR OURS?

1. J. Sidlow Baxter, *The Strategic Grasp of the Bible* (Grand Rapids, Mich.: Zondervan Publishing House, 1968), 18.
2. Ibid.

3. Marilyn Hickey, *Signs in the Heavens* (Denver: Marilyn Hickey Ministries, 1984), 21. Also *Marilyn Hickey Ministries*, Trinity Broadcasting Network, May 23-27, 31, 1994.

4. Ibid.

5. Ibid., 31, 37.

6. Ibid., 71-72.

7. Ibid., 89, 91.

8. Ibid., 111-12.

9. John Miller, *A Commentary on Proverbs* (New York: Anson D. F. Randolph, 1872), 533.

10. *Merchant of Venice*, Act 2, Scene 6.

11. R. Laird Harris, ed., *Theological Wordbook of the Old Testament* (Chicago: Moody Press, 1980), 1:259, #597.

12. *Bible Illustrator*, (Hiawatha, Iowa: Parsons Technology, 1990-1992). Also found in Jean Staker Garton, *Who Broke the Baby?* (Bethany House, 1979), 35.

13. *Bible Illustrator*.

14. Robertson McQuilkin, *Understanding and Applying the Bible* (Chicago: Moody Press, 1983), 18.

15. Ibid.

16. Ibid.

17. Ibid.

18. Eleanor Doan, *Speaker's Sourcebook* (Grand Rapids, Mich.: Zondervan Publishing House, 1960), 84.

19. Illustration adapted from Robertson McQuilkin, *Understanding and Applying the Bible* (Chicago: Moody Press, 1983, 1992), 42.

20. Henry A. Virkler, *Hermeneutics: Principles and Processes of Biblical Interpretation* (Grand Rapids, Mich.: Baker, 1981), 100.

21. Harris, ed., *Theological Wordbook*, 1:259, #597.

A DECISION TO MAKE

1. Herbert V. Prochnow, *Treasury of Inspiration* (Grand Rapids, Mich.: Baker, 1958), 23-24 (sermon by Rev. George Parker used by permission).

2. Charles Haddon Spurgeon, *Spurgeon's Expository Encyclopedia,* Vol. 3 (Grand Rapids, Mich.: Baker, 1985), 476.

3. My gratitude to D. James Kennedy for these principles and methods in Evangelism Explosion (Wheaton, Ill.: Tyndale House Publishers, 1977).